S0-AHR-217

BROADCAST/ CABLE REGULATION

Marvin R. Bensman

UNIVERSITY
PRESS OF
AMERICA

Lanham • New York • London

Copyright © 1990 by
University Press of America®, Inc.
4720 Boston Way
Lanham, Maryland 20706

3 Henrietta Street
London WC2E 8LU England

All rights reserved
Printed in the United States of America
British Cataloging in Publication Information Available

Library of Congress Cataloging-in-Publication Data

Bensman, Marvin R., 1937–
Broadcast/cable regulation / Marvin R. Bensman.
p. cm.
1. Broadcasting—Law and legislation—United States—Digests.
2. Mass media—Law and legislation—United States—Digests.
3. Cable television—Law and legislation—United States—Digests.
I. Title.
KF2763.36.B46   1990
343.7309'945'02638—dc20   89–21502 CIP
[347.303994502638]

ISBN 0–8191–7661–3 (alk. paper)

The paper used in this publication meets the minimum requirements of
American National Standard for Information Sciences—Permanence
of Paper for Printed Library Materials, ANSI Z39.48–1984.

Preface

With rapid technological advances in national and global communication; entertainment and communications have become very specialized fields. Within copyright, contracts, tax, labor law, antitrust and tort law are considerable issues which affect the electronic media. These issues are of increasing import to decision-making management, media practioners, and students, for they impact upon custom and practice in the electronic media industry.

The Communications Act of 1934, the empowering statute of the Federal Communications Commission, is unique in that it contains very little substantive law. The regulations and policies issued by the FCC respond to specific issues and procedures. It is difficult for station management and staff to keep up-to-date without the assistance of law firms or consultants. This publication is designed to provide an understanding of the basic development behind the changing face of regulation.

The first two versions of this work consisted of cases, decisions and memoranda in a strictly chronological order. This completely reorganizes and updates the material into topic or subject sections, alphabetically, adding more material on cable regulation and other areas of entertainment law affecting broadcasting and cable. There is now an complete and new index to help locate material across the topic areas.

While the Federal Communication Commission has recently eliminated many of its rules and policies in "deregulation," what has actually occurred is "re-regulation." Private causes of action generally do not arise from a Federal statute or the regulatory structure to implement that statute. But with the removal of many FCC policies and rules and the National Association of Broadcaster's self-regulatory code the FCC has made it very clear that private means should be used to continue to protect against the very abuses the FCC once controlled through specific rule and regulation.

This work shows the development of policies and rules. Each topic has a current example of how it still impacts on broadcasting-cable. As many license revocations as could be determined are included from the beginning of broadcast regulation.

In the field of communication, perhaps more than in any other, the statement of an abstract rule, divorced from the factual context, sheds little light. It hardly needs emphasis that without some knowledge of the developmental and historical factors operating in the field one cannot predict the future.

It is hoped that the readers will not make the same mistakes others have in the past and this work is both a guide and warning to all.

Appreciation is expressed to Lawrence W. Lichty and Joseph R. Riley for introducing me to broadcast regulation at the University of Wisconsin-Madison where early material originally compiled by students of Harrison B. Summers of Ohio University was utilized.

Thanks also go to the assistance and support of my loving and loved wife, Harriet, and my wonderful children, David and Lauren. I dedicate this and more to the memory of my late beloved parents.

Marvin R. Bensman, J.D., Ph.D.
Memphis State University
Department of Theatre and Communication Arts

Bitnet: BensmanM@MemStVx1
1990

BROADCAST / CABLE REGULATION

The Department of Commerce from 1921, when there were only a handful of broadcast stations, to 1927, when there were over 700 broadcasting stations, regulated radio under the provisions of the **Radio Act of 1912**. Because of the limited use made of radio prior to 1920 except for wireless telegraphy for safety at sea there had been no pressing need for further legislation. However, it became increasingly difficult to apply the law of 1912 to the new use of radio as "broadcasting." Twenty bills were placed before the 67th Congress (1921-23); 13 proposed laws were submitted to the 68th Congress (1923-25); and 18 bills introduced to the 69th Congress (1925-27); all to regulate radio communication. Of these 51 bills only one was to pass both houses of Congress—the **Radio Act of 1927**. The Secretary of Commerce, Herbert Hoover, called the radio industry together for annual conferences in 1922-25 to seek advice on regulation, obtain recommendations on legislation and to gain voluntary acquiescence for the activities of his department which was making an effort to control interference and determine the course of governmental control. The Department of Commerce, since it knew it had little specific authority to regulate, adapted its authority under the Radio Act of 1912. It (1) classified radio stations; (2) prescribed their service; (3) assigned frequencies; (4) cleared a broadcast band of other conflicting services; (5) regulated and tested apparatus; (6) established zones and wavelengths for those zones; (7) made regulations to prevent interference; (8) advocated freedom from censorship; (9) helped settle on the phrase "public interest, convenience and necessity" and (10) specified the role and makeup of its' successor agency, the Federal Radio Commission, formed by the Radio Act of 1927. The Department of Commerce staff discussed, devised and implemented the scheme of regulation which to this day impacts upon what "broadcasting" is in the United States.

When WJAZ, Chicago, pirated a Canadian frequency it was judicially determined that the Radio Act of 1912, gave no legal authority over determining frequency, power, etc. to the Sec. of Commerce, *US v. Zenith Radio Corp.*, 12 F. 2d 614 (1926). Congress had to act and passed a new law to regulate radio.

Congress's Right to Establish Radio Regulatory Agency. The Ct. upheld the *Radio Act of 1927*, which created a five-member Federal Radio Commission. The FRC was renewed annually until the *Communication Act of 1934* created a seven-man Federal Communication Commission, *G.E. v. Federal Radio Commission*, 31 F. 2d 630 (DC App. 1929). The *Act of 1934*, was essentially the same as the *Radio Act of 1927*. In 1983, FCC Commissioners were cut from seven to five members to decrease cost, *97-21, Second Session*, (Aug. 18 1982); and FCC bureaus reorganized into four new divisions: Audio Services; Enforcement; Policy and Rules; and Video Services, (Nov. 1983).

License to Broadcast. (§301, §303(1)—1934 Act); The first conviction under the *Radio Act of 1927* for operating a broadcasting station without a licence and illegally transmitting in interstate commerce was that of George W. Fellowes in St. Louis. Fellowes argued that "the air is free for anybody to use." The Ct. noted that radio could not be properly useful "...unless some regulation of this sort were enforced to stop every Tom, Dick, and Harry from getting on the air." Sentenced to one year and a day, Fellowes was instead deported over irregularities in his citizenship, *FRC., 4th Annual Report, p. 54*, (1930). Licensees must be US citizens; no more than 25% partly owned/or managed by foreign entities, *Citizen Requirements of License*, 61 RR 2d 298 (1986). FCC no longer requires stations to employ operators with third or first class licenses. Restricted Radio Telephone Permit (obtainable without test) is sufficient, 70 FCC 2d 2371, 44 RR 2d 1521 (1979), 87 FCC 2d 44, 49 RR 2d 1453 (1981). Remote

2

transmitter control requires a licensed operator during all periods of operation to terminate the station's operation should it become a source of harmful interference or be operating inconsistent with law or treaty, 57 RR 2d 302 (1984). The requirement that only US citizens can hold Radio Operator licenses was upheld as immigration is an incentive for aliens to become naturalized, and provided the President with an expendable token for treaty negotiating purposes, *Campos v. FCC*, 650 F. 2d 890 (7th Cir. 1981). Congress then amended §303(1) to allow the FCC to issue operating licenses to persons who are qualified by the FCC and who otherwise are legally eligible for employment in the US, (46 FR 35464, July 8, 1981). The only other cases of pirate broadcasting in the US took place in the 1970—80's. The FCC revoked Carl McIntire's Faith Theological Seminary licenses for violations of the "Fairness Doctrine," *Brandywine-Main Line Radio*, 473 F. 2d 16, (1972). McIntire began an off-shore broadcast operation, "Radio Free America" from a US registered ship on an unlicensed and extraterritorial basis. This type of activity had not been tested in the courts. After one day a permanent restraining order was obtained, 29 RR 2d 883, 370 F. Supp. 1301 (1974). In 1987, "Radio New York International," a rock station from a ship with Honduran registry began broadcasting on AM, FM, shortwave and longwave. After four days, boarded and arrested, the operators were charged with operating an unlicensed station, conspiring to impede the FCC, and violating the *International Telecommunications Union Convention*, Article 30, §1(1). Could net five years and a $250,000 fine. The operators argued First Amendment "constitutional right to freedom of expression over the public forum of the airwaves." Charges were dropped when they apparently agreed to cease operations, but the ship was then reregistered to the Principality of Sealand and resumed for four nights until a temporary restraining order was obtained. The authority of the FCC to extend its jurisdiction to any transmissions received in the US regardless of origination was upheld, *US v. Weiner and Rothstein*, EDNY, (July 28

1987). The Utah Supreme Ct. declared that the purchaser of a radio station had defaulted in its time payments, and therefore the purchaser's interest in the license and other assets was forfeited back to the seller, as provided in the sale agreement. The FCC would have to approve the license transfer, but as between purchaser and seller, the seller owned the license. If the FCC did not approve the transfer, the license could be terminated, *Themy v. Seagull Enterprises*, 595 P. 2d 526 (Utah 1979).

Federal Government Power over Intrastate Radio. Supreme Ct. found that the *Radio Act* requirement that broadcasters operate to a "public interest, convenience and necessity" standard was not unconstitutionally vague. The FRC had broad discretionary authority in applying that standard. Intrastate control is ancillary to authority over interstate control; as radio is devolved from the commerce clause of the Constitution. The federal government must license stations within state boundaries because radio waves inside a state affect radio waves crossing state lines, *FRC v. Nelson Bros.*, 289 US 266 (1933).

Federal Radio Commission Revocations. (§326); The FRC, and the later FCC were given the power to revoke licenses. The FRC in 1927, eliminated stations which were no longer operating, moved station frequencies and set power to lessen interference. They made considerations based on program content as well as with technical matters. Revoked licensee who used his station to campaign for public office, attack personal enemies, express personal views and used defamatory language, WCOT, *FRC., 2nd Annual Report, pp. 152-3*, (1928). Licensee Schaeffer responsible for the content of sponsored programs when candidate Duncan, during and after political campaign used profanity in vitriolic attacks, *Duncan v. US*, 48 F. 2d 128 (Cir. Ct. App. 9th, 1931). In first judicial affirmation of the FRC's right to revoke on the basis of past performance, Dr. John R. Brinkley's license revoked for undesirable programs; goat gland cure for impotence. Personal communication runs counter to definition of Broadcasting in §3(o). Also defined 1927 no censorship §109 clause (applies to §326—*Act of 1934*), *KFKB v. FRC*, 47 F. 2d 670, (DC App. 1931). Dr. Baker's license renewal denied on basis of defamatory attacks, undesirable program content, advertising a cancer cure, *FRC 5th Ann. Report*, p. 78 (1931) & *Baker v. US*, 115 F. 2d 533 (1940). "Battling Bob" Shuler's license renewal denied for attacks on Catholic church, the Jewish religion, Salvation Army, Christian Science, the courts and local Chamber of Commerce. Ct. of App. upheld FRC action as not prior censorship, *Trinity Methodist Church, S. v. FRC*, 62 F. 2d 850 (DC App. 1932).

The following topic areas are alphabetically arranged, and within each topic, in some chronological order.

Advertising. Broadcasters have been sued by purchasers of products, alleging fraud in the ad or claiming the product was allegedly defective. Many courts today generally hold that if the station itself did not make quality representations, product endorsements, or induce the public to buy the product other than the ad itself; the station does not have a duty to investigate an advertiser or to test the products in the advertisement. It makes no difference if the station produced the ad or simply broadcast a supplied ad. However, a station may be held liable for <u>knowingly</u> broadcasting a fraudulent commercial reasonably relied upon by the consumer. Station required to be aware ads for a product under Post Office Fraud Order, *Hammond Calumet Broadcasting*, 2 FCC 321 (1936). Revocation based, in part, on fraudulent advertising, *WGBZ*, 2 FCC 599 (1936).Responsibility of station to investigate accuracy of ads such as exaggerated claims of effectiveness and harmlessness, *Don Lee Broadcasting Co.*, 2 FCC 642 (1936). Local medical societies protested advertising for chiropractic and alcoholism cure as practising medicine without a license. It was station's responsibility to check accuracy of advertising claims, *KMPC*, 6 FCC 729; 7 FCC 449 (1939). A TV station was sued for fraud by a viewer who went to a doctor who had advertised a breast augmentation as "new, safe and painless." The surgery caused her permanent physical and emotional damage and the Ct. held the station could not escape liability if it is a knowingly fraudulent commercial reasonably relied upon, *Bullock v. RKO*, No. 51-82 (Cal. Supr. Ct. 1988). Stations should include an indemnity clause in contracts with advertiser or agency, holding station harmless against any claims resulting from acts of agency or advertiser. Companies may sue alleging defamation arising from comparisons of an advertiser's product with a competing product; trademark infringement from the content of the ad; and copyright claims arising from music or creative presentations used in the ad. (See "Trade—Service Mark—Unfair Competition"). Stations may be held liable for ad whose legality of purpose is questionable. Not permitted to use Mock-up to deceive viewer; substitution due to photographic process is OK, *FTC*, 22 RR 2043; 24 RR 2058; 310 F. 2d 89; 380 US 374; 6 RR 2d 2024 (1965). If station has either actual or constructive knowledge of copyright infringement, but proceeds to advertise illegal copy, without making adequate investigation, held liable for infringement, *Screen Gems-Columbia v. Mark-Fi Records*, 256 F. Supp. 399 (SD NY), 7 RR 2d 2191 (1966). FCC will defer to FTC as per formal memorandum of understanding, whether particular ads are false and misleading, *Reply to Center for Law and Social Policy*, 23 RR 2d 187 (1971); see also *Deceptive Advertising, Public Notice*, 32 FCC 2d 360, 23 RR 2d 1550 (1971). FTC given clear regulatory power over deceptive advertising reaching down to local level, *Magnuson-Moss Act*, PL 93-637, 88 Stat. 2183 (1975). FTC §255.1 requires endorsements reflect honest opinions, findings, beliefs, or experiences of the endorser and may not contain any representations which would be deceptive, or could not be substantiated if made directly by the advertiser. Ads which present experiences of consumers must be comparable to the performance consumers will generally achieve. If actors appear as actual consumers, then must be actual consumers or the ads must disclose as actors. FTC §255.2; any connection between endorser and seller which might materially affect weight or credibility must be disclosed, but payment to an endorser who is an expert or personality need not be disclosed as it would be expected. *Federal Trade Commission, Endorsements and Testimonials in Advertising,* 16 CFR Part 255 (January, 1980). The FTC also regulates broadcast contests. (See "Lotteries"). FTC has agreed to exempt marketers and users of games-of-chance promotions from the necessity of disclosing full prize and odds in broadcast advertising. FTC also no longer requires TV to disclose both aurally and visually. Other businesses not regulated as were grocery stores and gasoline stations, *FTC,* 16 CFR 419 (1983). FTC orders end to Anacin spots as unfair or deceptive. Cannot claim has unique pain-killing formula, is medically proven or established as superior in effectiveness, causes less frequent side effects, or has more active ingredients. Failed to reveal contained aspirin. Order justified by the potential health danger, past record, and wide dissemination in advertising, *American Home Products v. FTC,* 695 F. 2d 681 (3rd Cir. 1983). McNeilab (Tylenol) granted an injunction against American Home Products (Advil) from presenting allegedly false claims superior effectiveness and safety. Statement, "Like Tylenol, Advil doesn't upset my stomach," is more than puffery as Advil was not like Tylenol in terms of adverse effects on stomach, *McNeilab v. American Home Products,* 675 F. Supp. 819 (SDNY 1987). Stations and advertisers who run comparison ads are now more vulnerable to civil suits. The *Trademark Law Revision Act of 1988,* offers some protection for "innocent infringers," but prohibits companies from misrepresenting the qualities or characteristics of their competitors' products. Under prior law, advertisers could not misrepresent their own products. The new law applies to broadcast advertising, but stations must <u>knowingly</u> run problem ads. The law also affects station promotions slogans. Political speeches, consumer or editorial commentaries, parodies and satires are not limited by the law, *The Trademark Law Revision Act of 1988*, (effective Nov. 1989).

TV stations customarily hold ad agencies liable for payment for air time purchased on behalf of clients unless the stations are given prior notice of the agency's nonliability. If an ad agency gives prior notice of nonliability, a station might check the client advertiser's credit, require the advertiser to submit a letter of responsibility, and mail the bill for air time to the advertiser "in care of" the agency. When the client of an ad agency declared bankruptcy stations sought payment from the agency which denied liability. Some of the stations had incorporated the American Association of Advertising Agencies' nonliability clause which exempts an ad agency if nonpayment by client. Others had clauses that made agency solely liable for payment, and if it was insolvent, the client advertiser would be liable. One station stated that the agency was jointly and severally liable for payment in the event of its client's default. The Ct. ruled that industry custom and the stations' adherence to custom were established, and rebutted any presumption of nonliability. The agency had never notified the stations that it was acting solely as the agent of a disclosed principal, and therefore was liable to the stations for the payment of air time on behalf of its client, *Midwest Television v. Scott, Lancaster, Mills & Atha*, 252 Cal. Rptr. 573, 1988). (See "Right of Publicity," "Trade—Service Mark—Unfair Competition").

Alcoholic Beverage Advertising. FCC decried undesirable program materials such as alcoholic beverage advertising and fourteen other undesirable program types in the Blue Book of 1946; also see *Letter to Senator Edwin C. Johnson*, 43 FCC 446 (8/5/49). In 1983, FCC removed formal policy rule relating to alcoholic beverage advertising. FCC said, however, that alcoholic beverage ads raised serious public issue questions even in states where legal and were against the "public interest" where states had made illegal, *Underbrush*

8

Broadcast Policies, 54 RR 2d 1043 (1983).

Oklahoma banned alcoholic beverage advertising on cable TV in the state. State law prohibited cable systems from retransmitting out-of-state signals which contained such ads. Ruled unlawful as Federal Law preempts state regulation of cable TV signal carriage and there is no federal ban on liquor advertising, *Oklahoma Telecasters Association v. Crisp*, 699 F. 2d 490, 53 RR 2d 903 (10th Ct. App. 1983); *Capitol Cities Cable v. Crisp*, 104 S. Ct. 2694, 56 RR 2d 263 (1984). However, a Mississippi statute, banning alcoholic beverage advertising on broadcasting, was upheld by the Supreme Ct. as there was significant State governmental interest in controlling liquor ads within the state. The Ct. distinguished this situation from its' Oklahoma decision by noting that Mississippi did not include in its regulatory scheme out-of-state advertising. Therefore, it was not preempted by federal law and reached no further than necessary for a legitimate State interest, *Mississippi Tax Commission v. Lamar Outdoor Advertising*, 701 F. 2d 314 (5th Cir. 1983); *Dunagin v. Oxford*, 718 F. 2d 738 (5th Cir. 1983). General policy to only use retired sports figures in advertising beer. Soft drink advertisers use active sports personalities. Group petitioned the FTC to limit the advertising of alcoholic beverages as appealed to young people; should have health warnings on print ads; and should require public service announcements to discourage excessive drinking. FTC refused as "no reliable basis on which to conclude that alcohol advertising significantly affects alcohol abuse," (1985). (See "State Control of Interstate Advertising").

All—Channel TV Sets. In 1962, Congress passed a law requiring all TV sets sold in the US to be able to receive both UHF as well as VHF channels, 76 Stat. 150-151. The FCC eliminated the requirement that TV sets receive UHF Channels 70—83 and provided for licensees operating on those channels to transfer to lower frequencies, *UHF-TV Reception Improvements*, 90 FCC 2d 1121, 51 RR 2d 1628

(1982). When a Ct. decision removed the FCC's mandatory TV broadcast signal carriage rules for cable (see "Must—Carry Rule") the FCC required operators to make available equipment (A/B switch) that will allow subscribers to switch between cable and off-air TV reception, *Century Communications v. FCC*, 835 F. 2d 292, Cert. denied, 108 S. Ct. 2014, 64 RR 2d 113 (DC Cir. 1987). (See "Cable Regulation").

Antitrust—Advertising. Sponsorship of a TV program is not the sale of a commodity as defined by the Robinson-Patman Antitrust law, therefore, discounts do not have to be equal for all advertisers, *CBS v. Amana*, (CA 7th); 22 RR 2019; 295 F. 2d 375 (1961). On other grounds the following case achieved the same result. After founding of the American Association of Ad Agencies in 1917, the AAAA was successful in obtaining a standard 15% discount (rebate) for agencies from the media where they placed advertising for their clients. In 1956, a civil antitrust action by the Justice Department resulted in Consent Decrees enjoining the AAAA and other trade associations from preventing media from granting similar commissions directly to advertisers or with advertiser in-house advertising agencies. Among the prohibited practices were the fixing of the amount of compensation allowed or received from clients. The media may make independent judgments of who gets discounts. The FTC then reversed an earlier action which had required the same proportional discounts be given to small advertisers as were given to large advertisers or agencies under the Robinson-Patman Antitrust law. Smaller advertisers are not significantly harmed by a cumulative volume discount rate structure and any such order would raise prices to all advertisers; motivate media to refuse to sell to small advertisers; and would injure competition, *Ambook Enterprises v. Time*, 612 F. 2d 604 (2d Cir. 1979); *Times-Mirror Co. v. FTC*, CCH Trade Regulation Reports, Para. 21, 937 (July 1982). FCC repealed their policy which had barred sales representative firms owning radio or TV license from representing rival station in same market, 87 FCC 2d 668, 49 RR 2d 1705 (1981). However, such an arrangement is limited by Antitrust laws and stations should be aware when sales reps are selling time in combination. The FCC also eliminated its former prohibition against using combination rates and sales practices except if used to fix prices or otherwise restrain competition. Advertisers cannot be forced to purchase time on co-located, commonly-owned radio and TV stations to get time they want on one station, *Second Report and Order*, 59 RR 2d 1500 (1986). (See "Advertising").

Antitrust—Broadcasting. (§313, §314); Besides private law suits by individuals or companies to foster competition under the Antitrust laws (at treble damages if proven), the FCC's statutory mandate, while not requiring it to enforce the Antitrust laws directly, mandates that they must deny licenses if violation occurs and may consider any potential violation. The FCC has found an association of station's setting rates is price-fixing and violation of Antitrust law, *US v. Phil. Radio & TV Broadcaster's Assoc.* (ED Pa.), 18 RR 2009 (1958). Antitrust Consent Decree signed and NBC gives up Philadelphia stations acquired to avoid losing all licenses if it had lost, *US v. RCA* (ED Pa.), 17 RR 764 (1959). Conspiracy to require buyers to take exhibition rights to less desirable programs to get desirable series is a tying arrangement called block-booking. Block booking sales of motion pictures to TV is a violation of Antitrust laws, *US v. Loew's*, 24 RR 2032; 371 US 38 (1962). Requiring taking other, less desirable programs to get desirable series of <u>Bonanza</u> and <u>High Chaparral</u> is block-booking. The <u>per se</u> nature of the violation, if proven, is illegal and affected producers who were in the target area of potential injury, *Aurora Enterprises v. NBC*, 524 F. Supp. 655; 688 F. 2d 689; 52 RR 2d 693 (1982). After 10 years of litigation and three previous Ct. decisions, including a US Supreme Ct. decision, Ct. has affirmed dismissal of CBS's claim that the blanket licensing of copyrighted music for <u>networks</u> by ASCAP and BMI violates federal Antitrust law.

(See "Copyright—Performance Rights to Music"). A blanket license, usually for one year, permits a licensee to use any music controlled by a performing rights society as often as desired for either a flat sum or a percentage of user's revenue. CBS contended the agreement unreasonably restrained trade. The Supreme Ct. held that blanket license was not a per se violation of the *Sherman Antitrust Act* and there was no proof a restraint of competition. Under terms of a 1950 consent degree, ASCAP and BMI get only non-exclusive licensing rights from member-composers and may not restrict or interfere with those members right to issue directly to any user a per-program non-exclusive performing rights license. ABC asked ASCAP, rather than each composer, for a per-program license quote. ASCAP feared that ABC would then drop its blanket license and would use BMI music which might cause composers and publishers to switch from ASCAP to BMI licensing. ASCAP resisted giving a per-program quote and told network to get each per-program license itself from each composer. Under the 1950 Consent Decree a music user is allowed to petition the Fed. District Ct. in New York to judicially fix a reasonable fee if dissatisfied. ABC petitioned the Ct. to fix a reasonable per-program license fee through ASCAP. ASCAP countered with a motion to modify the Consent Decree to relieve ASCAP of the obligation to issue per-program licenses to TV networks holding blanket licenses from their competitor, BMI. The Ct. denied ASCAP's request on the assumption that networks, as ASCAP feared, would take a blanket license from one performing rights society but not both, provided per-program licenses were available. This would foster competition and lower prices to sell blanket licenses which is the purpose of Antitrust laws and Consent Decrees. BMI does not have to provide for judicial rate-setting in its Consent Decree, but must price per-program and blanket licenses so there is a realistic choice between them, *United States v. ASCAP*, 586 F. Supp. 727 (SDNY 1984). However, the Ct. determined that the feasibility of getting a direct license from each composer was established by evidence refuting allegations of barriers to direct licensing. If CBS makes the effort and has difficulty, only then would it be entitled to obtain a per-program license, see *Broadcast Music v. CBS*, 441 US 1 (1979); 620 F.2d 930 (2d Cir. 1980). Initially Ct. ruled that blanket licenses used by ASCAP and BMI with local TV stations violated Antitrust law. Reversed on appeal. Television producers could acquire music performance rights, *Copyright Act* §106(4), from composers at the same time the producers acquire synchronization rights and then pass on cost. (Synchronization rights are for use of music used with visual images on a soundtrack of a film or videotape which is a subset of the larger category of reproduction rights), *Copyright Act* §106(1). Synchronization rights are customarily obtained from the Harry Fox Agency. Reasonable source licensing availability was reason to allow the blanket license in the case of networks and the same reasoning was applied to local stations as no evidence to show that local stations could not get performance licenses directly from copyright owners and no evidence that per-program license fees were too costly, *Buffalo Broadcasting Co., v. ASCAP*, 546 F. Supp. 274 (SDNY 1982); 744 F. 2d 917 (2d Cir. 1984), Cert. denied. A small publisher filed a class action suit against ABC for using 19 seconds of one of their songs once as background to an assemblage of film clips in a sports feature. ABC argued covered by the blanket license, but publisher argued needed separate synchronization license. Ct. held there was an issue to adjudicate, but no final decision reported to date so likely settled, *Angel Music v. ABC Sports*, 631 F. Supp. 429 (SDNY 1986). Twenty-six independent producers sued ABC, NBC and CBS for Antitrust, First Amendment and Civil Rights violations. Charged that in-house documentary production froze independents out of market, monopolized, and denied access. Ct. dismissed, technically, as did not constitute State action; industry defies traditional antitrust analysis; percentage of market insufficient for networks to control prices or exclude competition; affiliates may take or reject product. If proof that independents can produce at one-half cost and as high a quality may be inter-network conspiracy, but needed further proof, *Levitch v. CBS*, 495 F. Supp. 649 (SDNY 1980); Upheld, 697 F. 2d 495 (2d Cir. 1983). Warner Amex CUBE, Columbus, Ohio sought order to allow cablecast of Ohio State Football games. NCAA had sold exclusive rights to ABC, but previous negotiations by Warner and threat of antitrust suit had allowed ten earlier sold-out games to be carried. ABC then refused to give up exclusivity on games not sold out and Warner filed second antitrust suit. Ruled must show irreparable harm as inadequacy of money damages for injunction. Warner could still carry sold-out games and buy tickets of those games not sold out to obtain coverage. Warner did buy out seats to show games, *Warner Amex v. ABC*, 499 F. Supp. 537 (SD Ohio 1980).

Since 1952, the National Association of Broadcasters trade association had a Code of Good Practices to which all members had to adhere. The Justice Dept. challenged Code's various standards. The multiple product standard prohibited the advertising of two or more products or services in a single commercial (piggy-back) if the spot was less than 60 seconds. Time standards limited the amount of commercial material to be broadcast each hour to 9 minutes per hour in prime time, plus minute for promotional announcements, and 16 minutes at all other times. Independent stations were allowed more time and children's programs were limited as to commercial time allowed. Standards also limited the number of consecutive interruptions of the program and announcements per interruption (clutter). Held the multiple product standard was a <u>per se</u> violation of §1 of the *Sherman Antitrust Act*, and ordered a trial on the time and program interruption standards. The NAB ceased enforcing the code (treble damages if they had continued and were found violating Antitrust) and appealed. A Consent Decree was agreed upon halting use of a general industry code and networks and stations were urged to adopt their own independent policies, *US v. NAB*, 51 RR 2d 175, 536 F. Supp. 149, 553 F. Supp. 621

(DC 1982). Martin Fine appeared from 1978 to 1982 on numerous game shows and won $11,000+. In 1982, he applied to become a contestant on Joker's Wild but was disqualified for previous game show appearances. NBC limits contestants to three game shows a lifetime; ABC to once in the past 12 months or twice within the past five years; and CBS to one show in the past 12 months or two shows in a lifetime. Barry and Enright, producers of Joker's Wild limited to one show within 12 months or two shows in past 10 years. Fine, a law student, sued. Held that Fine could not prove that limitations were group boycott which is a per se violation of §1 of the *Sherman Antitrust Act*. There was no concerted effort at a single market level and the Ct. noted the restrictions were developed partially in response to the 1950's quiz scandals; to prevent familiarity with selection and taping procedures, and the restrictions were not identical and were adopted at different times, *Fine v. Barry and Enright Productions*, 731 F. 2d 1394 (9th Cir. 1984). (See "Astrology," "Copyright—Performance Rights to Music," "Network Regulation," "Network Service Rights," "Comparative Qualifications," "First Amendment Rights for Broadcasting," "Clipping," "RKO Revocation").

Antitrust—Cable. The planned 1981 operation of a new pay cable company, Premiere, by Columbia, MCA, Paramount, 20th Century-Fox and Getty Oil was determined to constitute price-fixing and group boycott violating §1, *Sherman Antitrust Act*. Reasonable likelihood Premier was concerted action to make films available only to their own corporations thereby refusing to deal with, and to boycott, other services, thereby restraining competition, *U.S. v. Columbia*, 507 F. Supp. 412 (SDNY 1980). Case of wide-ranging effect on City Home Rule struck down city ordinances placing a permanent geographical limitation on cable system expansion. City can be held liable for violation of Antitrust law in restraint of trade by refusing to allow competition between cable companies. Exercising pervasive controls would violate First

Amendment and lose claim of antitrust exemption. More than one cable company can be on same poles without adversely affecting public ways, *Community Communications v. City of Boulder*, 630 F. 2d 704 (10th Cir. 1980); 496 F. Supp. 823 (D. Colo. 1980); 70 L. Ed. 2d 810, 50 RR 2d 1183 (Supr. Ct. 1981). In a case distinguished from the above *City of Boulder*, held that the State of Kentucky had granted cities the authority to issue franchises, while Colorado had a neutral position. Thus, Kentucky cities are immune from Antitrust law as approved State action, *Hopkinsville Cable v. Pennyroyal Cablevision*, 562 F. Supp. 543, 54 RR 2d 385 (WD Kentucky 1982). The usual practice in awarding a cable franchise is to evaluate competing companies and give to the most qualified applicant. In Houston the major told five local companies to divide the city among each other. New franchise applicant, Affiliated, was told to work with the five other entities which they chose not to do and filed Antitrust suit. The jury found the City of Houston, the mayor, and Gulf Coast TV had participating in a conspiracy in unreasonable restraint of trade and awarded $2.1 million to Affiliated. Held no legitimate city purpose overrode the "public interest" in competition. The mayor was found to have qualified immunity, in that he had not violated a clearly established law, *Affiliated Capital v. City of Houston*, 735 F. 2d 1555 (5th Cir. 1984).

From 1973 to 1978, the Directors Guild waived its requirement that members work only for signatories of Guild Agreement to enable HBO and other pay channels to become established. In 1978, the Guild sought a collective bargaining agreement from HBO, but were refused. Guild ordered members not to work for HBO. HBO sued alleging the Guild members were independent contractors and Guild's order was an illegal restraint of trade. Broad range of combined labor activity is exempt if union is able to establish acts are in self-interest and separate from non-labor group. For example, Actor's Equity upheld in licensing agents and regulating their fees, (101 S. Ct. 2102 (1982). Guild was also held exempt from Antitrust laws and HBO had not shown violation or loss or damage to its business, *Home Box Office, v. Directors Guild*, 531 F. Supp. 578 (1982); 708 F. 2d 95 (2nd Cir. 1983). In 1985, Rainbow Service Company and MGM/UA entered into a ten year contract in which Rainbow paid $45 million for cable rights to most of MGM library of films. Turner Broadcasting System then bought MGM/UA, sold off everything but $700 million dollar library for syndication and cable use on "TNT" which is 75% MGM product. Rainbow sued MGM/UA for breach of contract and Turner for antitrust violations. Settled for large cash amount; terminated MGM-Rainbow contract, (1985). In 1981, TCI Cablevision refused to bid for refranchise of Jefferson City, MO which it had acquired and managed from 1973, arguing it had a First Amendment right to continue to provide cable service. The City granted the franchise to Central Telecommunications, but the mayor vetoed and subsequently cast a tie-breaking vote in favor of TCI even though proposal provided fewer viewing channels and inferior picture quality at a higher monthly rate. Central sued TCI, and the jury held that TCI had conspired with the mayor and other officials to retain its franchise in violation of §1 of the *Sherman Act*; had pursued an illegal anti-competitive action to retain its monopoly in violation of §2; and that TCI tortiously interfered with Central's business expectancy in violation of state law. Antitrust law permits the trebling of damages so the Ct. entered judgment for $32.4 million on the antitrust claims or $35.8 million on the state law claim, aff'd, Cert. denied, *Central Telecommunications v. TCI Cablevision*, 800 F. 2d 711 (8th Cir. 1986). See "Cable Regulation").

Antitrust—Rights Sports. In 1952, the NCAA adopted by majority vote a plan that declared the NCAA was the exclusive representative of all member schools for the purpose of selling TV rights to football games. Colleges were not permitted to make their own contracts with networks or individual stations. NCAA rules also limited how many times on

TV and amount of money from TV. Large football schools formed the College Football Association and in 1981, negotiated a lucrative offer from NBC while the NCAA was negotiating with ABC, CBS and Turner. NCAA made public statements that violation of their rules would be dealt with and the Universities of Georgia and Oklahoma obtained temporary injunction barring NCAA from disciplinary action. CFA members opted out of NBC contract. Upheld by Supreme Ct. that since the vast majority of NCAA schools do not play football or play on TV and yet can vote to restrict the TV rights of the minority and obtain a substantially larger portion of TV money then they deserve, the NCAA has fixed prices and restricted the output of its members. These practices are illegal <u>per se</u> under Antitrust law. The Ct. also held the plan was illegal under the rule of reason and had no redeeming pro-competitive benefits, *Board of Regents of University of Oklahoma v. NCAA*, 546 F. Supp. 1276 (1982); 707 F. 2d 1147 (10th Cir. 1983); 104 S. Ct. 1268 (1984). In 1990, Notre Dame became the first single college or university to sign its own national broadcast network deal with NBC for all its 1991-95 home games for $30 million. CFA then had to renegotiate its 1991-95 contract with ABC-ESPN from $350 to $300 million. Professional basketball, baseball and hockey are exempt from some provisions of Antitrust law and are permitted to sell TV rights as single package, unlike college sports as noted above. Therefore, the teams may also "blackout" home coverage of games to keep ticket sales high. A TV station 96 miles from Miami was to carry Dolphin games, outside 75—mile radius of NFL rule. However, their new powerful transmitter would penetrate 75—mile limit and Dolphins refused TV coverage. Ruled that "black-out rule" can be based on signal penetration, rather than station location and the station was legally denied carriage, *WTWV v. NFL and Miami Dolphins*, 678 F. 2d 142 (11th Cir. 1982). Wichita State won injunction against KWKN preventing them from broadcasting away games in Wichita area as exclusive rights given by State to KAKZ. KWKN tried to get away games by signing contracts with the schools with which Wichita State was to play, but Ct. ruled State's opponents had no right to broadcast their games in Wichita and therefore could not sell rights in that community, *Wichita State University v. Tri-City Broadcasting, District Ct. of Sedgwick County, Kansas*, Case No. 81-C-130 (1981). Dispute over WTBS "SuperStation's" right to broadcast <u>NCAA Football</u> arose when NCAA altered exclusive affiliation with ABC to offering two networks rights and offered cable or pay series of football on a trial basis. In 1982, NCAA signed with Turner for two-year supplemental series. Turner did not operate cable or pay system, but WTBS on-air station is "SuperStation," over satellite, to cable systems. ABC affiliate in Atlanta and ABC sued on basis that they had contract with NCAA with understanding supplemental series would be carried on cable or pay only; not conventional over-the-air station. CBS contract with NCAA did carry provision allowing one over-the-air station to carry series but this was added after contract signed with Turner. ABC had attempted to obtain specific provision prohibiting any over-the-air coverage for supplemental series. However, ABC had been dilatory in seeking relief; Turner had substantially changed its position in reliance on its NCAA contract; schools in supplemental series would be harmed, therefore, TBS could carry 1982 games, but were enjoined broadcasting games in 1983 through 1985. To alleviate damage to WSB, NCAA ordered to permit broadcast of two University of Georgia and two Georgia Tech games in addition to regular 1982 games to be carried by ABC, *Cox Broadcasting v. NCAA*, C-89120 (Georgia Superior Ct. 1982). Turner, who owns both Atlanta Braves and WTBS wished to broadcast <u>National League Baseball Championship</u> games in which Atlanta Braves were playing under exception to ABC's rights which grants each club participating in series the right to permit its local flagship station to broadcast series in the team's home market. Ruled TBS would damage ABC as its signal is not just in home market, but reached 20+ million homes in US.

VERNON REGIONAL
JUNIOR COLLEGE LIBRARY

Injunction granted, *ABC Sports v. Atlanta National League Baseball Club,* C-82-6104 (SDNY 1982). Several NY sports teams entered into exclusive production and distribution contracts with Cablevision. In 1979, Cablevision created a subsidiary, SportsChannel, as a premium cable TV service. Cablevision later acquired a non-exclusive franchise cable company which operated in Huntington, Long Island. The other cable company in the same community, HTVC, approached some of the sports teams which had licensed rights in exclusive arrangement with Cablevision. Cablevision refused to allow HTVC the right to carry SportsChannel, while doing so itself. The Ct. held that the team's granting Cablevision exclusive rights was at most an indirect cause of alleged injury and HTVC did not have standing to assert antitrust violations against them. HTVC had not attempted to obtain exclusive metro-wide rights as granted Cablevision, *Nishimura v. Dolan,* 599 F. Supp. 484 (EDNY 1984).

Ascertainment of Community Needs. FCC required licensees to conduct a regular assessment of the problems and needs affecting their community. The broadcaster then was to construct an annual specific list of needs and document their specific programming which dealt with those needs. A license grant was refused on the basis of failure to ascertain or survey community needs and Ct. ruled FCC has statutory authority to require stations to do a community survey to determine those needs, *Suburban,* 112 US App DC 247, 302 F. 2d 191, 371 US 821, 83 S. Ct 37, Cert. denied; 20 RR 951 (1961—62). Rather extensive guidelines for the survey were provided by the FCC, *Primer on Ascertainment of Community Problems* (1971); revised, 74 FCC 942, 39 FR 32288, (1974). In 1975, added noncommercial stations. Licensees were then relieved of the obligation to provide a description and explanation of the methodology as method was not the FCC's concern. Public Service Announcements (PSA's) were allowed to help fulfill the issues/programs list requirement. The FCC earlier had turned down a proposal to impose specific obligations on broadcasters to present PSA's, but encouraged their airing, *Report and Order*, (1980). In 1981, the FCC announced that since stations for years had performed at levels considerably higher than those required by the rules the FCC was eliminating the complex, formal ascertainment requirement. Their random long form audit of programming logs was also eliminated. The formalized ascertainment requirements gave way to procedures requiring that all significant segments of a community are contacted regarding problems, needs and issues and a list setting forth five to ten issues that the station covered during the year had to be maintained annually in the public file, however, licensees could go beyond the maximum of ten issues. Licensees could be asked upon renewal what percentage of such programming they had aired, *Federal Communications Commission, Deregulation of Radio*, 84 FCC 2d 968, 49 RR 2d 1 (effective April 3, 1981); 53 RR 2d 805; 53 RR 2d 1371; aff'd, 706 F. 2d 1224, 53 RR 2d 1501; 707 F. 2d 1413, 53 RR 2d 1371; 719 F. 2d 407, 54 RR 2d 811, 1151 (DC Cir. 1983); *Deregulation of Commercial Television*, 98 FCC 2d 1076, 56 RR 2d 1005 (1984); 60 RR 2d 526 (1986). Short-term renewal, KGGM, Albuquerque for not meeting needs of Latin-American audience, *New Mexico Broadcasting*, 50 RR 2d 340 (1982). The FCC eliminated noncommercial Radio-TV formal ascertainment guidelines and program log requirements, 98 FCC 2d 746, 56 RR 2d 1157 (1984). Station technical logs still required (§73:1820). The Ct. of Appeals then ruled that the FCC's minimal public file requirement (decision did not involve TV stations) of an illustrative issues list showing community issues addressed by the station's programming and giving a brief description of the manner in which the issues were treated, was arbitrary and capricious. Since the FCC relies, in part, on public participation in discharging its regulatory responsibilities, the scarcity of information undercut the FCC's own regulatory policies, *Office of Communication of the United Church of Christ v. FCC*, 779 F. 2d 702 (DC Cir. 1985), 59 RR 2d 895 (US App. DCC 1986). Responding (in the radio context), the FCC amended the issues/program list rule. Radio licensees, like TV, must now prepare such lists on a quarterly basis rather than annually for inclusion in the public file, *Programming and Commercialization Policies (Reconsideration)*, 60 RR 2d 526 (1986); *Issues-Programs List for Public Broadcasting Licensees*, 64 RR 2d 667 (1988). Upheld replacing program logging requirements with quarterly lists of "issue-oriented" programming, *Action for Children's Television v. FCC*, 821 F. 2d 741, 63 RR 2d 440 (US App. DC 1987). (See "Public File," "Promise v. Performance")

Astrology. Advice programs are undesirable, if point-to-point communication. Astrology programs for which claims of accuracy are made and designed to take advantage of the credulity of listeners are contrary to "public interest." *Scroggin v. FCC*, 1 FCC 194 (1935). Advice programs which mislead public, objectionable, and not in the "public interest." *Broadcasting Corp.*, 4 FCC 125 (1937). Astrology advertisements and similar material were later controlled by the NAB Code. This raised an antitrust problem. NBC, as well as other networks, had policy of following NAB Code, including banning non-news material presented for purpose of fostering belief in astrology. WFMY-TV, NBC and NAB sued by astrological forecasting service for antitrust conspiracy to limit access for a program featuring forecasts. Held sufficient cause of action on theory of State action and First Amendment rights. Settled out of Ct., *Mark v. NBC*, 25 RR 2d 2083, 468 F. 2d 66 (Cal. 1972); *letter*, 34 FCC 2d 434 (1972); *Gemini v WFMY*, 70 F. Supp. 559 (MD NC 1979). With NAB Code now defunct, (see "Antitrust—Broadcasting") FCC might have been construed to have stronger interest. FCC thus eliminated policy on advice programs, §73:4030, leaving civil remedies and the FTC to determine, *Underbrush Broadcast Policies*, 54 RR 2d 1043 (1983).

Balanced Program Structure. The *FRC's 2nd Annual Report* noted that program service would be taken into account in the granting or withholding of a license, p. 161 (1928); Stations were required to carry diverse and balanced programming to serve the tastes, needs, and desires of the general public, *Great Lakes v. FRC* (D. 4900, 1928). Chicago station proposed to program only for minority groups; FCC stated must program to all groups in service area, *Essaness Assoc.*, 25 RR 479 (1963). Commercial TV stations were obligated to carry programs which fulfill educational needs whether or not noncommercial broadcasting stations exist in the community of license, *UHF Channel Assignment*, 2 FCC 2d 527, 6 RR 2d 1643 (1966). The FCC later stated that while licensees were required to offer programming responsive to public issues each station could take into account the services provided by other radio stations in the community rather than providing something for everyone, *Public Notice*, 44 FCC 2d 985, 29 RR 2d 469 (1974). A licensee has no obligation to divide its coverage of community problems according to the racial, ethnic or religious composition of the community. The licensee can rely on general programming to meet the specific needs of minority audiences, *Georgia Board of Education*, 70 FCC 2d 948, 44 RR 2d 1599 (1979). (See "Fairness Doctrine").

Broadcasting Re-creation. Re-creating an event is not "rebroadcasting" although it may be violation of another's property rights which are not jurisdiction of FCC, *Newton*, 2 FCC 281 (1936). When exclusive rights to Louis-Farr fight were sold to others (NBC) it is illegal to use information by paraphrase or original text for up-to-the-minute reports, *20th Cent. Sporting Club v. Transradio*, 300 NYS 159 (1937). Summary of race transmitted by phone to rival station by staff member listening to station which bought rights to race; re-created at station, is permitted as became part of history upon happening, *Loeb v. Turner*, 9 RR 2018 (1953). May do re-creation if news summaries and at end of each round, *Int. Boxing v. Wodaam*, 9 RR 2050 (1953). Re-creations not re-broadcasts says FCC, McClendon sues Major Leagues for stopping his re-creations—settled out of Ct., *Liberty Broadcasting System v. National League Baseball*, 7 RR 2164 (1952); *Trinity*, 10 RR 279 (1954). Right to broadcast fight Summaries' from Press Association as news, *WOR, WINS, WOV, Broadcasting*, (8/25/58, p. 60.) (See "Rebroadcasting").

Broadcasting Telephone Conversations. (§73:1206); The FCC requires licensees to notify anyone of their intention to broadcast their telephone conversation prior to recording and/or broadcasting the conversation. This is two-party consent. The party can be presumed to be aware if an employee or reporter employed by the station or from the circumstances of the conversation that it will be broadcast, (a call-in show). The notification must be at the beginning of the broadcast, or as part of, the recorded portion of any call, *Recordings of Telephone Conversations*, 61 RR 2d 1658 (1987), 65 RR 2d 444 (1988). The FCC has also held that broadcasting the conversation and then asking permission is unacceptable. One way to notify the other party is to use a beeptone on the phone line (§64:501). (See "Secret Recording").

Cable Regulation. (Part §76, FCC Rules); Cable TV began around 1949, when there was a TV license "freeze" by the FCC to redraw their flawed allocation scheme introducing UHF TV. Cable brought TV to communities that did not have stations or had limited number. At first the FCC refused to regulate cable, leaving it to cities to contract franchise agreements directly with cable operators. Then cable systems began to import distant TV signals via microwave over state lines which competed with local TV stations in their markets. The FCC decided to assert jurisdiction over cable, *Carter Mountain Transmission Corp.*, 32 FCC 459 (1962), aff'd, 321 F 2d 359 (DC Cir. 1963), Cert. denied, 371 US 951 (1964). Starting in 1965, the FCC required all cable systems to carry all local stations, (Must—Carry Rule), then effectively stopped cable growth by prohibiting distant TV signal importation into the top one hundred markets, *Midwest TV v. Southwestern Cable*, 88 S. Ct. 1994; 392 US 157; 13 RR 2d 2045 (1968). Satellite distributed subscription services (HBO) began in 1975, when the FCC was prevented from restricting pay cable programming or barring cablecasters from showing channels where programs were presented for a direct charge, *Home Box Office v. FCC*, 567 F. 2d 9 (DC App. 1977), 40 RR 2d 283, 434 US 829, Cert. denied (1978). Dissatisfaction with the pro-broadcast stance of the FCC resulted in the Supreme Ct. holding the FCC did not have statutory authority to adopt cable TV public channel access rules which it had adopted in 1976. These rules required a system with 3,500 or more subscribers to make as many as three channels, (public, educational, governmental) [PEG] available to the general public. In *Southwestern*, the Ct. held that access rules transferred control of the content of access channels from cable operators to the public. §3(h) of the *Communications Act* prohibits the FCC from treating persons engaged in broadcasting as common carriers (one who provides communications facilities to all persons who wish to use them to communicate messages of their own design and choosing). Access rules might have violated the due process clause of the 5th Amendment by exposing cable operators to criminal prosecution for offensive broadcasts by access users over which operators had no control, *FCC v. Midwest Video*, 99 S. Ct. 1435; 45 RR 2d 581 (1978). However, cities were then allowed to require PEG access channels in their franchise bid requirements. Bases of regulation were that cable requires right-of-way, is monopolistic and therefore must abide by government regulations. Regulation was content neutral as all individuals had access to channels on first-come first-served basis. Rules did limit cable operators' editorial control but had substantial government purpose and only minimally interfered with free expression. Requirement to serve all religious institutions and parochial schools served valid secular purpose by promoting broad public access. Reasonable fees could be charged, *Berkshire Cablevision v. Burke*, 571 F. Supp. 976 (DRI 1983). The transmission of pay TV programs of interest to the general public constitutes "broadcasting" even though one cannot view without paying a fee for special equipment, (See "Subscription TV"), *Orth-O-Vision, Inc., v. Home Box Office*, et. al., 46 RR 2d 628 (SDNY, 1979); therefore FCC jurisdiction supersedes local Cable TV Commission, *NY Cable TV Comm. v. FCC*, 669 F.2d 58 (2d Cir. 1982). Cable systems were then allowed to carry as many distant signals as desired (if escalating scaled copyright fee paid) "which will foster competition and add diversity as does not affect materially the quantity of local programming." At this time, cable systems were still required to carry local signals as well, *Cable Television Syndicated Program Exclusivity Rules*, 45 Federal Register 60186 (Sept. 1980); upheld, *Malrite v. FCC*, 652 F. 2d 1140, 49 RR 2d 1127 (2d Cir. 1981). Networks permitted to own cable systems if not in same market as stations and aggregate number of subscribers less than one-half of one percent of total of US subscribers, *CBS*, 87 FCC 2d 587, 49 RR 2d 1680 (1981). In a case where an FCC rule conflicts with a provision of a franchise agreement between a city and a cable operator the appropriate conduct for a District Ct. is to recognize the primary jurisdiction of the FCC and stay proceeding pending resolution of validity by the agency, *City of Peoria v. GECCO v. FCC*, 690 F. 2d 116, 52 RR 2d 787 (1982). FCC expresses intention to use tax certificate authority, to promote additional minority ownership in the cable field, 52 RR 2d 1469 (1982); 710 F. 2d 492, 53 RR 2d 1711 (8th Cir. 1983). (See "Sale or Transfer of License"). FCC requires that cable systems "black-out" network programming broadcast by a distant station that is being broadcast by a local station, (§76.67). Sports Programming Rules require cable to black-out live local sporting events if all of the tickets are not sold and the event is not being televised by a local broadcast station. Teams might refuse to allow broadcast of sporting events generally if not protected from the impact of local broadcasting on attendance, *In the Matter of Cable TV Syndicated Program Exclusivity and Carriage of Sports Telecasts*, 56 RR 2d 625 (1984). FCC fined cable system $2,000 for not blacking out four NBA and one NHL game, *In re National Basketball Association-Storer*, CSC-344 (1985). Restaurant owners' use of satellite dish to intercept transmission of St. Louis Cardinals football games where blacked out violated *Copyright Act*, *National Football League v. McBee & Bruno's*, 792 F. 2d 726 (8th Cir. 1986). Must—Carry Rules were still supported by FCC at this time; for example, sole empty channel must go to local religious station even if subscribers uninterested. Deleting must—carry signal when system saturated was at operator's own risk, *New Milford Cablevision*, 52 RR 2d 617 (1982); *Rockland Cable*, 53 RR 2d 253; *KSDK*, 53 RR 2d 283 (1983). However, in 1985, a federal court found that "Must—Carry Rules" violated the First Amendment editorial discretion rights of cable operators and programmers but apparently left open the possibility that more limited rules might pass constitutional muster, *Quincy Cable TV v. FCC*, 768 F. 2d 1434, 58 RR 2d 977 (DC Cir. 1985). In 1986, the FCC released new Must—Carry Rules, requiring cable systems which would drop local channels to supply an A/B switch and perform cable consumer education on how to reactivate their antennas, 61 RR 2d 792 (1986). But, Ct. again found the new rules still violated the First Amendment for cable operators and felt that cable operators would probably not drop local channels, *Century Communications v. FCC*, 835 F. 2d 292, Cert. denied, 108 S. Ct. 2014, 64 RR 2d 113 (DC Cir. 1987). Ct., however, allowed FCC to mandate an A/B switch and cable consumer education requirements if local channels not carried. (See "All—Channel TV Sets").

Broadcasters competition with cable, allied with producers for over-the-air programming, moved from attempting to obtain FCC control to Copyright control and First Amendment challenges. (See "Syndicated Exclusivity," "Antitrust—Cable")

In an effort to overcome uncertainty and inconsistency, Congress passed a national policy for cable television after long negotiations between the National League of Cities and the National Cable Television Association. However, the passage of the *The Cable Communications Act of 1984,* did not settle the major constitutional issues in cable. The *Cable Act* affirmed the authority of municipalities to award exclusive franchises to cable operators, and made cable TV the only mass medium required to provide access to its facilities by any member of the public through PEG channels. The statute limits the franchise fee that municipalities may obtain to 5% of gross annual revenues and ended local regulation of basic cable rates two years later. Regulation by cities of other than basic services was preempted. The law bans co-located cable-broadcast TV cross-ownerships and prevents telephone companies from entering cable business in their service areas unless rural and not likely to be served by cable operators, 58 RR 2d 1 (1985). Law also prohibits treatment of cable as common carrier. Procedures for renewing cable franchises are also set forth. There is no ban on newspaper ownership, *Cable Communications Policy Act of 1984;* 98 Stat. 2779 (1984). Congress, under complaints from constituents and cities is reconsidering cable regulation.

A case, striking down all or parts of the 1984 cable act, on the basis of constitutionality has yet to be heard by the Supreme Ct. However, the Supreme Ct. ruled that Cable operators had First Amendment rights. With this, lower Cts. have begun to nibble at the law by application of the First Amendment to cable regulation by cities. The First Amendment does not allow the State (government) to pass any law which restricts freedom of expression. A Los Angeles ordinance establishing an exclusive cable franchise area was found to violate the First Amendment, even though the Ct. recognized the *Cable Communications Act of 1984* supported a franchising model similar to that utilized by LA, *Preferred Communications v. City of Los Angeles,* 754 F. 2d 1396 (9th Cir., 1985). A number of District Courts have been deciding that there is no substantial governmental interest in support of a policy of granting only a single cable franchise to serve the community. Cts. have been viewing the assertion that cable as a natural monopoly justifies exclusive franchising policy as irrelevant to the First Amendment since economic efficiency and consumer welfare may not override constitutional imperatives, *Group W v. City of Santa Cruz*, 63 RR 2d 1656 (ND Calif. 1987). The *Cable Act* grandfathered cities who had PEG requirements. A District Ct. declared a new franchise agreement requiring an exclusive franchise, three educational and two governmental access channels, universal service (wiring entire city, not just selected areas) and "state-of-the-art" installation requirements unconstitutional. Violates the First Amendment rights of the cable operator to have to carry material by speakers that they might choose not to present, thereby dampening the vigor and limits the variety of public debate and intrudes into the cable operator's editorial functions. On ruling in a cross-motion the Ct. held the franchise fees levied unconstitutional under the First Amendment. The fee requested was the maximum amount permissible under the *Cable Act*. Ct. also invalidated post construction and performance bonds, *Century Federal, Inc. v. City of Palo Alto*, 63 RR 2d 1736 (1987); 65 RR 2d 875 (ND Ca. 1988). The Supreme Ct. ruled FCC authority preempts local franchise authorities from imposing more stringent technical standards governing the quality of cable signals than those of the FCC, *City of New York v. FCC*, 108 S. Ct. 1637, 64 RR 2d 1423 (1988). A case which might relieve some cities of the constitutional attack which has been leveled at their control is a ruling that arm's length negotiations, and the contract (franchise) which specified these negotiations was "valid, binding and of full force and effect." Such activity was a waiver of constitutional and statutory challenges to the fee and public access provisions of the franchise agreement. The argument that the evolving body of case law concerning the First Amendment standards applicable to cable should be considered was not dealt with by the Ct., *Erie*

Telecommunications v. City of Erie, 853 F. 2d 1084, 65 RR 2d 1 (3rd Cir. 1988).

Cable—Pay Signal Piracy. (§705); *Communications Act* prohibits unauthorized interception of broadcasts unless for the use of the general public. Ct.'s have ruled that Pay-TV is broadcast only for use of paying subscribers; that to determine otherwise would threaten economic vitality; and violates FCC consumer protection policy in investment in equipment by public, *Chartwell v. Westbrook*, 637 F. 2d 459 (6th Cir., Dec. 1980); *National Subscription TV v. S. & H TV*, 644 F.2d 820 (9th Cir., May 1981); *FCC Public Notice, Manufacturers and Sellers of Non-Approved Subscription TV Decoders are Cautioned* (August 15, 1980); *AT&C v. Western Techtronics*, 51 RR d 85 (1982); *Hoosier Home Theatre (TVQ) v. Adkins*, 595 F. Supp. 389 (SD Ind. 1984). Manufacture and sale of equipment allowing unauthorized interception of Multipoint Distribution Service of Pay-TV is violation of §605 of *Communications Act* and permanent injunction granted, *Home Box Office v. Advanced Consumer Technology*, 549 F. Supp. 14 (SDNY 1981); *American Television and Communications v. Manning*, 651 P. 2d 440 (Colo. App. 1982); *American TV and Communications v. Western Techtronics*, 529 F. Supp. 617 (D. Colo. 1982). More than $1 million in damages awarded Cablevision Systems in company's action against supplier of decoders, descramblers, converters and other devices used to intercept Cablevision's services. Previous injunction ignored and sales continued. This was largest damages granted under FCC Act to that date, *Cablevision Systems v. Annasonic* (1984). Using external visual and electronic inspection of antenna to determine if homeowner is pirating the signal is no violation of First Amendment right of privacy, *Movie Systems, Inc., v. Heller*, 52 RR 2d 1483 (D. Minn. 1982); 710 F. 2d 492, 53 RR 2d 1711; *Movie Systems v. MAD*, 54 RR 2d 932 (8th Cir. 1983).

Congress amended §705 of the *Communications Act*, to allow owners of backyard satellite dishes to legally receive unscrambled TV signals. Program suppliers must choose between negotiating agreements with representatives of the "backyard" home dish industry to receive compensation for signal use or scramble their signals. The FCC issued reports that the number of services with scrambled signals has increased; a greater number of discounted program packages have been made available to home dish owners by programmers, cable operators and third-party packagers at prices comparable to and, in some instances, less than prices charged to cable subscribers. Signal piracy, however, remains "the biggest single problem facing the industry today," and recommended increasing the penalties for signal theft. FCC decides to rely on free market forces to resolve continuing complaints of home dish owners, *Scrambling of Satellite TV Signals (Second Report)*, 64 RR 2d 910 (1988). There are severe penalties for unauthorized reception of scrambled signals through the use of "blackboxes" for commercial or private gain. Copyright holders may bring civil actions seeking injunctive relief to restrain violation of the statute with damages of up to $50,000 for willful violation, *Cable Communications Policy Act of 1984.* A motel owner intercepted, exhibited and retransmitted from his satellite dish and after the proverbial law book was thrown at him was found to have willfully misappropriated audiovisual works, for commercial advantage, in violation of §705(a) of the *Communications Act.* This violation was not exempt as a use by the general public and was not private home viewing as defined in §705(c)(4). It also violated the *Copyright Act* (§501) and infringed the tradename and marks of HBO in violation of §1125(a) of the *Lanham Act,* $40,000 fine assessed, *ESPN v. Edinburg Community Hotel* (SD Tex., 1985), also *California Satellite Systems v. Nichols,* 216 Cal Rptr. 180 (Ca. App. 1985). The FCC reiterated its concern over satellite signal piracy as it issued citations to 19 vendors who sold equipment to defeat the scrambling system used by satellite programmers to encrypt their signals. Otherwise legal integrated circuits and computer software can be used to illegally intercept so the

FCC is working with the Dept. of Justice to obtain "a more coordinated and effective enforcement effort." The FCC also strongly encourages the initiation of civil actions by persons aggrieved by such theft, *Theft of Satellite Programming*, 65 RR 2d 36 (1988). The cases pursued by the industry are so numerous that further citations are not included, (See "Syndicated Exclusivity," "Cable Regulation," "Copyright—Broadcast Rights," "Home Recording and Viewing").

Cable TV Installation. A number of delivery technologies compete to bring pay TV into apartment complexes; Cable, Multipoint Distribution, SMATV, etc. A landlord sued Teleprompter and the City of NY challenging constitutionality of a statute which allowed cable to install facilities to service tenants and limited compensation to apartment owner (usually $1 unless damages shown). Cable had been giving 5% of the gross revenue from building to the landlord. Supreme Ct. agreed that any permanent physical occupation authorized by the government is an illegal taking without regard to the "public interest" it may serve, even if only minimal economic impact on the owner. Remanded. NY Ct. then held statute proper exercise of State's police power provided more appropriate compensation paid subject to Ct. review, *Loretto v. Teleprompter Manhattan*, 459 NYS 2d 743; 102 S. Ct. 3164 (1982); 446 NE 2d 428 (1983). FCC then announced it preempts all state and local entry regulation of satellite master antenna systems (SMATV), *NY State Comm. on Cable TV v. FCC*, 749 F. 2d 804, 57 RR 2d 363 (DC App. 1984). Three federal district Cts. and now an appellate Ct. have ruled that an implied "private right of action" based on §621(a)(2) of the *Cable Act* allows a cable operator to bring suit to enjoin property owners from barring the operator from laying cable along utility easements and rights of way, *Centel Cable of Florida v. Admiral's Cove*, 835 F. 2d 1359, 64 RR 2d 411 (1988). However, a unanimous Ct. ruled the *Cable Communications Act of 1984*, does not give cable TV operators a right of access to wire the interiors of privately owned multi-unit dwellings for the purpose of providing service to the tenants without compensation, *Cable Investments v. Woolley*, 65 RR 2d 1490 (3rd Cir. 1989).

Call—In Poll Policy. Call-in polls had to be clearly noted as to their nature and their scientific basis or lack thereof. This policy was eliminated as FCC concluded that market forces and licensees' self-interest in their own credibility would ensure an adequately informed public concerning such poll results, *Underbrush Broadcast Policies*, 54 RR 2d 1043 (1983).

Call Letters. The FCC determined that it would no longer assign call letters to stations. If a dispute arises the FCC recommended that local Ct.'s be sought under state laws of "unfair competition." Permits identical call signs if stations operate in different services and are not commonly owned if station seeking sign obtains written permission from any stations in the nation already using the call. The FCC also would not be an arbiter of good taste in choice of call signs when local communities could enforce. Also, prohibition from using call letters of initials of former or current Presidents is eliminated. Will not eliminate "K-W" geographic use as traditional historically, *Call Letters*, 54 RR 2d 1493 (1983), 63 RR 2d 1625 (1987). USA Network, a national sports oriented cable channel was denied a preliminary injunction against a Denver TV station which had applied to change its call letters to KUSA-TV. "Likelihood of confusion" was unlikely because the primary product sold by both was advertising time and ratings companies would not be confused, and, therefore, advertisers using ratings to purchase time would not be confused, *USA Network v. Gannet*, 584 F. Supp. 195 (D. Col. 1984). A Fed. Dist. Ct. ruled the likelihood of confusion between radio call letters WMEE and WMCZ warranted the issuance of an injunction on behalf of WMEE. Found phonetically similar; similarity in targeted audience; overlapping service area; lack of close attention by audience in selecting stations; strength of WMEE's mark in market through long-term use; funds spent to promote call letters; status of station as number one in market and evidence of some intent to trade on the goodwill and reputation of competitor. Pending issuance of new call letters station must use disclaimer, "Not to be confused with WMEE, FM-97," *Pathfinder v. Midwest*, 593 F. Supp. 281 (ND Ind. 1984). The Patent and Trademark Office holds that the licensee of an AM station may register station's call letters (obtained in 1925) as a service mark. Not the property of the FCC, *Dept. of Commerce Pat. & Trmk. Off., In re WSM, Inc.*, 58 RR 2d 548 (1985). (See "Station Identification").

Censorship of Non—Political Speaker. (§315); When the Republican National Committee wished to use pre-recorded excerpts from Roosevelt's speeches which non-candidate Senator Vandenburg would debate, CBS censored the Roosevelt recorded material. FCC held stations have right to reject, or censor, political speech by non-candidate, *Broadcasting*, (11/1/36, p. 87). Chairman of local Republican Party, on behalf of the Republican candidate, gave a speech on radio and implied Democratic candidate Felix was a communist. Stations argued they could not censor candidate "or spokesman" and should not be liable for defamation. Ruled FCC Act §315 applies to candidate personally and does not apply to a noncandidate speaking on or in behalf of candidate, *Felix v. Westinghouse Radio*, 6 RR 2014 (1950); 6 RR 2086 (1950); *West. v. Felix*, 89 F. Supp. 740, reversed 186 F. 2d 1 (1950); 341 US 909, Cert. denied (1951). (See "Censorship of Political Candidate").

Censorship of Political Candidate. (§315, §76:205); Station cannot censor talk by political candidate even if defamatory and so is not liable for such remarks, *Port Huron Broadcasting*, 12 FCC 1069, 4 RR 1 (1948). Candidate's talk cannot be censored even when it does not deal with candidacy, *WMCA*, 7 RR 1132 (1952). Supreme Ct. decided station cannot be held liable for defamatory broadcast by political candidate since cannot censor, *Farmers' Union v. Townley* (ND Dist. Ct.) (1957), 15 RR 2058 (1957); *Farmer's v. WDAY* (ND Sup. Ct.), 89 NW 2d 102, 17 RR 2001 (1958), 360 US 525, 18 RR 2135 (1959). Only known instance of ruling that candidate who is (a) communist (b) in jail, and (c) could not appear in person still had right to time as candidate, *Yates v. Associated Broadcasting,* 7 RR 2088 (1951). Licensees' immunity from civil action for libelous statements made by candidate extended to statements made by those appearing on program with candidate, *Gray Comm.,* 14 FCC 2d 766, 14 RR 2d 353 (1968). Candidate sought to purchase time for political ads using hypnotic techniques. Station requested exemption from FCC from any obligation to present as subliminal advertising is illegal (§73:4250), but FCC refused to issue a declaratory ruling. Station rejected ads and candidate sued for damages for violating §315 and First Amendment. Federal Ct. of Appeals dismissed on grounds §315 did not create private cause of action for damages and no governmental action was involved giving rise to First Amendment. Should have sought further action from FCC as it is Congress' intent for FCC supervision, *Belluso v. Turner Communications,* 633 F. 2d 393 (5th Cir. 1980). However, in 1984, the FCC Staff issued a memorandum resulting from the plans of Magazine publisher Larry Flynt to run for the Presidency and include X-rated film clips in his political commercials, that U.S. Criminal Code §1464, prohibits the broadcast of obscene or indecent material and it is unreasonable to exempt broadcasters from criminal prosecutions by allowing them, even in political ads, to broadcast obscenities. They noted that any violation of <u>criminal law</u> would not be covered by the no-censorship provision of §315. The spirit of the law is to promote public access to political debate, not to break criminal laws, 1/6/84, FCC. (See "Censorship of Non—Political Speaker," "Indecency—Obscenity").

Censorship by State. State cannot have right to pass on films shown over TV as interstate commerce and preempted by Federal law, *DuMont v. Carroll*, 5 RR 2053 (1949); 6 RR 2045 (1950); 86 F. Supp. 813, aff'd, 184 F. 2d 153 (1950), 340 US 939, Cert. denied (1951). In 1980, the PBS network ran a docudrama, <u>Death of a Princess,</u> about a Saudi Arabian princess and her commoner lover who were executed publicly for adultery. The program was critical of Saudi religious, cultural and political life. Saudi government protested noting it might endanger American citizens in Middle East. Alabama ETV and University of Houston cancelled broadcast. Challenge by subscribers and viewers of stations. Resulting appeals affirmed Alabama and reversed Texas decisions. Although public broadcast licensees, stations possess same programming discretion as commercial broadcasters. While State is subject to First Amendment constraints not applicable to private licensees, FCC has determined licensees have sole right and independent responsibility to select programming. (See "Licensee Control Over Programs," "First Amendment Rights for Broadcasting") Public stations are not public forums and not required to provide right of access to viewers. The First Amendment does not preclude the government from exercising editorial control over its own expression thus did not have to present program. On an unrelated issue (see "Defamation") a class action suit was filed against the program's producers, PBS and others on behalf of alleged class of nearly one-billion followers of the Islamic faith and Americans who respect Islamic traditions. Damages of $20 billion were sought. Ct. dismissed as law of defamation protects individuals, and group that sued was so large that program could not have defamed any individual members. To permit action by such a large group would render meaningless First Amendment rights to explore issues of public import, *Muir v. Alabama ETV Commission*, 688 F. 2d 1033, 52 RR 2d 935 (CA 5th, 1982); *Khalid v. Fanning*, 506 F. Supp. 186 (ND Cal. 1980); Cert. denied.

Changes in Entertainment Formats. A series of Ct. of Appeal decisions required the FCC to grant petitions-to-deny from listeners' wishing to preserve unique if profitable formats for the greatest good of the greatest number, *Citizens Committee to Preserve the Voice of the Arts in Atlanta v. FCC,* 436 F. 2d 263 (DC Cir. 1970). The FCC adopted a policy statement refusing to consider such petitions. The US Supreme Ct. upheld the FCC policy against reviewing past or proposed changes in a radio station's entertainment programming during license renewal or transfer proceedings. Under §309(a) and §310(d) of the *Communications Act of 1934,* the FCC must consider the "public interest, convenience and necessity" when assigning broadcast licenses. Neither the language nor the legislative history compel FCC supervision of format changes, and such supervision would not advance the welfare of the listening public, would pose substantial administrative problems and would deter innovation in radio programming. The FCC's policy did not conflict with the First Amendment rights of listeners, since the "Fairness Doctrine" decision of *Red Lion Broadcasting,* 395 US 367 (1969) did not imply that the First Amendment grants individual listeners the right to have the Commission review the abandonment of their favorite entertainment programs, *FCC v. WNCN Listeners Guild,* 506 F.2d 246; 101 S. Ct. 1266 (1981), aff'd, 813 F. 2d 465, 62 RR 2d 866 (1987). Efforts have since been made to preserve formats under contract principles. Listener's petitioned FCC to deny license of owner who promised to retain jazz format when bought the station but then dropped. FCC refused to hear on ground that petition did not set forth "clear, precise and indubitable evidence" of misrepresentation. Ct. remanded for evidentiary hearing as "peculiar" to require, as a precondition for a hearing, that the petitioner fully establish what it is the very purpose of a hearing to determine. "The statute [Communications Act] in effect says that the Commission must look into the possible existence of a fire only when it is shown a good deal of smoke; the Commission has said that it will look into the possible existence of a fire only when it is shown the existence of a fire," *Citizens for Jazz on WRVR v. FCC*, 775 F. 2d 392, 59 RR 2d 249 (1985). Ct. upheld FCC approval of transfer as reasonable even though "big band" format would be lost, *Committee to Save WEAM v. FCC*, 808 F. 2d 113, 61 RR 2d 1444 (US App. DC 1987). National Drug Free Council signed $6,000 contract for advertising and on-air promotion of concert with KCPW-FM pop station. Eleven days later station changed to oldies format and did not carry out contract and did not accept $6,000. NDFC sued as sold 1,700 tickets of 17,000, losing $250,000, contending too late to carry out effective campaign and station deliberately failed to notify of planned change in format, *Variety*, (9/27/89, p. 70).

Character Qualifications. (§308(a), §319, §73:24(d)); Ct. upheld the FCC's right to refuse a transfer of license where denial was based on purchaser's character qualifications, *Arde Bulova, Transferor, Mester Bros. Transferees*, 11 FCC 137 (1946); *Mester v. FCC*, 70 F. Supp. 118; *Mester et. al. v. US*, 392 US 749, Cert. denied, aff'd, 332 US 749, rehearing denied, 332 US 820 (1947). News slanting, if proven, reflects on character qualifications, *Frances S. Richards, KMPC*, 7 RR 788 (1951). The FCC has stated that it will look into charges of rigging and slanting the news only if there is extrinsic evidence, in writing or otherwise, from insiders or persons who have direct personal knowledge of an intentional attempt to falsify the news. Of concern would be orders from the broadcaster, its top management, or its news management to falsify the news. No such evidence was presented in this complaint, *Salazer*, 54 RR 2d 731 (1983). Sufficient remedial and deterrent effect to deny one license out of seven where misconduct limited and individual who did misconduct no longer with licensee, *Faulkner Radio*, 88 FCC 2d 612, 50 RR 2d 814 (1981). Any station whose renewability appears to be affected by misconduct of joint license will be designated for hearing at the same time as the original station. Any stations not affected by the alleged conduct will be freely transferable. The FCC also affirmed its authority to revoke the licenses in one service on the basis of egregious violations of the rules of another service, *Public Notice*, 53 RR 2d 126; *Bernard Winner*, 53 RR 2d 215 (1983). In 1985, the FCC issued a statement that many areas of conduct previously considered in a character evaluation of a licensee or applicant would no longer be considered, except for disqualification purposes, unless it involves: (1) violations of the Act or rules; (2) instances of fraud or misrepresentation in programming or in actions before the FCC; (3) adjudicated instances of fraud before another agency of government; (4) criminal convictions involving fraud or deceit; (5) criminal convictions involving dishonesty or false statement; (6) other felony convictions bearing significantly upon proclivity to be truthful or to comply with FCC rules and policies (burden on challenging party); or (7) adjudicated instances of anticompetitive behavior. Misconduct by a corporate parent may also be assessed against a broadcast subsidiary. (See "RKO Revocation"). But misconduct in multiple ownership situations will be presumed that conduct at one station is not necessarily predictive for other licences owned unless evidence otherwise. A licensee will also be held responsible if one of its employees violates FCC rules in the course of employment, (See "Program Service Contracts"). Willfulness, frequency and currency will be relevant to the predictive value of applicant misconduct. This does not signal any relaxation of FCC oversight of network practices, *Character Qualifications*, 102 FCC 2d 1179 (1985), 59 RR 2d 801, 61 RR 2d 619 (1986). ALJ should have added as hearing issue prevailing applicant's 50% partner's failure to pay income taxes for two years, *Las Americas Communications*, 60 RR 2d 1366 (1986). FCC clarified that licensees or their principals drug trafficking convictions will be considered in license renewal and will initiate license revocation proceedings. The adoption of drug counseling, drug education, and other similar programs by licensees and permittees is encouraged.

Licensees and permittees should also prohibit the use of drugs by employees while at work. (1989). FCC denied renewal of WKSP-AM, Kingstree, S.C. following conviction of the station's principal on drug trafficking charges, (Feb. 1990). (See "Misrepresentation," "Sale or Transfer of License").

Children and TV. Action for Children's Television petitioned the FCC to limit ads on children's programs. The FCC refused, but adopted other items, *Children's TV Report and Policy Statement*, 50 FCC 2d 1, 31 RR 2d 1228 (1974), aff'd, 564 F. 2d 458 (1977), 40 RR 2d 1577 (1977). The FCC also refused to adopt a 14 hr. a week minimum standard for children's programs, 546 F. Supp. 872 (DDC. 1982). FCC also declined to redefine children's programming to include programs viewed by children, but intended for adults. Broadcasters are not relieved of their obligation to provide programming for children in three age specific groups for if challenged will still be required to justify concentration on limited segments of the child audience or on particular needs of that audience. Also adopted a policy of prohibiting program host or other personality to promote products in the program on which he or she appears, 63 FCC 2d 26, 39 RR 2d 1032 (1977); Upheld, 712 F. 2d 677, 54 RR 2d 293, 55 RR 2d 199 (DC Cir. 1983), 57 RR 2d 1406 (DC Cir. 1985). FTC declines to adopt prohibition on all ads directed to or viewed by children which contain premium offers, 40 RR 2d 1 (FTC 1977). However, state law may be a remedy (or a pain, depending on your point-of-view). In 1977, a State class action suit was brought alleging fraudulent, misleading and deceptive advertising by General Foods, two ad agencies and a supermarket chain. The TV ads stated that children who eat candy breakfasts' "are bigger, stronger, more energetic, happier, more invulnerable and braver." The ads also noted that sugared cereals are grain products that are healthful and nutritious. The California Supreme Ct. held that causes of action for injunctive relief and restitution under State's "unfair competition" and false advertising laws had been made but denied other elements of the suit. The case was settled, *Committee on Children's TV v. General Foods*, 197 Cal. Rptr. 783 (Cal. 1983). Since program-length commercials are no longer prohibited one can broadcast them if proper sponsor identification is made that "program" is a commercial. (See "Sponsor ID"). FCC ruled that the sponsorship requirements of §317 do not apply to programs targeting child audiences unless the broadcast is so interwoven with commercial matter and so devoid of significant entertainment value that the entire program is commercial in character. One way to avoid having to label as a program-length commercial is to provide separation "bumpers" before and after each commercial interruption differentiating program and advertising segments. Later, FCC rejected argument that <u>Thunder Cats</u> offering to TV stations a share in the profits from sales of toys to carry programs was a violation of "public interest." FCC called such profit-sharing "an innovative technique to fund children's programming; advantageous to the continuation and growth of children's TV offerings, which is clearly in the public interest." <u>He—Man</u> and <u>Masters of the Universe</u> were then produced and provided to stations on straight barter basis for two minutes of non-prime air time. Appellant contended two minutes for commercials was only a token payment, given expense of production, and that producers were obviously just advertising the toys. The station claimed the barter deal was not nominal payment, with two minutes worth $300M and now $400M. It was up to the station to make good faith determination series had significant entertainment value and whether the program "constitutes a single commercial promotion for the sponsor's products or services." Or, which came first; the program or the toy, *Action for Children's Television*, 58 RR 2d 61 (1985). Ct. reversed FCC elimination of commercialization guidelines for children's TV for its failure to articulate a reasoned basis for the decision. FCC's established policy was to single out children's TV programming for special regulatory scrutiny because of lack of sophistication of audience. Removing such scrutiny on basis that commercials help support children's programming inadequate justification for entrusting regulation to market forces alone, *Action for Children's Television v. FCC*, 821 F. 2d 741, 63 RR 2d 440 (US App. DC 1987). The Ct. reversed the FCC on its' sponsor ID ruling relating to Mattel and Group W programs. The unanimous panel held §317 is clearly a barrier. Nothing in the legislative history, according to the court, indicated that the requirement is limited to broadcasts purely commercial in character and the decision by the FCC was a departure from the agency's own past practice, *National Association for Better Broadcasting v. FCC*, 63 RR 2d 1501 (1987). Responding to the court, the FCC reiterated its view that KCOP in Los Angeles did not violate the sponsor ID requirements of §317 and provided a new rationale. It now says that sponsorship identification will not be required where, as in the case of KCOP, the licensee has paid what is clearly more than a nominal charge even though the charge may be less than the fair market price of the programming. Requiring the FCC to determine in a detailed review the adequacy of payment every time a program discount is alleged would be beyond Congress' intent, *National Association for Better Broadcasting v. FCC*, 66 RR 2d 889 (1989). FCC has proposed rulemaking under consideration on Children's TV issues and Congress has passed legislation removing antitrust barriers, allowing broadcasters to get together to voluntarily agree on commercial limitations, (1989).

Clipping. The FCC issued a statement warning stations that substituting local ads or programming for network or syndicated ads or programming, in violation of the supplier's contract may be a fraudulent action. Network clipping can also be a violation of sponsorship identification requirements. *Public Notice*, 40 FCC 2d 136, 26 RR 2d 1253 (1973). License revoked for clipping parts of network shows to insert local ads, misrepresentation to network and FCC. Not excusable that corporate licensee did not know—manager of station was officer and on board of directors to achieve local integration, *Las Vegas Valley*, 589 F. 2d 594, 44 RR 2d 683 (DC App. 1978). The FCC then deleted the rule and policy statement, leaving such matters to private resolution through civil litigation or enforcement of local laws relating to fraud, racketeering, unfair trade and antitrust, *Second Report and Order*, 59 RR 2d 1500 (1986). (See "Network Regulation," "Sponsor ID").

Community of License Determinations. §307(b) requires equitable distribution of radio service (this also has justified a preference for local ownership.) The "Suburban Policy," enacted by FCC in 1965, was to discourage applicants from filing applications for small communities near large cities but to identify with the larger community. Burden was on applicant to show they really wished to serve their local suburban area. The "Berwick Doctrine" applied the same "public interest" considerations to FM &TV as to AM by requiring an evidentiary hearing determining whether programming would be for larger or smaller community specified as the community of license. In a number of cases the FCC review board favored licensing the station for the larger, unserved community over smaller, served community, *Cornwall*, 89 FCC 2d 704, 51 RR 2d 389 (1982). FCC's first priority in assigning FM stations was to assure the availability of at least one full-time station for as many people as possible. FCC then attempted to provide either a first local or second non-local signal depending on which would reach greater audience. The FCC allowed a relaxation of policy to allow a competing application to obtain a second channel in community if available, thus avoiding comparative hearings over the first license, *In the Matter of FM Assignment Policies and Procedures*, 90 FCC 2d 88, 51 RR 2d 807 (1982). A "Defacto Reallocation Policy" affected only FM and TV when a channel assignment for one community was to be moved to establish a service to another community.

One had to request removal of channel from one city and show effective use to provide service to another community unless one could show station to be licensed to unlisted community would be within 10 miles of a community listed in the Table of Assignments. Applicants needed to only submit a petition for rulemaking to add an unlisted community to the Assignment Table, 53 RR 2d 681 (1983). The main studio of the station was required to be in the community of license (§73:1125), however, the FCC now allows at any location within the "city grade" contour. Also eliminated was the requirement that broadcast stations originate a majority of their non-network programming from the main studio or other points within the principal community, *Main Studio and Program Origination Rules*, 62 RR 2d 1582 (1987), 65 RR 2d 119 (1988). A new policy of major significance announced by the FCC applied the "Huntington Doctrine" to radio applicants. The general rule, as noted above, is that a broadcast applicant that proposes to be licensed to a community to which no other station has been licensed should be awarded a decisive preference over an applicant proposing a community that already has its own local station. Under "Huntington," if the competing applicants specify separate communities that are dependent upon, and contiguous to, a central city, and the applicants propose sufficient power to serve the entire metro area, the entire area is to be treated as a single community and none of the applicants will be given a preference. Evaluation will be under standard comparative criteria without reference to the proposed communities of license. In the absence of persuasive evidence that two communities share needs and interests, there is no basis for inferring that one's need for local service will be satisfied by a station licensed to the other community. To determine if a proposed community and a nearby central city are interdependent the following will be considered: (1) the extent to which specified community residents work in the larger metro area, (2) whether specified community has its own newspaper or other media that cover needs and interests, (3) whether community leaders and resident perceive the specified community as integral part of, or separate from, the larger metro area, (4) whether the separate community has its own local government, (5) whether the smaller community has its own telephone book and/or zip code, (6) whether it has its own commercial establishments, health facilities and transportation systems, (7) the extent to which they are part of the same advertising market, and (8) the extent to which the specified community relies upon the larger for municipal services; police, fire protection, schools, libraries, etc., *Faye & Richard Tuck,* 65 RR 2d 402 (1988). The FCC then adopted a new procedure allowing FM and TV broadcasters to request a new community of license without risking losing their license to competing applicants unless such a move would deprive a community of its only local transmission service and is not a nonadjacent channel upgrade, *Modification of FM and TV Authorizations to Specify a New Community of License,* 66 RR 2d 877 (1989).

Comparative Qualifications. (§309, §311, §73:3525, §73:3597); The FCC must give reasonably equal consideration to competing applicants for a new license and upon renewal give other applicants a reasonable opportunity to apply, *Ashbacker Broadcasting v. FCC,* 326 US 327 (1945). The criteria used to assess new license applicants has been diversification of control of media, full-time participation in station operations by the owners, local residence, minority preference, past broadcast record if any, efficient use of frequency, proposed program service and other factors. Some examples are: Applicant which proposed less network use wins, *WADC-Simmons,* 169 F.2d 670, 4 RR 2023; 335 US 846, Cert. denied (1948). Applicant proposing 60% limit on sponsored time superior, *Bay State v. FCC,* 171 F. 2d 826, 4 RR 2109 (1948). FCC not engaged in censorship when comparing promises of rival applicants, *Johnston Broadcasting,* 3 RR 1784 (1947); 175 F. 2d 351, 4 RR 2138 (1949). Congress urged the FCC to allow competitors to arrive at settlements of comparative hearings because of costs. A broadcaster may not assign or transfer his license if issues concerning his basic qualifications to remain a licensee have been designated for hearing but not yet resolved, except if minority distress sale. (See "Sale or Transfer of License," Minority Ownership"). The FCC ruled it must approve any payment agreements when a competing applicant settles for withdrawal of his application, (1963). Protection for licensees from frivolous ("greenmail") competing applications by prohibiting payment to other applicants in exchange for withdrawal of their applications was added to *Communications Act* (§311) in 1981. Amended by Congress, (See §73:3525; §73:3597) to only allow payment of "legitimate and prudent out-of-pocket expenses," strengthened by the FCC for both competing applications and petitions-to-deny, *Rule Amendments*, 53 RR 2d 823 (1983); 65 RR 2d 1734, 66 RR 2d 708 (1989). FCC refuses to permit contractual obligation to pay $500M for "consulting service" of competing applicant as veiled attempt to avoid §73:3597, *Central Television*, 60 RR 2d 1297 (1986). FCC stated where on quantitative basis applicants equal, the qualitative comparison based on broadcast experience becomes decisive, *Rockland Broadcasting*, 2 RR 2d 39, 36 FCC 303 (1964); and *1965 Policy Statement on Comparative Hearings*, 5 RR 2d 1901 (1965). It is more difficult to compare an incumbent with a new applicant in a renewal situation. The FCC at first gave a decisive preference to the renewal applicant; *Hearst Radio-WBAL*, 15 FCC 1149 (1951). Then, a newspaper owned station in Boston was filed against by a group which promised better programming, integration and diversity of local media control. The newspaper incumbent claimed not fair as only promises and the Herald-Traveler paper would fold. The FCC revoked their license and the newspaper ceased publication shortly thereafter—actually decreasing diversity of media in the community, *WHDH*, 444 F. 2d 841 (DC App. 1970); 403 US 923, Cert. denied, 15 RR 2d 411 (1971). The FCC then devised a policy to lay to rest the WHDH effect on comparative renewals, 22 FCC 2d 424, 18

RR 2d 1901 (1970). The DC App. Ct. overturned the FCC stating that full comparative hearings must be held, with the incumbent license judged on evidence, all relevant criteria, including integration of minority groups into station operation. In judging the past performance of the licensee, "superior performance, which means far above average" is to be a plus of major significance. It included elimination of excessive and loud advertising, quality programs, re-investment of profit, diversification and independence from governmental influence to promote First Amendment objectives, *Citizens Communications Center. v. FCC*, 447 F. 2d 1201; 24 RR 2d 2045 (DC App.1971). About the same time in 1969, Cowles-Florida, sought renewal of its license. Central-Florida applied for same frequency. After comparative hearings between the applicants the FCC gave Cowles its renewal. The DC App. Ct. remanded on the grounds the FCC had inadequately investigated anti-renewal factors and the renewal process was unclear. By determining without much evidence that this licensee's past performance record was "superior" the FCC had apparently created an irrebuttable presumption of "renewal expectancy," contrary to the full-hearing requirement of the *Communications Act*. The FCC then reconsidered and again ruled for Cowles. It was agreed that an incumbent licensee is entitled to some degree of renewal expectancy in a comparative hearing. "Renewal expectancy" is to be weighted with all the other factors, and the better the past record, the greater the renewal expectancy weight. This should prevent paper promises by challengers from being given equal weight with proven performance; licensees will be encouraged to insure quality service and; this will prevent the comparison of incumbents as though just new applicants which would result in the haphazard restructuring of the broadcast industry. The Ct., however, warned the FCC that renewal expectancy may not be harmful to the "public interest," noting that so far no incumbent television station licensee has ever been denied renewal (except WHDH) despite the filing of many such challenges, *Central*

Florida Enterprises v. FCC, 598 F. 2d 37 (1979), Cert. dismissed, 99 S. Ct. 2189, 44 RR 2d 345 (1978), 44 RR 2d 1576 (1979); aff'd, 683 F. 2d 503, 51 RR 2d 1405 (DC Cir. 1982). FCC stated that character qualifications would be excluded from comparative consideration as seldom of decisional significance in comparative proceedings, *Character Qualifications*, 59 RR 2d 801 (1986). Renewal of license delayed for nearly a decade was finally approved when the ALJ's renewal denial was reversed by the Review Board. Board applied renewal expectancy because of more than minimal non-entertainment programming and substantial record of responsiveness in the most recent fourteen years of holding the license, *Intercontinental Radio*, 56 RR 2d 903 (1984). Review Board of FCC reemphasizes primary importance of ownership diversification in comparative hearing, *Communications Properties*, 52 RR 2d 981 (1982). Where an applicant proposed 36.3% local programming the opponent raised the question of whether licensee could afford to so program. A slight demerit was given the applicant for failure to prove he could. The premise, "local needs can be met only through programming produced locally" was rejected by the FCC, *WPIX*, 68 FCC 2d 381, 43 RR 2d 278 (1978). Then, RKO-General, KHJ-TV, was filed against by Fidelity in 1966. In 1967, the Justice Dept. filed an antitrust action against RKO-General for fixing prices on tires. FCC said would take into consideration when finally decided. A Consent Decree, not admitting guilt but agreeing not to continue activity, was signed in 1970; so legally not a factor in the renewal proceeding, but Fidelity requested adding as issue. The Administrative Law Judge (ALJ) found that RKO was lacking in past performance in programming and community relations; presenting old films of excessive violence. RKO station WNAC-TV Boston subsequent to KHJ decision challenged also. FCC reversed ALJ on KHJ and granted renewal based on; RKO had promised in 1962 old films and had provided old films. RKO was one of many stations in market and credit should be given to an existing service. DC App. Ct. stated, the FCC when faced with a fairly and evenly balanced record may, on the basis of the renewal applicants past performance, award a renewal. RKO had agreed to sell WNAC upon condition FCC renewed license, (1978). FCC could determine that both applicants were poor or minimally acceptable, *Fidelity TV v. FCC*, 515 F.2d 684 (DC App. 1975); 44 FCC 2d 149, 16 RR 2d 1181 (1969); 32 RR 2d 1607 (DC App. 1975). The Fidelity case led to following Policy Statement, "Until Congress acts no quantitative standards will be adopted and applicant must continue to run on its record measured by whether programming was sound, favorable, and substantially above a level of mediocre service. Case-by-case basis," (see "RKO Revocation") *FCC Report & Order*, 66 FCC 2d 419, 40 RR 2d 763, aff'd, 44 RR 2d 547 (DC App. 1977). Reversing its' Adm. Law Judge, FCC denied "renewal expectancy" and decided a one man locally owned-and-operated classical music FM station license should be given to challenger. Various grounds were cited; FCC gave a diminished preference for diversification (he owned no other station or media) and integration; stressed failure to conduct community survey and to do news. Ct. remanded to FCC on basis that diversification does not mean actual diversity of views, but ownership. Thus, FCC had abandoned presumption that "diversity of ownership is the litmus test in seeking diversity of viewpoints." The FCC's conclusion that programming was of no value to community was contrary to the testimony (public outcry had ensued on license renewal denial) and was the type of content evaluation prohibited by §326. The competing applicant owned other stations and would not be increasing the diversity of viewpoint even with more informational programming. Active participation is a significant factor in determining whether programming is likely to be in the "public interest" by assessing how involved ownership will be in the day-to-day operations of the station (quantitatively). The Ct. felt the FCC had not explicitly weighted or explained its departure from precedent. Therefore, the FCC's decision was set aside as unreasonable and remanded, *Simon Geller*, 90 FCC

2d 250, 51 RR 2d 1019, 52 RR 2d 709 (1982); *Committee for Access v. FCC*, 737 F. 2d 74, 56 RR 2d 435 (DC Cir. 1984). The FCC then reversed its decision and granted renewal. FCC determination that no "renewal expectancy" as devoted less than 1% to nonentertainment programming and presented no programming responsive to community needs was reaffirmed, and upheld by Ct. of App. (56 RR 2d 435 (1985). However, 100% fulltime integration earned an enhanced preference over opponent which proposed "only" 66% fulltime participation. Also won substantial preference for diversification as owned no other interests, *Simon Geller*, 59 RR 2d 579 (1985). A pledge by an owner to actively supervise his station is considered important, comparatively. An applicant had on file two applications for TV stations. One was in Sacramento, California and the other in Orlando, Florida. In each application he claimed a high level of integration (owner involvement). When challenged on how he could work at both stations on two coasts, applicant reported he was in process of negotiating a settlement agreement which would result in dismissing his Sacramento application. Therefore, was, in a sense, a hypothetical application so ALJ dismissed Orlando application for misrepresentation on integration question. Review Board overturned as found a complete absence of intent to deceive or conceal required for misrepresentation disqualification, *Metro Broadcasting*, 57 RR 2d 440 (1984). FCC refused to give license to either party in comparative hearing even though the community will remain without TV service after years of expensive litigation. One application was described as "a consummate hoax, and one of the most unsavory cases of applicant dishonesty ever encountered in a broadcast licensing case held before the FCC," and the competing application was "a virtually unending series of misrepresentations and perjuries so flagrant and opprobrious as possibly to warrant other action." The community "will in the long run be immeasurably better served than it would have been by the manifestly unjust enrichment of either of these poseurs, whose counterfeit credentials we hereby renounce and dismiss," *California Broadcasting*, 63 RR 2d 1220 (1987).

In an unexpected move, the FCC used its review of a case to establish a new method for comparative evaluation of ownership-management integration proposals. Once a 20 hour per week threshold requirement for integration consideration is met a new sliding scale method of calculating integration credit will be used for proposals to work at a station for less than 40 hours per week. A modified <u>Hirschman-Herfindahl Index,</u> used by the Dept. of Justice in assessing antitrust implications of corporate mergers, will be applied to reflect the relationship between number of hours per week worked by owner/managers and quality of service to the public. Divide the number of proposed hours per week by 40 hours, multiply the resulting fraction by 100, then square the product. This figure will then be multiplied by the integrated principal's percentage of ownership integration into management. For example, a 75% owner, 36 hours per week: Integration score of 6075 (100 x (36/40))^2 x .75 = 6075), and a 90% owner working only 28 hours per week would score 4410 ([100 x (28/40]^2 x .90 = 4410). The ownership shares of other integrated managers would be calculated and added to obtain an aggregate score for judging integration. This will remove ambiguity, reduce comparative hearing costs, reduce imprecision and uncertainty, *Omaha TV 15*, 65 RR 2d 1019 (1988). A decision to facilitate settlements of multi-party comparative licensing proceedings was later overturned internally by the FCC. The Fowler FCC held §311(c) does not prohibit a qualified non-party from being awarded any forthcoming construction permit (CP) as part of a settlement agreement. The anti-trafficking provisions of §73:3597 were inapplicable where the CP is granted after a settlement, and the dismissing applicants could receive compensation exceeding their legitimate and prudent expenses in prosecuting their applications. This created a <u>de facto</u> private auction for broadcast spectrum and is inconsistent while FCC prohibits the right to sell for a profit after CP is granted, *Rebecca Radio of Marco*, 65 RR 2d 1408 (1989), overturned, (Feb. 1990). The FCC issued a public notice designed to deter abuses of the comparative renewal process by eliminating the "Cameron Policy," under which a challenger to a renewal applicant could specify the incumbent's existing transmitter site as its own proposed site, *Docket 81-742*, 66 RR 2d 708 (1989). The FCC's Review Board reviews decisions of the Administrative Law Judges. It clarified five elements it will consider for a licensee to get "renewal expectancy" as, (1) the licensee's efforts to determine the problems, needs and interests of the community; (2) the licensee's on-air response to the ascertained problems, needs and interests; (3) the licensee's reputation in the community for serving problems, needs and interests; (4) the licensee's record of compliance with the Communications Act and the FCC's rules and policies; and (5) any special effort at community outreach or providing a forum for local self-expression, (Nov. 1989). (See "Promise v. Performance," "Character Qualifications," "Sale or Transfer of License").

Conflict of Interest. Station promotions of non-broadcast off-air concerts while other non-station connected concerts are not nearly so well promoted may be "unfair competition," *Radio WCMQ*, 62 FCC 2d 487, 39 RR 2d 506 (1976). FCC decides not to propose a formal rule against plugola (mentioning product for personal gain). Reasonable diligence should be used and FCC will deal with on a case-by-case basis, *Broadcast Announcement of Financial Interests of Broadcast Stations and Networks and their Principals and Employees....*, 76 FCC 2d 221, 46 RR 2d 1421 (1980). Generally, employer is responsible for acts of employees. A talk show host received money in exchange for his promise to promote a product. Employee might be liable, the Ct. found that employee's acts were not in furtherance of his employer's business and were outside scope of employment so MBS not responsible, *Friedman v. MBS*, 380 So. 2d 1313 (Fla. App. 1980).

Short-Term Renewal for using station to further private interests in anti-competitive manner, *E. Boyd Whitney*, 86 FCC 2d 1133, 49 RR 2d 1240 (1981). The FCC no longer restricts telling the audience to call particular groups or individuals, even if such broadcasts are made to promote the private interests of the license. Such conduct subjects owners to the personal attack rule, invasion of privacy or nuisance, or criminal sanctions under federal and some state laws, *Policy Statement and Memorandum Opinion and Order*, 54 RR 2d 1043 (1983). FCC deletes the policy asking licensees to exercise special diligence to avoid improper use of facilities by employees whose private outside interests might conflict with their responsibilities. FCC noted this policy was covered by the sponsorship identification requirements. Stations are still required to avoid "plugola" and "payola," *Policy Statement and Order*, 57 RR 2d 913 (1985), aff'd, *Telecommunications Research and Action Center v. FCC*, 800 F. 2d 1181, 61 RR 2d 61, (DC Cir. 1986). (See "Sponsor ID").

Copyright—Broadcast Rights. In the absence of any definite contractual provision about <u>Painted Dreams</u> to the contrary, literary materials developed by Irna Phillips, employee, on company time are considered property of employer, *Phillips v. WGN*, 307 Ill. App. 1, 29 NE 2d 849 (1940). Rights to <u>Mr. District Attorney</u> program developed by employee <u>prior</u> to employment belong to employee, *Cole v. Phillips H. Lord*, 28 NYS 2d 404 (1941). Rival station restrained from using title of program identified with station after hiring away personality, *Bremer Broadcasting v. NJ Broadcasting* (NJ Sup. Ct), Docket C-793-49 (1949). Character created by employee is owned by station, however, now former employee has right to portray character on another station using different name, *Broadcasting*, (8/20/62, p. 76). Rights to title are abandoned after 5 years of non-use, *Screen Test, Inc., v. ABC*, 97 NYS 2d 372 (1950). Although separate elements were not new or novel, if the combination is the program format is protected, *Stanley v. CBS*, 221 P. 2d 73 (Calif. 1950). Person can have right to idea even though not patentable nor subject to copyright if reduced to concrete detailed form and in some way novel, *Belt v. Hamilton Bank*, 108 F. Supp. 689, 8 RR 2046 (1952). Unsolicited submission of program idea without a contractual agreement maintaining the confidential basis of submission cannot be basis for recovery if idea or parts of idea are same as another's, *Carneval v. William Morris Agency*, 9 RR 2048 (1953). If a producer accepts a submitted idea with full knowledge that the offeror expects payment in the event of use, California Cts. impose liability under a theory of implied-in-fact contract, *Desny v. Wilder*, 46 Ca. 2d 715 (1956). Commercial values in name created by TV series belong to owners of series, *W. Earp Enterprises v. Sachman* (SDNY), 16 RR 2034, (1958). CBS used parts of an article published by Life in 1949, for a <u>Playhouse 90</u> production. The material had been submitted to CBS earlier, but rejected. Ct. awarded damages, *Broadcasting*, (6/25/62, p. 62). In 1964, Faris conceived, prepared and registered a format for a sports quiz show. Six years later, he discussed with KTLA personality. Some time later similar show was started. In order to prove existence of an implied-in-fact contract, one must show; that he or she prepared the work; that he or she disclosed the work to the offeree for sale; unless agreed otherwise, it can be concluded that the offeree knew the conditions under which it was tendered (<u>i.e.</u>, the opportunity to reject the attempted disclosure if the conditions were unacceptable); and a reasonable value was placed on the work. An implied contract is not created just because a phone call is returned or a request is made to read a work unconditionally submitted. A confidential relationship is not created just by submission. There must be evidence of communication of confidentiality, *Faris v. Enberg*, 97 Cal. App. 3rd 309 (1979). In 1959, Szczesny submitted to WGN an idea for a TV show consisting of filmed horse races and the use of prenumbered cards to determine home winners. WGN acknowledged receipt of submission but stated no new program material was being solicited. In 1967 the plaintiff viewed WGN's program <u>Let's Go</u>

<u>To The Races</u> which showed films of horse races. Viewers could obtain coded tickets at sponsors for cash prizes. (This took place before the introduction of new *Copyright Act of 1976*, effective 1978; USCA Title 17 (1976.) All work created prior to 1978 is protected under *Copyright Act of 1909* which would protect any material put into concrete form—such as his submitted concept. *Act of 1976*, protects from the moment of creation. Independent producer began to work on idea in 1955; no one from WGN spoke to producer about plaintiff's idea; denied knowledge of plaintiff's idea. Lack of timely objection but noted that requiring element of novelty (originality and concreteness) was traditional; although this requirement has been rejected in California, (*Blaustein v. Burton*, 9 Cal. App. 3rd 161 (1970) *Szczesny v. WGN*, 201 USPQ 703 (Ill. App. 1977). Burke filmed a dramatic fight between a zebra and a lioness and sent by request to naturalist Grzimek who used for lectures and broadcast on German public TV. Grzimek later gave film to British company which included it in nature program. NBC purchased nature film from British and broadcast it in 1977. Burke sued NBC. Common law copyright no longer exists except for works created prior to 1978, and all protection is now by federal statute. Prior to new *Copyright Act*, the creator of an artistic or literary work had the common law right to copy and profit from that work; could distribute or show it only to a limited class of persons for a limited purpose without losing that right. This common law copyright continued until general publication and then specific requirements had to be met to protect under 1909 Law. Burke had never applied for statutory copyright and NBC argued that Burke had lost his common law right because of general publication when used over German public TV. Held that was not general publication as used only for lectures and on noncommercial TV; specific and limited. TV use, under 1909 law does not constitute a publication. Judgment for Burke, *Burke v. NBC*, CCH Copyright Reports, Para. 25,075 (1st Cir. 1979) Cert. denied. A summary judgment is not possible when two films have

the same title, as liability may be imposed by a jury if they find the use results in confusion as to the origin of plaintiff's product, *Capital Films v. Charles Fries*, 628 F. 2d 387 (5th Cir. 1980); see *Narwood v. Lexington*, 541 F. Supp. 1243 (SDNY 1982). Paramount waived its right to object to the use of "Goodbar" from its film <u>Looking for Mr. Goodbar</u> in the title of a made-for-TV movie <u>Trackdown: finding the Goodbar Killer</u> broadcast in 1983, by CBS. The word could not be emphasized in the title; the movie could not be a factual account of the same murder; and the advertising could not state a sequel or derived from the original novel or film. The author of the original novel alleged unfair competition and false designation of origin. Since CBS's movie started where <u>Goodbar</u> movie ended, actual police search for killer, not infringing. Characters were historical. Disclaimer, however, should be in credits, *Rossner v. CBS*, 612 F. Supp. 334 (SDNY 1985). In 1935, late Clarence Mulford (Hopalong Cassidy) granted right to make films based on books. Copyrights to films expired and a company sought to license 23 for TV exhibition as public domain material. Ruled exhibition would violate existing copyright in books as substantial similarity, *Filmvideo Releasing v. Hastings*, CCH 25,222 (SDNY 1981); aff'd, 668 F.2d 91 (2d Cir. 1981). The *1909 Copyright Act* did not permit owners of copyrights in scripts to copyright separately any sound recordings produced from the scripts. Since 1965, Charles Michelson has held an exclusive license in the <u>Lone Ranger</u> episodes for radio play. In 1979, Jim Lewis, without a license, began leasing recorded <u>Lone Ranger</u> episodes to radio stations. In 1982, <u>Lone Ranger TV</u> sued for copyright infringement and conversion. The *Copyright Act of 1976* protects sound recordings, but does not extend to scripts "fixed" by recording prior to 1978. The Ct. however, found that valid copyrights in the underlying scripts gave the company the right to control derivative works which had been infringed by Lewis. Under California law, <u>Lone Ranger TV</u> had an intangible property interest in the performances from the time of their recording and conversion is the illegal

taking of something of value. In another Lone Ranger decision, Clayton Moore's right to wear the Lone Ranger mask
was reinstated after a Ct. in 1981 had enjoined his public use
of the device, *Lone Ranger TV v. Program Radio Corp.*, 740 F.
2d 718 (9th Cir. 1984). In 1972, Iowa State offered ABC rights
to film made by students about Olympic wrestler Dan Gable.
ABC refused to buy. During Munich Olympic's, two segments of 12 seconds and two and one-half minutes were
used. Iowa State notified ABC of its copyright claim. ABC
then used another eight-seconds on Superstars' show. Ct.
awarded total damages because ABC had initially denied in-
fringements and had defended lawsuit vigorously, *Iowa State
Univ. v. ABC*, 475 F. Supp. 78 (SDNY 1979); 621 F.2d 57 (2nd
Cir. 1980). ABC obtained exclusive rights for 1981 World
Figure Skating Championships to be held in Hartford.
Agreement called for local stations not to broadcast footage
until ABC finished entire broadcast if they wished entry into
arena where event staged. If arena were privately operated,
such a contract provision is valid, however, since city-owned
constituted State action so attention directed to capacity in
which city was functioning. Ruled city not operating as government but in proprietary private manner and restrictions
were not arbitrary, but minimal, and allowing local TV coverage would diminish commercial value to ABC, *Post
Newsweek v. Travelers, Skating Club and City of Hartford*, 510 F.
Supp. 81 (1981). First Refusal Rights (option for next use) to
televise sporting events are essential, for without them a
network is placed in the position of promoting an event and
enhancing its value one year without sufficient security to
prevent the future benefit from being reaped by another
broadcaster. CBS refused French Tennis Open deal requiring
it to promote Wimbledon or pay additional fee and NBC
agreed since it already had rights to Wimbledon. Odious and
unconscionable demand and not bonafide proposal, *CBS v.
French Tennis Federation* (NY Cty., Special Term, Jan. 1983).
Between 1966 and 1968, Star Trek was distributed without a
copyright notice and a company claimed it had therefore en-

tered public domain. Ruled this was not a publication under *1909 Copyright Act*, as license agreements restricted access, *Paramount v. Rubinowitz*, Case CV 81-0925 (ED NY 1981). Larry Seller's told Geraldo Rivera in 1978, he had exclusive story on cause of Elvis Presley's death. Insisted Rivera sign agreement that Sellers owned copyright and required ABC to credit him. Two theories were then given; that doctor and bodyguard had slowly replaced medication with placebos causing cardiovascular failure; alternatively, Presley murdered to prevent seeking repayment of loan. Rivera informed Sellers needed verification. Sellers called once but did not divulge further information. Nine months later Rivera conducted two-month investigation and broadcast two-hour special stating Presley died of interaction of prescription drugs. Sellers sued for misappropriation, breach of contract and copyright infringement. A vague or indefinite contract will not be enforced under NY law. The ideas was neither specific, novel or unique enough to support misappropriation or copyright claims. Claim of misappropriation requires: (1) novelty, (2) disclosure made in confidence for sale, and (3) adopted and used by defendant, *Sellers v. ABC*, 668 F. 2d 1207 (11th Cir. 1982). Day after Chaplin died, Dec. 26, 1977, CBS broadcast half-hour retrospective comprising 40% of footage from copyrighted Chaplin films. CBS defended on basis of "fair use." Found could have used public domain material; excerpts were quantitatively substantial and qualitatively great overall; had been denied such use previously; was not sufficiently newsworthy in themselves for exemption as original compilation was used in 1972 Academy Award show, *Roy Export Co. v. CBS*, CCH Copyright Law Reports, Para. 25, 212, 208 USPQ 581 (SDNY 1980); aff'd, 672 F.2d 1095 (2d Cir. 1982); Cert. denied. <u>Greatest American Hero</u> does not infringe <u>Superman</u>, since expression of ideas was dissimilar and only theme or general idea had any similarities, *Warner Bros. v. ABC*, 654 F. 2d 204 (2d Cir. 1981); 523 F. Supp. 611; 530 F. Supp. 1187 (SDNY 1982); 720 F. 2d 231 (2d Cir. 1983). A TV series commissioned by the Federal

Government, produced by a public TV station, and broadcast by PBS is copyrightable and not in the public domain notwithstanding §105 of the *Copyright Act of 1976* which provides that there is no protection for any work of the US Government. The production was not prepared by a government employee; would not deprive the public of access; and did not conflict with First Amendment interests. The Ct. assumed that an assignment to the government had taken place and agency had a copyright interest. Government was not precluded from receiving and holding copyrights transferred to it by assignment, *Schnapper v. Foley*, 667 F. 2d 102 (DC Cir. 1981), Cert. denied, (1982). Distinction between unprotectable "idea" and its "protectable expression" at issue when in 1976, four-page radio script and sales proposal copyrighted which featured staff of fictional radio station involved in remote broadcast from business when interrupted by armed robber. WKRP in Cincinnati in 1978, also featured episode involving remote broadcast from business interrupted by armed man. Copyrighted script never submitted to MTM and CBS, but became question of substantial similarity. Ct. relied upon abstractions test; essence of infringement lies in taking not a general theme, but particular expression in treatment, details, scenes, events and characterizations. Episode not infringement because only an idea, and handling of scenes, details and characterization were not substantially similar. Implied contract also requires direct submission, *Giangrasso v. CBS*, 534 F. Supp. 472 (EDNY 1982). David Merrick to produce Blood and Money for CBS. Under the Rights Agreement CBS agreed to pay for his right, title and interest and to budget $10 million for the project. Merrick hired a writer and director and one year later Merrick was told by them the project could not be completed on the date in the Production Agreement. CBS was not informed. CBS' agreement provided that if photography did not begin by August 1979, would terminate, with rights reverting to Merrick and CBS committed to pay balance on rights provided no breach of contractual obligations. CBS and Merrick agreed to delay, but Merrick then repudiated oral modification. Oral modification was upheld by actions and later repudiation constituted breach of contract. Ordered to return advance and monies paid to his agents. Writer and Director may retain their fee, but physical property rights to screenplay belong to CBS, and other rights revert to Merrick, *CBS v. Merrick*, 716 F. 2d 1292 (9th Cir. 1983). Production Contractors, organizer and promoter of Chicago 1985 McDonald Charity Christmas Parade sold exclusive TV rights to ABC, owner and operator (O&O) of WLS-TV, and to 25 other TV stations throughout the US. Chicago's WGN-TV then announced it would do a simultaneous telecast of the parade and Production Contractors sought declaratory judgment on copyright infringement and unfair competition. Held no violation of copyright as idea of a Christmas parade is a common one. WGN planned on using own equipment and directors to create its own work of authorship which would be separately copyrightable when "fixed" at time of broadcast. Producers had not obtained copyright registration for floats, *Production Contractors v. WGN*, 622 F. Supp. 1500 (1985). Alan Landsburg Productions, without authorization, used 90 seconds of National Geographic footage from The Sharks in the 1983, Sharks Don't Die: The Making of Jaws 3-D. Sharks was the most popular prime-time show ever on public television. Seen on 98 stations, then Landsburg and MCA were liable for 98 statutory damage awards. Settled, (1986). The Amos 'n' Andy Show was created by Freeman Gosden and Charles Correll in the 1920's; in 1948, they assigned all rights to CBS, continued to create scripts, and broadcast on radio until 1955. CBS presented as a TV series from 1951 to 1953; with nonnetwork syndication until 1966, which ceased under protest from NAACP. In 1985, author Silverman sought a declaration that the radio broadcasts from 1928 to 1948 were in the public domain as not re-registered as required under *Copyright Law of 1909*, and he was free to use in a Broadway musical comedy. CBS counterclaimed as infringing copyright of radio shows broadcast after 1948, TV programs and for trademark infringement and unfair competition. Ruled CBS was entitled to prohibit unauthorized copying, distribution or exhibition of sound recordings of the post-1948 radio programs. CBS held valid copyrights in the scripts although not registered until early 1985. While TV programs were broadcast without a copyright notice, CBS did properly register when syndicated. CBS also asserted trademark rights to the name Amos 'n' Andy, and fifteen phrases, such as "The Mystic Knights of the Sea." Barred from using copyrighted portions of post-1948 radio and TV programs, but CBS had not used the trademarks for twenty years and Appeals Ct. ruled CBS had abandoned its trademarks and pre-1948 characters were public domain, *Silverman v. CBS*, 830 F. 2d 40 (SDNY 1986); cert. denied, *Supr. Ct.* (1989). Ingo Preminger, producer of the 1970 film, M*A*S*H, yielded certain rights for $500 each TV episode to MASH TV series to 20th Century-Fox. Fox, holder of the literary property rights, should have paid Preminger for spinoff Trapper John, M.D. Fox was considered by Ct. to be trustee for Preminger on a three-to-one basis and must pay Preminger. May be as much as $15 million, based on recent syndication sales, *Preminger v. Twentieth Century-Fox*, NYLJ (NY Cnty., 1987). In a decision which will affect freelance reporters and artists, the Supreme Ct. has ruled that copyright was owned by the creator, rather than an organization that had commissioned and paid for the work, even though the organization actively controlled and influenced the work. Usually one person or company owns the exclusive right to copy a work, distribute it, perform it publicly, and create new works using it. In this case, the parties were operating under an oral agreement that never considered copyright ownership. A free-lance reporter or artist will be the legal owner of his or her work unless: (1) he or she is, in effect, an employee, (2) there is a written contract that explicitly states the work is "considered a work made for hire," (3) the freelancer assigns whatever rights he or she might have, in writing, to the organization. Requests for such agreements will usually lead to requests for additional payment, (See "Employment"), *Community for Creative NonViolence v. Reid,* 846 F. 2d 1485 (DC Cir. 1988), overturned, US Sup. Ct. (1989). Studios and producers will tighten procedures for dealing with unsolicited program ideas. Many already do not open unsolicited material. Writers will push claims more vigorously, leading to more lawsuits. Studios will be more careful in contractual negotiations. The accounting procedures of studios will be exposed to greater public scrutiny. All because Art Buchwald submitted "King for a Day" in 1981, to Paramount and was allegedly rejected by Eddie Murphy's people. After spenting $750,000 to develop it released their rights. Buchwald was paid $17,500 for his contribution. Ct. ruled Murphy mega-hit was based upon a material element or was inspired by the earlier original treatment by Buchwald. This allowed Buchwald to recover contract claims of $250,000 plus 19% of net profits. Buchwald's lawyers spent $750,000 to sue, *Buchwald v. Paramount,* (1990). Case will impact broadcast concept rights, as in suit where Morgan Creek and 20th Century Fox are suing ABC-TV and MGM-TV for using feature film <u>Young Guns</u> as basis for the tv series <u>Young Riders</u>. Makers of hit movie pitched idea behind film to network which rejected it. Several months later series went into production. Key will be definition of terms "based upon" or "inspired by" used in Buchwald case. (See "Trade—Service Mark—Unfair Competition").

Copyright—Performance Rights to Music. ASCAP and BMI have been vigorous in protecting the music rights licensing for which they collect for music performance. Broadcasts, even non-sponsored, are Performance for Profit as department store which owned station received publicity value and audience through use of music, *WOR-Witmark v. Bamberger,* 291 Fed. 776 (D-N. Jer., 1923). However, Ruled a small Restaurant does not "perform" copyrighted music when playing radio through less than four speakers. However, *Copyright Act of 1976,* §110(5) imposes liability where proprietor has commercial system installed or converts standard home receiver into equivalent of commercial sound system and must pay copyright royalty. Another factor is whether establishment is of sufficient size to justify subscription to commercial background music service, *20th Century v. Aiken*, 422 US 151 (CA 3rd 1975), 30 RR 2d 1053 (1974) and *Sailor Music v. Gap Stores*, Cert. denied, 1982; and 668 F.2d 84 (2d Cir. 1981); *BMI v. US Shoe*, 678 F.2d 816 (1982). However, a miniature golf course using a radio wired to six separate speakers but only audible without distortion at close proximity in a noisy area and where the business was not of sufficient size to justify a subscription to a commercial background music service is exempt, *Springsteen v. Plaza Roller Dome*, 602 F. Supp. 1113 (MDNC 1985).

Memphis ad writer H. Jackson Brown composed jingle for new car dealership and sold to two other dealers. An employee of the last dealer to obtain the jingle bought a dealership, substituted his name and used the jingle. After Brown learned of this use he registered his work and brought an action for infringement. Ruled Brown's jingle had entered the public domain prior to the *Copyright Act of 1978* as its use was neither limited in purpose nor limited to a definitely selected group, *Brown v. Tabb*, 714 F. 2d 1088 (11th Cir. 1983). A Connecticut station broadcast 23 musical compositions without paying ASCAP fees and without permission of copyright holders. The station while operating at a loss was not a non-profit use. Ct. enjoined further infringement and awarded statutory damages of $1,000 per infringement and attorney's fees, *Boz Scaggs Music v. KND Corp.*, 491 F. Supp. 908 (D Conn. 1980); another case $54,000 damages—$26,400 attorney fees; *Rodgers v. Quests*, 213 USPQ 212 (ND Ohio 1981). Copying a song for purposes of parody constitutes a "fair use," and while permission may be sought "parodists will seldom get permission from those whose works are parodied. Self-esteem is seldom strong enough to permit the granting of permission even in exchange for a reasonable fee [and] the parody defense to copyright infringement exists precisely to make possible a use that generally cannot be bought." Did not meet demand for original song so parody, "When Sonny Sniffs Glue," had no economic effect on the original, *Fisher v. Dees,* 794 F. 2d 432 (9th Cir. 1986).

When music is used in an advertisement, specific special clearance must be obtained as the blanket music license does not cover use in an ad. Schlitz applied for a one-year license to use Cream Records Theme from Shaft in a TV commercial. Cream quoted a price of $100,000 and Schlitz refused but used anyway. Damages became the major issue with Cream contending its opportunity to license the music to other advertisers had been significantly decreased. Separate damages against ad agency to prevent unjust enrichment, *Cream Records v. Jos. Schlitz,* 754 F. 2d 826 (9th Cir. 1985), 864 F. 2d 668 (1989). In the contract to run an ads stations and networks should make certain they are indemnified if litigation occurs. (See "Antitrust—Broadcasting").

Defamation—Ad-libbed. Affiliate station is held liable for defamatory statement in CBS' March of Time network program. Station is not a common carrier and must be responsible for what it broadcasts, regardless of the source of the material, *Coffey v. Midland,* 8 F. Supp., 889 (West D-Mo., 1934). Extemporaneous non-scripted defamatory remarks in radio show are slander, not libel, as not written, *Locke v. Gibbons,* 164 NY Misc. 877 (1937). District Attorney's remarks in broadcast of actual murder trial are privileged and not actionable slander, *Irwin v. Ashurst,* 158 Ore. 61 (1938). No network liability for ad-libbed defamation by Al Jolson on sponsored program if "all due care" taken by network to prevent statement, *Summit Hotel v. NBC,* 336 Penn. 182 (1939). Unless "due care" proof offered, station liable for remarks made by newspaper sponsor's newsman, *Kelly v. Hoffman,* 137 NJL 695, 4 RR 2047 (NJ Ct. App. 1948). NBC neither malicious nor negligent in ad-libbed defamation and removed from action, *Wagner v. Finkelstein (Sally Rand),* 8 RR 2016 (ND Ill., 1952). Baltimore D.J. stated humorously, following looting by blacks during blizzard, that a local black TV commentator was seen entering a hospital for a bad knee, caused by carrying a TV. Although a public figure the jury awarded $30,000 from DJ, and $35,000 punitive damages from station. The Ct. rejected the "due care" general rule that limits situations in which punitive damages may be awarded against an employer when the remarks have been ad-libbed, *Embrey v. Holly*, 429 A. 2d 251 (Md. App. 1981). A theatre manager held a televised news conference in which ad-libbed statements were made about the part-owner's finances. A bank called in a loan, repossessed equipment and the theatre closed. Ruled part-owner was a private figure as not an individual of fame or notoriety and not an issue of public controversy as to statements about personal finances so only negligence, not malice, need be proven, *Bichler v. Union Bank*, 715 F. 2d 1059 (6th Cir. 1983). A talk show host and callers made ad-libbed remarks concerning a state senator who leased his building to a state committee. Ruled that the disparaging remarks were opinions and as a public official the remarks were related to the senator's fitness and qualifications so no cause of action results, *Hawkins v. Oden*, 459 A. 2d 481 (R.I. 1983). Author of <u>The French Connection</u>, Robin Moore appeared on a live radio call-in program and was asked about a former FBI agent who had participated. Moore stated was doing "40 years in the slammer" and "had ripped him off for $10M." The agent then called the program and claimed the statements were false. At request of Candy Jones, the host, Moore apologized on the air. But agent sued. Held that host could not be aware, or should have been aware of the probable falsity of the statements and had elicited a retraction. The seven second delay prior to the broadcasting of the statements was an insufficient period of time to conduct a full investigation into statements which were not obviously false, *Waters v. Moore*, NYLJ (NY Cnty 1985). WBZZ-FM, Pittsburgh, was found quilty of defamation of character, intentional infliction of emotional distress and invasion of privacy and was ordered by Ct. of Common

Pleas to pay $694,204 in damages to Liz Randolph, former station news director. Case revolved around sexual jokes made by station's morning team at Randolph's expense. As result of jokes, said she suffered anxiety attacks before delivering news, *Broadcasting*, (2/19/90, p. 97). (See "Defamation").

Defamation. Common law and state statutes recognize the right to be protected from publication, spoken or written, which tend to lower one's reputation among responsible and respectable people, or causes one to be shunned or avoided, or to become the object of contempt, hatred or ridicule. Just because program is sponsored is insufficient for station to claim qualified privilege and avoid responsibility, *WMCA*, 15 NY Supp. 2d 193 (1939). Held that certain radio broadcasts, if defamatory, taped by a church pastor at a station, constituted libel rather than slander. The Ct. relied upon decisions from most other jurisdictions and upon the <u>Restatement of the Law of Torts, Second</u>, which states: "Libel consists of the publication of defamatory matter by written or printed words, or its embodiment in physical form or by any other form of communication that has the potentially harmful qualities characteristic of written or printed words. Defamatory material broadcast by radio or otherwise is libel whether or not it is read from a manuscript," *First Independent Baptist Church of Arab v. Southerland,* 373 So. 2d 647 (Ala. 1979); *Gray v. WALA,* 384 So. 2d 1062 (Ala. 1980). Since *NY Times v. Sullivan,* 376 US 254 (1964), *Curtis v. Butts,* 388 US 130 (1967), and *Gertz v. Welch,* 418 US 323 (1974), the standard by which fault will be determined often revolves around whether a person is "private," and therefore only negligence need be proved or a "public official or public figure" which requires proof of "actual malice." Following are cases which illustrate the difficulties of determination: Name and place of business of man found guilty of crime broadcast, just after appeal had his conviction overturned; damages found, *Purcell v. Westinghouse,* 1 RR 2d 2016 (1963).

Station reporter named plaintiff as suspect in robbery. The individual was not involved; not a public figure; had not injected himself into a matter of public interest; although officers had mentioned the plaintiff as being the suspect under investigation. Relying primarily on Oklahoma law, held that the station should have exercised that degree of care which ordinarily prudent persons engaged in the same kind of business usually exercise under similar circumstances. Reporter had reasonable basis, displayed no indifference or negligence and the need to report matters as quickly as possible is not merely good competition but serves a paramount concern of society to have access to information of public concern as soon as possible, *Benson v. Griffin TV*, 593 P. 2d 511 (Okl. App. 1979). Showed a videotape of an alleged bank robber in handcuffs, and reported he would be charged with bank robbery. His name was not mentioned. He was soon released. Ruled story was privileged as a fair report. Was substantially accurate and station later correctly gave names of men who were formally charged with the crime. The matter was of legitimate public interest so soon after the incident took place and was constitutionally protected, *Williams v. WCAU-TV*, 555 F. Supp. 198 (E.D. Pa. 1983). Two men were arrested at a shopping mall when police responded to a robbery call. A report on the TV evening news was based upon information from the police scanner, a store clerk, and "no comment" from the police with footage of the arrest. No names were used. The men were later released when officers decided no crime had been committed. The Ct. noted that an award of punitive damages can only be made where proven that the story was broadcast with actual malice, *KARK-TV v. Simon*, 656 SW 2d 702 (Ark. 1983).

A Florida Ct. went to some length to note both parties had been unfaithful but still awarded alimony to Mrs. Firestone. Florida law does not allow alimony on grounds of adultery and Ct. did not specify reasons for granting divorce in its decision. Time Magazine reported divorce had been granted on grounds of cruelty and adultery. Mrs. Firestone was a private figure because she had not thrust herself to the forefront of any particular public controversy and was held defamed, *Time v. Firestone*, 424 US 448 (1976). A TV station broadcast charges of sexual harassment against a college financial aid officer. Held he was a public official as college was state-supported, used federal money for scholarships and the charges bore directly upon fitness and qualifications to hold his position, *Van Dyke v. KUTV*, 663 P. 2d 52 (Utah 1983). An investigation of a police officer is reported on TV; later resolved for the officer. The Ct. rules that this is not defamation as he is a public figure by virtue of his duties which are governmental and highly charged with the "public interest," *Pierce v. Pacific & Southern*, 303 SE 2d 316 (Ga. App. 1983). A slander action was brought against ABC's KGO-TV and the Better Business Bureau for quote that close-out sale was deceptive as promises of bargains not bargains at all. Ruled: merely doing business with parties to a public controversy does not elevate one to public figure status which requires greater malice proof. "...[A] person in the business world advertising his wares does not necessarily become part of an existing public controversy. It follows those assuming the role of business critic do not acquire a First Amendment privilege to denigrate such an entrepreneur." *Vegod Corp. v. ABC*, 88 Cal. App. 3rd 95; 25 Cal. 3rd 763 (1979), Cert. denied. However, in another state an opposite result. Broadcast that steak sale ads mentioned neither grade of meat nor price per pound; that commercial grade meat was lowest grade available; and that store allowing sale terminated endorsement. Held steak company became public figure when they voluntarily involved themselves in sale by managing and advertising it, *Steaks Unlimited v. Deaner*, 468 F. Supp. 779 (WD Pa. 1979); Upheld, 623 F.2d 264 (3rd Cir. 1980).

$1000 fine for personal attack on landlord as slum-lord etc. News documentary is not exempt from personal attack rules (see "Fairness Doctrine") as broadcast over 3 times in a year, *WNET, Ed. Broadcasting Corp.*, 65 FCC 2d 152, 40 RR 2d 1676 (1977); however, in similar case, referring to a land-lord as a "slum-lord" was not strictly defamatory under the innocent construction rule. Term can be construed to mean a person who owned buildings in a poor-dirty neighborhood. Under innocent construction rule, allegedly libelous statements must be taken as a whole, and if capable of any innocent construction, the statement is not defamatory, *Rasky v. CBS*, 431 N.E. 2d 1055 (Ill. App. 1982). There is no private cause of action if a personal attack, however, the Federal District Ct. may hear both State and Federal claims in state libel case combined with personal attack charge, even if personal attack claim fails, so long as Federal claim not frivolous. However one cannot obtain damages based just on personal attack FCC rule violation, *Lechtner v. Brownyard*, 50 RR 2d 609 (WD Pa. 1981); 679 F. 2d 322, 51 RR 2d 953 (1982); and same result, *Cyntje v. Daily News*, 53 RR 2d 299 (6th DC 1982). Harry Levinson, not a public figure but a jeweler of worldwide prominence, was linked with mob boss "Anthony Big Tuna" Accardo in numerous telecasts. Following the rule of innocent construction the Ct. ruled the publications could be construed innocently as not reflecting adversely on Levinson's abilities in business and were not actionable as libel per se, *Levinson v. Time, et. al.*, 411 NE 2d 1118 (Ill. App. 1980). Public figure, retired Army officer Anthony Herbert, sought damages for allegedly defamatory segment on 60 Minutes. To meet burden of proof of "actual malice" wished to inquire into the state of mind of Producer Barry Lando (co-defendant with Mike Wallace, CBS, Atlantic Monthly Magazine). Supreme Ct. held "...courts across country have long been accepting evidence going to the editorial process of the media without encountering constitutional objection." Ct. distinguished between this case and *Tornillo*. Newspapers are not required to allow reply to an attack, *Miami Herald v. Tornillo*, Sup. Ct. 418 US 241, (1974), as this involved efforts to control publication in advance and not post-publication inquiries. Principal concern is to balance First Amendment protection of press and need to protect individuals from defamatory publications, *Herbert v. Lando*,

99 S. Ct. 1635, 441 US 153 (1979). Fed. Dist. Ct. then left two of eleven allegedly defamatory statements for trial, 596 F. Supp. 1178 (SDNY 1984); 603 F. Supp 983 (SDNY 1985), and Ct. of Appeals dismissed remaining statements as not actionable, 781 F. 2d 298 (2d Cir. 1986).

A Media Buying Service sent letters to TV stations that an agency had breached contracts and failed to pay bills. Letters were libelous per se because they tended to injure reputation by disparaging integrity in agency's business dealings, *Matthews, Cremins, McLean, Inc., v. Nichter*, 256 SE 2d 261 (NC App. 1979). In 1975, Muhammad Ali was critical of referee Perez in Ali-Wepner fight as Howard Cosell pursued subject provocatively. Perez sued Ali for libel. Ali won but it cost $193,352 in legal expenses. AFTRA, which has a agreement which ABC has signed, provides that the producer of any program would indemnify performer against acts done or words spoken by performer at producer's request. Ali, a member of AFTRA, had been paid $5,000 for interview and claimed his statements made at Cosell's request. ABC refused to pay and Ali instituted arbitration proceedings under AFTRA collective bargaining agreement. Arbitration panel found ABC liable. The Supreme Ct. has held that courts should not review the merits of arbitration decisions because they should be binding and final if agreed to in collective bargaining agreements. But, ABC appealed. Review of record found decision rational even though ABC claimed AFTRA Code did not require indemnification for ad-libs. Arbitrators had found remarks induced by Cosell and it had been taped, reviewed, and edited by ABC, *ABC v. Ali*, 489 F. Supp. 123 (SDNY 1980).

In the case of a docudrama of the Scottsboro rape trial, NBC thought one of participants was deceased. After broadcast she wrote NBC that she considered broadcast libelous but NBC then proceeded to rebroadcast. Ruled that NBC had not negligently broadcast any untruths and had not broadcast with malice as she was public figure. Movie contained literal falsehoods. Appeal settled; *Street v. NBC*, 645 F. 2d 1227 (6th

Cir. 1981).

<u>60 Minutes</u> interviewed the wife of Richard Alfego who had taken their children in violation of a child custody order. Although not named or shown his identity was obvious and his reputation was injured. News must be substantially complete and accurate and not distorted, but not every fact and detail sympathetic to every side need be presented. Wife's charges were opinion and not libelous so long as not based on undisclosed falsehood. There is a distinction between a false statement of fact and an opinion, *Alfego v. CBS,* 7 Media Law Reporter 1075 (D. Mass. 1981).

WMC-TV broadcast report on starving cattle. Ct. of App. ruled that owner was private individual but he had burden of proof reports were false, *Wilson v. Scripps-Howard,* 7 Media Law Reporter 1169 (6th Cir. 1981).

The Village of Grafton, Ohio, identified on crawl used on <u>The Killing Ground</u> documentary which listed 54 locations of hazardous chemical waste dumps. Ruled the statement was privileged because made about a city; the city had no reputation to be defamed as did a person; and the information came from a federal agency though erroneous, *Grafton v. ABC,* 435 NE 2d 1131 (Ohio App. 1980).

Segment on <u>20/20,</u> had Geraldo Rivera reporting on alleged arson-for-profit scheme where he stated he had found circumstantial evidence and then interviewed manager of building alleged to have been burned for profit. In many states, it is <u>libel per se</u> to impute a criminal offense to an individual. Seven statements were made about the manager, which when viewed in context, charged him with such criminal activity. Even if in the form of an opinion not constitutionally protected to accuse of a crime. Manager was private figure who had not thrust himself to the forefront of any particular public controversy, *Cantrell v. ABC,* 529 F. Supp. 746 (ND Ill. 1981).

In 1977, ABC broadcast documentary <u>Sex for Sale</u> about effects of sex businesses on local communities. In a voice-over commenting on street prostitution an accompanying visual was three women walking down local street. Suit brought by one of women. Since her appearance was capable of defamatory meaning; no privilege; not public figure; defamatory, *Clark v. ABC*, 684 F. 2d 1208 (6th Cir. 1982).

<u>60 Minutes</u> alleged a medical insurance fraud. The issue was whether Dan Rather and his producer had acted with reckless disregard for the truth by not checking information sufficiently and, whether the interviews were staged. Plaintiff was required to show by clear and convincing evidence that there were serious doubts about the truth of the statements to the level of reckless disregard. Even though the report was not truthful, CBS did not have serious doubts, *Galloway v. CBS*, 55 RR 2d 573 (1984); was not personal attack as not discussion of a controversial issue of public importance, 59 RR 2d 587 (1985); 14 Med. L. Rptr. 1161 (Ca. App. 1987).

Report on a bomb squad injured officer in which he stated his wife and five children had "deserted" him since accident. The Ct. held for the wife. Opinion can be determined by cautionary phrasing used, such as "in my opinion" or from context of statement. In this case, a reasonable person could have believed that the reporter had inside information or that the statement was fact. The reporter, who relied upon an interview with the husband, should have known likely to be a one-sided view and other sources should have been consulted. The word "deserted" in a marital relationship is emotional, derogatory and obviously pejorative, *Burns v. McGraw-Hill Broadcasting*, 659 P. 2d 1351 (Colo. 1983).

Police officer impounded talk show host's car for various violations. Host then verbally abused and ridiculed the officer on-the-air. The Ct. found the host had disclosed nondefamatory facts (car impounded by officer) upon which "opinion" was based, *Fleming v. Benzaquin*, 454 NE 2d 95 (Mass. 1983).

A California statute recognizes the privilege, in the absence of malice, of "fair comment on matters of general public interest." Showed the arrest of an auto shop owner for not giving required written estimates prior to beginning repairs. Car shown to be in good working order except for broken

VERNON REGIONAL
JUNIOR COLLEGE LIBRARY

spark plug, but repair charge $160, *Rollenhagen v. City of Orange,* 116 Cal. App. 3rd 414 (Cal. Ct. App. 1981).

In 1979, an attorney for ABC charged that top network executives and <u>Charlie's Angels'</u> producers Spelling-Goldberg had defrauded Robert Wagner and Natalie Wood of their profit participation by inflating expenses. ABC interviewed George Reeves, Senior VP of ABC on <u>World News Tonight</u>. He then sued his own company for libel, claiming that the excerpt used did not reflect his denial of the charges. The Ct. held for ABC on grounds the story was fair and true, the facts were undisputed, it was a matter of law and did not have to go to a jury, and the average viewer would conclude charges were refuted from the context. Protected by California's statutory "absolute privilege law" of a fair and true report of judicial or other public official proceedings, *Reeves v. ABC,* 719 F. 2d 602 (2d Cir. 1983). (See "Judicial Coverage").

WCPO-TV did two news broadcasts linking a supper club with gambling and organized crime following a raid on the club based on a police report. However, the club officer testified that no one from the station ever contacted him to verify the facts. The Ohio Supreme Ct. applied the ordinary negligence standard—whether the station acted reasonably in attempting to discover the truth or falsity or defamatory nature of the publication—and did not accept station's argument that it was privileged to publish government reports without liability, because the broadcasts contained information not in the official records, *Embers Supper Club v. Scripps-Howard,* 457 NE 2d 1164 (Ohio 1984).

<u>60 Minutes</u> aired a report that an owner of vocational schools in Texas had defrauded the federal government and students. CBS upheld as guilty verdicts on that issue won by Federal and State governments confirmed truth. The Ct. applied federal standards of collateral estoppel; determine if the judicial proceedings against the owner were identical to the issue at stake in the libel suit; if the issue had been actually litigated; and was the issue a critical and necessary part

of the previous judgment. If so, then stopped from contesting again, *Wehling v. CBS*, 721 F. 2d 506 (5th Cir. 1983). A series on medical quackery specifically referred to and pictured Chiropractor Spelson with statements "really borders on the criminal," "cancer con artist" and "unscrupulous charlatans victimizing cancer patients." Ct. declared expression of opinion and commentary; facts were presented for viewer's evaluation; criticism of acts only—not personal; and matter of vital public interest. CBS was entitled to hold the view that treatments were contrary to the beliefs of medical and chiropractic thought and were therefore worthless or even dangerous, *Spelson v. CBS*, 581 F. Supp. 1195 (ND Ill. 1984).

In 1978, ABC News obtained copies of General Services Administration documents from a confidential source. (See "News Sources"). These documents discussed serious deficiencies in the performance of a security company along with unconfirmed suspicions that the company's president had links to organized crime. Despite the GSA reports the contract was renewed. ABC broadcast a story based primarily on these documents. ABC asserted it had broadcast a fair and accurate report of governmental action and was protected by constitutional or common law privilege. Company argued the documents were internal memos not for public disclosure. The Ct. ruled that ABC was protected by the "fair report privilege" for if it had waited until the GSA made an official finding the report would never have aired. It had been made clear by ABC that the documents contained only charges and allegations which had not been proven. Summary judgment granted ABC, *Salvatore J. Ingenere, & Exelon v. ABC* (D. Mass 1984).

General William C. Westmoreland withdrew his $120 million libel suit against CBS in 1985, for the documentary <u>The Uncounted Enemy: A Vietnam Deception,</u> The agreement between CBS and the General did not involve either a payment or retraction and no recovery of CBS's court costs estimated at several million dollars, 596 F. Supp. 1170; 601 F.

Supp. 66 (SDNY 1984). The Mass Media Bureau of the FCC also rejected a "Fairness Doctrine" complaint by the American Legal Foundation against the documentary. Although CBS admitted the broadcast contained breaches of its own standards of newsgathering the FCC distinguished between mistakes which did not diminish overall accuracy and deliberate commission of mistakes or errors in judgment, (1985). Lyndon H. LaRouche, Jr., right-wing presidential candidate, unsuccessfully sued NBC for libel in connection with two broadcasts which described him as the head of a "political cult" with an anti-Semitic bias. The jury awarded $2,000 actual damages and $3 million punitive damages to NBC on it's counterclaim of business interference. Verdict upheld but reduced punitive damages to $200,000 as too high in relation to actual damages, *LaRouche v. NBC*, 780 F. 2d 1134 (4th Cir. 1984).

Newscaster made critical comment regarding restaurant serving of lion and hippopotamus meat. Shortly afterward, restaurant received threatening letters, the property was vandalized, and establishment closed. Held the statement was true and was opinion of newscaster, *New Deal Restaurant v. WPIX*, NY Law Jr. (NY Cnty., 1985).

WLS-Chicago broadcast a consumer report segment about an appliance repair company, Action. Found that certain comments were capable of innocent interpretation; others were true; and caution "Buyer Beware" was not actionable as honest opinion. However, a statement concerning a judge's belief about an upcoming customer suit, if false, was potentially defamatory as were allegedly inaccurate references to unfavorable Better Business Bureau reports and unsubstantiated allegations that Action was under investigation by the Attorney General's office, *Action Repair v. American Broadcasting Co.*, 776 F. 2d 143 (7th Cir. 1985).

ABC's documentary, <u>The American Inquisition</u>, about the McCarthy era, related an encounter Victor Lasky had with the former head of an college art department who had been fired for being a security risk and a communist, in which there was an exchange of name-calling. In a followup on ABC News, Lasky declared that he never labeled Mundel a communist. Lasky sued claiming the network failed in the documentary to publish his unequivocal denial. ABC's claim that it was protected by the privilege of neutral reportage was rejected as inapplicable since no raging and newsworthy controversy existed. Jury then apparently concluded that although documentary harmed Lasky, he failed to prove was false, *Lasky v. ABC*, 631 F. Supp. 962 (SDNY 1986), App. 1987. <u>Saturday Night Live</u> broadcast a segment featuring a character "Fast Frank" with the same name as and allegedly a noticeable physical resemblance to tax consultant Maurice Frank. Ruled that although identifiable, it was unlikely anyone would take the skit seriously as obvious figment of comic imagination. If humor were to disguise an intent to injure character or reputation would not be protected from liability, *Frank v. NBC*, 506 NYS 2d 869 (NY App. 1986).

Wayne Newton awarded $22.8 million, later reduced to $5.3 million (largest in history stemming from a news report), as NBC knew or should have known that broadcasts linking Newton to alleged crime figures were untrue, *Newton v. NBC*, 14 Med. L. Rptr. 1914 (D. Nev. 1987). If a matter is of genuine public interest, the Ct. may apply a "gross irresponsibility standard," (*Chapadeau v. Utica Observer-Dispatch*, 38 NY 2d 196 (1975). WNBC reported about a homeless and mentally retarded young man who claimed he was abandoned and mistreated by his family. Because Delaney was observably mentally impaired, did NBC have reason to doubt the accuracy of its source and would the truth have been easily accessible upon a proper investigation? Upheld family's right to determine if NBC grossly irresponsible, *Delaney v. NBC*, NYLJ (Queens Cnty. 1987).

In 1981, an independent auditor questioned the accounting practices of barter time controlled by J. Walter Thompson ad agency, claiming it should be substantially reduced in value. Marie Luisi had the responsibility for barter; the obtaining of certain amounts of commercial time in return for the programs. The time would then be sold by J. Walter Thompson, for a fee, to advertising clients. After internal and external investigations, JWT announced in a press release, that Luisi was responsible for irregularities which resulted in a $30 million loss, and she had been dismissed. She sued for $20 million for libel. Held that by the "gross irresponsibility standard," JWT had acted carefully in gathering and disseminating information, *Luisi v. JWT Group*, NYLJ (NY Cnty. 1987). WBBM's newscast co-anchor Jacobson did a feature report on the marketing practices of the cigarette industry. He said, in part, Viceroy adopted a market strategy to attract young smokers by relating the cigarette "to pot, wine, beer, and sex. Do not communicate health or health-related points....They're not slicksters. They're liars." Not considered opinion as the intro and promotional spots would lead reasonable viewers to believe they were hearing a news report. Did not find that B&W Tobacco actually did conduct such a campaign. Held that B&W had proved with clear and convincing evidence that CBS and Jacobson knew was false or in fact entertained serious doubts as to its truth, and acted with malice; (researcher destroyed critical documents while litigation pending). $3 million verdict let stand by US Supreme Ct., *Brown & Williamson Tobacco v. Jacobson*, 827 F. 2d 1119 (7th Cir. 1987). (See "Defamation—Ad-libbed").

Direct Broadcasting Satellite. FCC permits nonlocal broadcast service from satellite direct to the home with six-year construction permits. Multiple Ownership regulations rejected in favor of minimalist regulatory approach to encourage rapid development. DBS operator, if did not retain control, would not be treated as broadcaster, *DBS*, 90 FCC 2d 676, 51 RR 2d 1341 (1982). Ct. upheld regulations but vacated part of ruling that those parties who lease from DBS common carrier would not be treated as broadcaster as "forbidden statutory experimentation." Ct. declared that when signals go directly to homes with the intent that those signals be received by the public such transmissions fit the definition of broadcasting if a common carrier satellite leases its channels to a customer-programmer who does not own any transmission facilities. Someone is broadcasting and application of broadcast restraints to programmers, although infrequent, has been upheld. The Ct. cautioned the FCC to remain alert to diversification of media viewpoints and control as multi-channel use is a contingent right subject to "public interest" considerations, *NAB v. FCC*, 740 F. 2d 1190, 56 RR 2d 1105 (DC Cir. 1984). However, financial and launch difficulties following "Challenger" disaster prevented start of services so FCC granted two companies four-year extensions for construction. FCC in May 1988, issued a public notice accepting the filing of new applications for direct broadcast satellite systems. The FCC served notice it would not be so forgiving of future failures to comply with the timetable for construction and implementation, *United States Satellite Broadcasting*, 65 RR 2d 916 (1988).

Economic Injury. "Sander's Economic Injury" was a policy by the FCC to consider economic injury to other stations in market when deciding to grant another a license in the same community. Not a separate and independent element of consideration, *Sanders v. FCC*, 103 F. 2d 395 (1939); 309 US 470 (1940). "Carroll Doctrine" on economic injury required the FCC to hold a hearing to consider an existing broadcast licensee's allegations that it would suffer economic harm from the licensing of a new station, and, upon presentation of substantial evidence, was likely to result in a net loss of service to the public, *Carroll v. FCC*, 258 F. 2d 440 (1958), 27 FCC 161 (1959). FCC refused to grant VHF tower height increase based almost entirely upon probable economic injury to existing UHF stations in proposed coverage area, *WHAS*, 31 FCC 273; 21 RR 929 (1961). Contrary to precedent, the FCC also denied an application in non-competitive hearing for probable interference and for failure to establish need for a third station in market of 18,000, *Dixie Radio*, 22 RR 345 (1961). The FCC has now laid to rest the "Carroll Doctrine" and other economic doctrines by stating the original premise—that competition can disserve the "public interest" because of limited advertising revenue in a market—is no longer valid in individual licensing and allotment proceedings. The FCC noted that while frequently invoked, doctrine never had produced the basis for denying an application, *Policies Regarding Detrimental Effects of Proposed New Broadcast Stations on Existing Stations*, 64 RR 2d 583 (1988), 66 RR 2d 19 (1989).

Editorializing. Banned partisan editorials, *Mayflower*, 8 FCC 333 (1941). "Fairness Doctrine" formed when Mayflower Opinion reversed. (see "Fairness Doctrine") Broadcasters may editorialize on condition facilities available to spokesman of opposing viewpoints. FCC set the basic grounds for the treatment of "controversial issues of public importance," 13 FCC 1246, 1 RR 91, 201 (1949). Licensee obligated to "Seek Out and Encourage" opposing viewpoints when editorializing, *New Broadcasting*, 6 RR 258 (1950). Station has no right to insist on two-sided discussion of controversy when one side refuses to air its viewpoint, *Detroit Evening News*, 6 RR 282 (1950). Don't use own employees to give opponents position when editorializing if you can get opposing viewpoint from others, *Alabama Broadcasting, Inc.*, 17 RR 273 (1958). Station expected to seek out opposition even when editorial by outsider, *Metro*, 19 RR 602 (1959). No obligation to editorialize, *McPherson Broadcasting*, 54 FCC 2d 565, 34 RR 2d 785 (1975). Four Calif. stations presenting editorial advertising sponsored by a utility company failed to afford reasonable opportunity for contrasting viewpoints. Although the amount of time was proportionate, the frequency and extent of presentations during peak audience listening periods showed disparity, *Public Media Center*, 72 FCC 2d 776, 45 RR 2d 1751 (1979). The "Cullman Doctrine" is when presenting one sponsored side of an issue licensee cannot reject a presentation of the other side simply on the grounds that he cannot obtain sponsorship for that presentation thus leaving the public uninformed. However, the broadcaster is not precluded from obtaining payment if it is able to do so, *Cullman Broadcasting,* 25 RR 895 (1963). Commentary by news anchorman, written by station news director differs from opinion of licensee; even if the opinion held by news people is also held by the licensee. Commentary does not become an editorial subject to personal attack rule unless licensee authorizes commentator to speak for the station, *Let's Help Florida Committee,* 74 FCC 2d 584, 46 RR 2d 919 (1979). Station editorial on conduct of mayor not news-slanting as no evidence of deliberate falsification and editorials did not relate to honesty, integrity or like personal qualities so not personal attack, *Mayor Maier v. WTMJ,* 50 RR 2d 73 (1981); 53 RR 2d 377 (1983); 55 RR 2d 1603 (1984). Held unconstitutional §399 of *Communications Act* which prohibited noncommercial stations from editorializing as no compelling governmental interest for restriction on free speech. Relatively small percentage of governmental funding (16%), *League of Women Voters v. FCC,* 547 F. Supp. 379, 52 RR 2d 311 (1982); Supreme Ct. upholds, 52 LW 5009, 56 RR 2d 547 (1984). (See "Licensee Discretion on Selling Time").

Emergency Broadcast System Rules. (§73:901—§73:962); An entry in the station log is required even if the weekly test of the Emergency Broadcast System equipment reveals no defect in the station's own EBS Weekly Transmission Test Signal, *EBS System,* 66 RR 2d 196, (1989).

Employment. Many businesses that rely upon unique talent or skilled individuals include noncompetitive covenants in employment contracts. One such clause was that D.J. would not work in the same county for a broadcast station for one year after leaving his present job. Within six months of being fired he went to work for another station. Even though stations broadcast different music their audiences overlapped to a significant degree. "Covenant not to compete" was enforceable as long as three elements satisfied: (1) employer must have substantial protectable right unique in his business; (2) the restriction is relevant and reasonable to the protection of that right; and (3) there is no imposition of undue hardship on employee. In this instance, the fact that station is personalized and identified by listeners by its announcers is a substantial business right. The restraint on employment for one year within county is relevant and reasonable as applied to same type of job and there was no hardship. Damages upheld, *Cullman Broadcasting v. Bosley*, 373 So. 2d 830 (Ala. 1979); also *Murray v. Lowndes*, 284 SE 2d 10 (1982); *Beckman v. Cox*, 296 SE 2d 566 (Ga. 1982). Ct. refused to uphold newscaster contract where employee was restrained from any type of on-air work and restricted from the market area of the station. Too overbroad and denied employee ability to make a living, and the term market was too vague as a geographic designation, *Capitol Cities v. Sheehan*, CV-83-0218242-S (New Haven Dist. Ct. 1983). Employee's contract was assigned to a new owner and bound the employee for the remainder of the contract. He could not quit and go to work for a competing station. But, where an employee is fired, the station cannot hold employee to non-competition clause as it would deprive employee of his livelihood, *Evening News v. Peterson*, 477 F. Supp 77 (DDC); *Orion Broadcasting v. Forsythe*, 477 F. Supp. 198 (WD Kty. 1979). FCC, in approving settlement agreements, also considers contract provisions such as covenants not to compete. These provisions are inherently suspect unless limited in duration and geographic scope, *Intercontinental Radio, Inc.*, 62 RR 2d 1565 (1985). NLRB found TV station committed unfair labor practice in violation of §8(a)(3),(1) of *National Labor Relations Act* when eliminated six o'clock news and discharged certain employees. Stations claimed low ratings but board found actions were effort to avoid unionization election of newsroom staff and were reprisals for union victory, *RJR Communications, Inc., and Local 346, Teamsters*, 1980 CCH Labor Law Reports, Para. 16,914 (1980). After volunteer producer for noncommercial

FM started sexual and racial harassment suit station refused use of facilities. Volunteer brought action claiming deprived right of access under *Civil Rights Act of 1964* and violation of First Amendment. Ct. dismissed; access to broadcast media not constitutional or statutory right and station not public accommodation, *Bridges v. Pittsburgh Community Broadcasting*, 491 F. Supp. 1330 (WD Pa. 1980). ABC suffered agony of defeat when sportscaster Warner Wolf breached good faith negotiated contract to join CBS. Wolf violated first refusal provision of ABC contract at CBS' instigation, but denied injunction as Ct. cannot easily supervise the performance of a personal services contract. First refusal right was not restrictive covenant but only three month moratorium on like employment, *ABC v. Wolf*, 430 NYS 2d 275 (App. Div. 1980); 438 NYS 2d 842; 420 NE 2d 363 (NY 1981). Contract between sports director and station allowed either party to terminate agreement voluntarily by payment of six months salary. Memo was given to employee listing tasks to be performed within next 30 days. Employee responded that he considered memo a constructive discharge as duties were new and more burdensome without an increase in compensation. Employee then sued for six months salary as liquidated damages. Upheld that 30 day requirement was a substantial contract change and was designed to make employee resign. Station required to pay $17,996 salary, *Sanders v. May Broadcasting*, 336 NW 2d 92 (Neb. Sup. Ct. 1983). Society of Composers and Lyricists attempted to get approval from National Labor Relations Board to form a bargaining unit (union). The NLRB used the "right of control" test and did not approve. Where company or employer for whom services are performed retains the right to control the manner and means by which the result is obtained; this is employment. Where control is reserved only as to the result sought; this is an independent contractor. Artists may decline offer to work; generally work at home; use their own equipment; choose their own hours; work concurrently for others. After work is complete studio may assume legal ownership and even if not used composer/lyricist still receives fee, (See "Copyright—Broadcast Rights"), *Aaron Spelling Productions and Society of Composers and Lyricists*, NLRB, 31-RC-5755 (1984). The American Federation of Television and Radio Artists required talent agents who represented AFTRA members be franchised by the union and pay an annual fee of $50. AFTRA members are prohibited from using agents not franchised. Sued that fee was a violation of the Antitrust laws. Supreme Ct. had found the franchise system protected by the statutory labor exemption (See "Antitrust—Cable"), but reversed and remanded on the fee. That case and the Screen Actors Guild class action suit settled by agreeing to end the practice of collecting franchise fees, *H.A. Artists v. Actors' Equity*, 451 US 704 (1981); *Talent Representatives v. AFTRA*, 593 F. Supp. 576 (SDNY 1984). Stations were required to announce if sports announcers were employed by the station, team, etc., and the manner of their selection. The FCC has determined that this is an unnecessary intrusion into business operations of licensees and deleted the requirement, *Policy Statement and Order*, aff'd, *Telecommunications Research and Action Center v. FCC*, 800 F 2d 1181, 61 RR 2d 61, (DC Cir. 1986). News anchor Hunter asked to take a leave of absence sued for breach of contract and won a temporary restraining order. Appellate Ct. declared that First Amendment protects the rights of broadcasters to make editorial and programming decisions without government interference and ordering the company to reinstate Hunter had impaired that right. Hunter had failed to prove the existence of immediate and irreparable injury which could not be compensated for by money damages, *Hunter v. Gaylord Broadcasting*, 12 Med. L. Rptr. 1591 (La. App. 1985). In 1985, actress Tia Carrere entered into a three year contract with ABC guaranteeing an average of 1 1/2 performances per week in General Hospital at $600-$700 for each show. During the ABC contract she was hired to be in Steven J. Cannell's A-Team. In 1986, Carrere filed for voluntary Chapter 11 bankruptcy, and the next day sought to reject her ABC contract. Ruled §365 does not apply to a personal services contract in a bankruptcy case under Chapter 7 or 11. As a bankruptcy court is a court of equity (right) as well as law, it would be inequitable (not right) to allow a greedy debtor to seek the protection of the Court when her major motivation is to cut off the equitable remedies of her employer to obtain a more lucrative contract with another. ABC may seek a negative injunction against her taking the other job, *In re Tina Carrere*, (CD Ca. Bankruptcy Ct. 1986). In 1975, Western Media bought station from William Merrick, who agreed not to operate or work for any other radio or TV station within 50 miles for ten years for $50,000, payable monthly for ten years. In 1984, he accepted a position with the public radio station of Montana State University. The noncompetition covenant was upheld and Merrick was required to return monthly payments received after the breach, *Western Media v. Merrick*, 727 P. 2d 547 (Mont. 1986).

Equal Access to Justice Act. Rules are adopted providing for the award of attorney's fees and other expenses to qualified parties who prevail over the federal government in certain administrative and court proceedings, *Subpart K*, §73:1501—§73:1530, 50 RR 2d 1338 (1982).

Equal Employment. (§73:2080, §76:71-79); *Title VII of the Civil Rights Act of 1964*, and various other federal laws prohibit discrimination on the basis of race or color, religion or creed, sex (including sexual harassment and pregnancy discrimination, national origin, age, physical or mental handicap, or veteran status). Most of these laws are applied not by the FCC, but by private action. State laws also exist. Most of the federal laws are administered and enforced by the Equal Employment Opportunity Commission (EEOC). However, due to the rules of the FCC, broadcasters are held to a higher EEO standard than other private employers. Licensees are required to take specific, systematic and positive steps of affirmative action on behalf of women and minorities. The

FCC reviews station compliance as part of the license application and renewal process. An employment practice that has a substantial adverse impact on women, blacks or other minorities is discriminatory, and therefore, illegal, unless it can be justified as a job-related business necessity. In the area of where a religion prohibits working at certain times courts have ruled that an employer must make reasonable accommodations for the religious practices of employees, unless it can establish that the accommodation would cause undue hardship. Should offer voluntary swaps, flexible scheduling or lateral transfers or changes of job assignments.

A licensee is not obligated to participate in negotiations concerning employment practices and programming, *WKBN,* 30 FCC 2d 958, 22 RR 2d 609 (1971). FCC must conduct hearing when a petition-to-deny renewal raises substantial and material questions of fact or when renewal will not serve "public interest." Where statistical disparity in minority employment substantial and licensee's minority employment is outside zone of reasonableness (flexible concept comparing employment with availability of minorities in area and recruitment policies of station) FCC conducts own inquiries, but if it cannot or does not wish to do so itself it should permit discovery by petitioners, *Chinese for Affirmative Action v. FCC and Bilingual Coalition v. FCC,* 595 F 2d 621 (DC Cir. 1978). The FCC and EEOC plan to cooperate as FCC holds that discrimination by licensee is against the "public interest." Broadcasters have unique problems and responsibilities in the area of Equal Employment, *Memorandum of Understanding,* 70 FCC 2d 2320, 43 RR 2d 1505 (1978). Suburban stations EEO efforts will be evaluated on work force data from city and county of license including larger metropolitan area nearby, *Suburban Wash. DC Renewal,* 77 FCC 2d 911, 47 RR 2d 417 (1980). FCC uses a two-step approach in evaluating EEO efforts. The FCC will look first to EEO record, including; program and policies, complaints, composition of station's work force and available labor force in station's area as reported on Form 396. If satisfactory, no further analysis or investigation. If, however, the initial evaluation indicates station did not meet EEO obligations, those areas that appear deficient will be investigated further. Although numerical comparisons of station's work force with available work force will be means of identifying stations for further investigation, each station's overall record will be fully examined even if within processing guidelines. Processing guidelines are not "safe harbors." §73:2080 incorporates EEO requirements and suggested practices. Broadcasters must file a modified version of the 5-point Program Report, Form 396-A, as part of all initial and transfer applications. An Annual Employment Report, Form 395-B requires stations to identify employees by race/national origin and sex in nine job categories, with statistical tables conforming to the EEOC's Form EEO-1. Form 396 for EEO reporting at license renewal is designed to reduce paperwork burden. Broadcasters should have been collecting job referral data by race and sex since 1976 in order to comply with EEO obligations. Processing guidelines used: Stations with fewer than five full-time employees will only have to complete the identification and certification portions of Form 396; stations with five to 10 employees will have further investigation if minority group or women do not number, in comparison with local workforce, 50% over-all and 25% in top four job categories (officials, manager, professionals, technicians, sales); stations with 11 or more full-time employees must reach 50% parity over-all and in top four categories, *Equal Employment Opportunity Rules for Broadcasters*, 63 RR 2d 220 (1987), 65 RR 2d 1697 (1989). The US Ct. of Appeals ruled that it was unreasonable for the FCC to short-term renew the license of an FM-AM broadcaster without first conducting an evidentiary hearing concerning allegations of intentional racial discrimination and affirmative action deficiencies that had been raised in a petition-to-deny. The FCC did not obtain the necessary information to determine whether a very substantial discrepancy between black employment at the station and the number of blacks in the workforce was of benign origin and was an abuse of discretion by the agency. Case remanded, *Beaumont Branch of the NAACP v. FCC*, 854 F. 2d 501, 65 RR 2d 367 (DC Cir. 1988). One year later the Ct. upheld the FCC's decision to short-term renew two TV stations without first conducting investigations or holding hearings. The difference was a reasonable determination based on a well-established and consistently applied policy by the FCC that neither licensee had exhibited signs of intentional discrimination although their EEO program was in some respects defective,*Tallahassee Branch of the NAACP v. FCC*, 870 F. 2d 705, 66 RR 2d 186 (DC Cir. 1989). Private causes of action are also used in discrimination situations. In 1976, class action alleging employment discrimination on the basis of sex in violation of *Title VII* filed against network O&O station. Consent decree approved by Federal District Ct. had CBS agreeing to increase women in upper managerial and production positions when vacant through 1984; scholarship at USC for women; Career Development Training Seminar; station EEO officer; technical training for women employees, etc. Employee who sued received $30M, but agreed to resign. Consent Decree is not an admission of violation; merits of case not tried and CBS does not have to promote or hire unqualified nor promote or hire best qualified applicant, *Cotton v. CBS, Inc.*, Case No. 76-2215 HP (CD Cal. July 9, 1980); see also *Walker v. KFGO*, 518 F. Supp. 1309 (DN Dak. 1981). A former talk show hostess awarded $21M in damages and back pay as she was paid less than a male colleague performing equal work. The disparity in salaries was sex-based and violated the *Equal Pay Act of 1963* and *Title VII of the Civil Rights Act of 1964* which entitled her to the difference between what earned and amount should have earned. She was also asked to perform certain clerical tasks the male host was not required to perform and then was fired in retaliation for her refusal to perform such work, *Futran v. Ring Radio*, 501 F. Supp. 734 (ND Ga. 1980). FCC denied license renewal after investigation based on complaints by citizens group. Substantial shortfall in amount of time station devoted to non-entertainment; lack of good faith effort to do programming representations proposed in 1970; lack of candor in dealings with FCC; no effort to comply with EEO requirements and even fired some black employees, *Leflore Broadcasting v. FCC*, 636 F.2d 454, 47 RR 2d 901 (DC Cir. 1980). TV anchorman sought reassignment as anchor from reporting assignment. Alleged violated *Fair Labor Standards Act* which makes it illegal for employer to retaliate against employee who files charges or participates in labor dispute. Denied as failed to prove action had discriminatory motive. Station contended reassignment was due to ratings and unfavorable consultant's report. Ct. refused to interpret ratings or report and news director and station manager simply had to think ratings were too low, *Haines v. Knight-Ridder*, CCH Labor Law Reports, Para. 33,976 (D. RI 1980). Christine Craft charged sex discrimination, equal pay violation and fraud. Ct. dismissed sex discrimination and equal pay claims as actions taken were not the result of a general animus toward women or Craft in particular, and pay was attributable to several other factors other than sex. Overturned on appeal; not fraudulently induced into accepting employment as a co-anchor and reassignment to news reporter based upon a discriminatory application of an appearance standard, *Craft v. Metromedia*, 572 F. Supp. 868 (WD Mo. 1983); 766 F. 2d 1205 (8th Cir. 1985). Licensee which failed to communicate minority employment needs to sources of qualified minority applicants and failed to evaluate the effectiveness of its recruiting was given short-term renewal. Denial of renewal was considered inappropriate because sporadic hiring of minorities suggested absence of intent, *KDEN*, 55 RR 2d 1311 (1984). Periodic EEO reports were required where none of the ten persons hired in a year was a minority. Reporting conditions were also imposed on the noncommercial FM station where no minorities were represented in full-time positions, *University of Tulsa*, 55 RR 2d 1601 (1984). Stations whose 1980-83 license term employment of minorities was consistently below FCC guidelines and whose EEO programs revealed few <u>active</u> techniques to increase applicant flow were subjected to EEO reporting conditions and/or short term license renewals, *Texas Broadcast Renewals*, 57 RR 2d 13 (1984). The *Cable Communications Act of 1984*, mandated EEO guidelines to be applied to cable. The FCC's new cable rules also are applicable to SMATV systems. For the first time a prohibition on age discrimination. Cable operators with more than six employees will have to file and make available for public inspection for five years an annual Form 395A. Cable operators who fail to file or are found to discriminate will be denied certification, face fines, or other sanctions, *Cable Communications Policy Act Rules (Equal Employment Opportunities)*, 58 RR 2d 1572 (1985).

D.J. sued station that his discharge violated the *Age Discrimination in Employment Act*. Because of post-1975 hiring practices, by the end of 1981, station did not employ a single announcer over the age of 40, and the jury could conclude this was not merely coincidental nor a byproduct of the natural age progression of the labor market. Held, back pay of $97,000, but denied pay to be figured from firing to retirement age. The radio industry provides only tenuous job security for D.J.'s and animosity, distrust, disagreement and conflict had developed between station and Rengers. The US Supreme Ct., then, vacated judgment and remanded for retrial, *Rengers v. WCLR Radio*, 661 F. Supp. 649 (ND Ill. 1986), 825 F. 2d 160 (7th Cir. 1987), 857 F. 2d 363 (7th Cir. 1988). License revoked for engaging in racially discriminatory hiring practices, harassing persons attempting to review the station's public file, and numerous other abuses, *Catoctin Broadcasting of NY*, 62 RR 2d 1132 (1987), 66 RR 2d 131 (1989). In eleven situations since EEO rules were revised the FCC conditioned renewal upon the filing of periodic EEO reports demonstrating progress in compliance efforts, since no evidence of intentional discrimination, *Carolina Christian Broadcasting*, 64 RR 2d 1201 (1988). The Supreme Ct. issued two decisions tending to blunt the ability to prove discrimination in employment disputes brought under *Title VII of the Civil Rights Act of 1964.* (See "Handicapped," "Minority Ownership").

Equal Opportunity. (§312, §315, §73:1920, §73:1930, §73:1940, §76:205); Equal opportunities for political candidates means equal quality of time as well as quantity, *Stephens,* 11 FCC 61, 3 RR 1 (1945). Equal opportunities applies only to same office and same election, *Sam Morris,* 4 RR 885 (1948). Reports by official not actively running for office do not automatically entitle opponents to time for reply, *Fitzpatrick,* 6 RR 543 (1950). Even fringe candidate with less than 1% of primary vote entitled to equal opportunity, *CBS,* 7 RR 1189 (1952). Once candidate has announced for re-election equal opportunity provision is in effect including reports if opponent makes request within one week of broadcast, *KGNS,* 7 RR 1130 (1952). State paper-type talk by Pres. Eisenhower does not entitle opponents to equal opportunity even during campaign, *CBS,* 14 RR 720 (1956). No right to equal time on basis of appearance by candidate in news if not initiated by candidate, *Letter to Blondy,* 6 Feb. (1957). Debate between candidates for governor, rebroadcast two and one-half days after original broadcast was not exempt on-the-spot news coverage. "One-day rule" governs on-the-spot treatment, *New Jersey Public Broadcasting Authority,* 73 FCC 2d 808, 46 RR 2d 558 (1979); however, rebroadcast of news interview after six months, in regularly scheduled interview show hour but during election campaign does not deprive show of exempt status as still newsworthy, controlled by station, not unreasonable, *Robert Hanna,* 88 FCC 2d 346, 50 RR 2d 781 (1981). Some time must be afforded for appropriate spokesman to reply to Presidents speeches on Vietnam, *Committee for Fair Broadcasting of Controversial Issues,* 19 RR 2d 1103 (1970), reversed on other grounds, *CBS v. FCC,* 454 F. 2d 1018; 23 RR 2d 2019 (1971). Automatic right of reply by spokesman of opposing party to Presidential addresses rejected, *Democratic National Committee v. FCC,* 460 F. 2d 891, Cert. denied, 409 US

843; 23 RR 2d 2165 (1972). FCC upheld when denied DNC right to some time to reply to Presidential addresses on economic policy, *DNC v. FCC*, 481 F. 2d 543 (DC App. 1973). "Lowest Unit Charge." Amendment to §315; 45 days before primary election and 60 days before federal or special election stations can only charge candidate lowest unit charge for same class and amount of time for the same time period, 47 USCA 315(b), *Pub. L. 93-225* (1972). Stations must provide candidates lowest unit rate for a given class of time, but there is no requirement to offer the cheapest class of time, but must apply all discounts notwithstanding amount of time purchased, *Warren J. Moity, Sr.*, 46 RR 2d 399. State law attempted to prescribe rates that radio and TV could charge for political spots for state and local candidates by requiring lowest unit charge regardless of time of year. This, Ct. ruled, went beyond requirements of §315 and therefore intrudes upon federal government. Potential obstacle to the underlying reasoning of the federal statute that campaign periods should be shortened and excessive campaign spending should be curbed, *KVUE v. Moore*, 709 F. 2d 922, 54 RR 2d 224 (5th Cir. 1983); aff'd, 52 LW 3679 (Supr. Ct. 1983). The 45-days before the primary election and 60-days before regular election rules deal only with the lowest unit rate that may be charged, not with the dates during which a candidate may or may not be granted access, *Carter-Mondale*, 74 FCC 2d 631, 46 RR 2d 829 (1979). FCC $5,000 fine for repeatedly charging political advertisers rates in excess of lowest unit rate and for practice of requiring one candidate to pay with certified check while not requiring this of other candidates, *Alpha Broadcasting*, 57 RR 2d 469 (1984). FCC issued a public notice resolving a recurrent controversy, holding that preemptible spot time is to be considered a single class of time for purposes of calculating the lowest unit rate charge, and that the relevant period of time is to be the broadcast week. "Preemptible with notice" time and "run of schedule" time should also be treated as separate classes of time. Thus, the lowest unit charge for a preemptible class of time is calculated on a week-to-week basis according to the lowest price any advertiser has paid for a spot which has cleared a particular time period or daypart. Moreover, prices paid for "making good" spots which air in the daypart must be considered in establishing the lowest unit charge because "make goods are an integral part of preemptibility in today's marketplace." A "make good" is an offer by the station to air an advertiser's preempted spot at another, usually later date, in the same daypart as originally purchased, rather than make a refund. If a station sells preemptible time on a weekly rotation basis, and a commercial advertiser's "make good" spot airs during the daypart of a particular weekly rotation, the price paid for the "make good" spot counts in determining the lowest unit charge for that time period during that entire week, even if the political spot to which the lowest unit charge is applied is not itself a "make good." The same applies where stations sell preemptible spot time during prime time on a program-by-program basis, except that the lowest unit charge would apply only to the program or adjacency in which the particular spot runs. If fixed rates for non-preemptible spots station or cable operator may not increase those rates during the pre-election period unless the rate change is attributable to business factors unrelated to the pending election (audience ratings increase or normal seasonal variation), *Lowest Unit Charge Requirements*, 65 RR 2d 85 (1988).

"Employee—Candidate." Candidate A newscaster, Candidate B applies for equal opportunity; FCC gives equal time (several weeks) as used by A; B can't use all; FCC says must use personally, no representative, *Grace*, 17 RR 697 (1958). In 1959, Congress passed legislation exempting from equal opportunity "bona-fide" newscasts, news interviews, news documentaries and on-the-spot news coverage; §73:1940(g). However, appearance of employee—candidate is use under equal time rule, *WMAY*, 4 RR 2d 849 (1965). TV News reporter Branch ran for City Council and was taken off the air during the campaign. He sought a declaratory ruling from the FCC when told he could not work on-air. The FCC concluded that being a newscaster did not exempt the station from the obligation to provide equal opportunity to opposing candidates. On appeal, Ct. determined the only exemption was an intrinsically newsworthy on-air appearance by a candidate who was the subject of the news coverage. The Ct. rejected the claim that the statute unconstitutionally prevented Branch from seeking political office by imposing an undue burden (requiring him to take an unpaid leave). Since Congress' intent was ambiguous the Ct. deferred to the FCC opinion, *Branch v. FCC*, 824 F.2d 37, 63 RR 2d 826 (DC Cir.1987), Cert. denied (1988).

"Zapple Doctrine or Quasi—Equal Opportunities," requires that when a station gives or sells time to supporters or spokesperson of a candidate during an election campaign, the licensee must afford comparable time to the spokesperson for an opponent, *Nicholas Zapple*, 23 FCC 2d 707, 19 RR 2d 421 (1970). Political editorial regulations apply even in a recall election, even when incumbent's name is not on ballot. If an editorial endorses one candidate, spokesperson for all those not endorsed must be given chance to reply and the original editorial does not need to be rebroadcast to balance the numerous replies against the one time endorsement, *Friends of Howard Miller*, 72 FCC 2d 508, 45 RR 2d 1142 (1979).

"Political Debates." Congress passed, in 1960, temporary legislation permitting televised debates between Nixon and Kennedy, excluding all minor candidates. The FCC, in 1962, decided that coverage of a debate by major candidates invited by a Press Association is not news coverage so equal time applied, 24 RR 401 (1962). After Congress did not pass debate enabling legislation for the 1976 presidential campaign the FCC ruled that press conferences and debates of candidates are exempt news events where broadcast live, in entirety, and not sponsored or controlled by licensee or candidate and are exempt from equal time requirements. This allowed the Carter-Ford debates, *Aspen Institute*, 55 FCC 2d 697 (1975), aff'd, *Chisholm v. FCC*, 538 F. 2d 349 (DC App.);

Cert denied, 429 US 890 (1976); 36 RR 2d 1437 (1976). The FCC refined that decision by deciding debates between political candidates are bona-fide on-the-spot news coverage and the former policy requiring that broadcast debates between political candidates must be sponsored by a third party not connected with the licensee was eliminated, *Henry Geller*, 54 RR 2d 1246 (1983) aff'd, *League of Women Voters v. FCC*, (US App DC 1984). Thus, minor party candidates excluded from debates televised by the major networks was not in violation of the "Fairness Doctrine," First Amendment nor equal opportunities, *Sonia Johnson*, 56 RR 2d 1533, aff'd, 63 RR 2d 1492 (1984). US Ct. of Appeals affirms no minor-party candidates for president and vice-president have First Amendment right to be included in TV debates with major-party candidates, *Johnson v. FCC*, 829 F. 2d 157, 63 RR 2d 1492 (1987). Candidate-sponsored debates can be a "bona-fide news event" exempt from the equal opportunities rule. Therefore, can exclude all but two candidates. There is no meaningful distinction between debates sponsored by broadcasters and those sponsored by candidates. Neither gives unbridled power in a single candidate to advance his or her candidacy as adversarial nature of the debate format reduces greatly the opportunity for broadcasters to use their coverage to advance the candidacy of a particular candidate unfairly, *WCVB-TV*, 63 RR 2d 665 (1987); also applies to major political party sponsored debates, *Lenora B. Fulani*, 65 RR 2d 644 (1988). The FCC was ordered to reconsider a declaratory ruling that separate, back-to-back, in-studio presentations of position papers without any press interaction are not "on-the-spot coverage of bona-fide news events" as more akin to candidate advertising. In-studio interviews do not fall into exemption because the segments are not part of "regularly scheduled" programming. Ct. asked FCC to use its traditional two-part test; (1) is program newsworthy, and, then (2) is it the exercise of good faith news judgments, *WEBE-108 Radio*, 63 RR 2d 1748 (1987); *King Broadcasting v. FCC*, 860 F. 2d 465, 65 RR 2d 732 (1988).

"Personal Attack Rules." §315(I), §73:1920, and §76:209 are amended to exempt all §315 uses of broadcast and cable facilities by candidates for public office, and to eliminate all applicability of the "Fairness Doctrine" to §315 uses, *Personal Attack Rules and Applicability of the Fairness Doctrine,* 78 FCC 2d 457, 45 RR 2d 1635 (1979). (See "Fairness Doctrine"). FCC ruled that a paid ad in which a U.S. Congressman was described as fiscally irresponsible was not a personal attack, particularly since the Congressman was given an opportunity to purchase equal time for a response, *Hon. Les AuCoin,* 53 RR 2d 1024 (1983). State election laws and state election officials' decisions prevail concerning who is a legally qualified candidate, unless such determinations are overturned in Ct., *John J. Marino,* 71 FCC 2d 311, 45 RR 2d 356, and candidates under the *Federal Election Campaign Act* are not necessarily candidates under §73:1940, *National Citizens Committee for Broadcasting,* 75 FCC 2d 650, 46 RR 2d 1 (1979). FCC affirms that someone is not a legally qualified candidate for equal opportunity purposes unless certified under applicable state law, *Mayor Bergin,* 90 FCC 2d 813, 51 RR 2d 1535 (1982). A noncommercial TV station did not act unreasonably in refusing time to a self-proclaimed write-in candidate for Federal office. Under §312(a)(7) and §73:1940(a) must demonstrate substantial campaign activity after denial of access to ballot, *Michael Levinson,* 61 RR 2d 1306 (1986). A station denies reasonable access by not selling prime time, but does not have to sell political time within any news show, *Anthony R. Martin-Trigona,* 42 RR 2d 567, 42 RR 2d 1599 (1978). An opponent who requests time more than seven-days after another candidate for the same position has appeared must not be turned down if request is for "reasonable access" and not equal opportunities, *Kennedy for President Committee,* 80 FCC 2d 93, 46 RR 2d 1539 (1980). Then-President Carter held a news conference on the eve of the New Hampshire primary and held was exempt from equal opportunity requirements of §315 as on-the-spot coverage of a bona-fide news event. The FCC is only required to consider whether or not the broadcaster intends to promote the interest of a particular candidate in presenting such coverage. Four days before Illinois 1980 primary Carter gave a press conference and speech on the economy. The FCC affirmed that neither §312(a)(7) nor the "Fairness Doctrine" entitled Kennedy to free response time when time was available for purchase. The Ct. again upheld the FCC noting that while §315(a) sets forth a right of equal opportunity when there has been a prior use by another candidate; §312(a)(7) is not dependent upon prior use but requires the broadcaster to provide reasonable access to a candidate or to sell the candidate time at prescribed rates. The "Fairness Doctrine" claim was denied as Kennedy had not identified the particular controversial issue involved and no evidence that broadcasters had failed to present contrasting viewpoints on the economy, *Kennedy for President Comm. v. FCC*, 636 F. 2d 417, 636 F. 2d 432; 47 RR 2d 1521, 1537 (DC Cir. 1980). Since federal candidates access is personal right no such right is afforded Political Action Committee's (PAC's). Broadcaster obliged to give free response time to candidates if PAC obtains time, 89 FCC 2d 626, 51 RR 2d 233 (1982). NJ Sup. Ct. holds §315 does not preempt state statutes requiring public broadcasting to promote full discussion of issues consistent with balance, fairness and equity, in state race for governor, *McGlynn v. NJ Broadcasting Auth.*, 439 A. 2d 54, 50 RR 2d 867 (1981). FCC declines to question network's pre-address decision that Reagan's last minute plea for support of policies and party scheduled shortly before mid-term election of 1982 was a bona-fide news event, *Democratic National Committee,* 91 FCC 2d 373, 52 RR 2d 713 (1982). §312 states that a station must not deny access to any candidate for federal office, regardless of what form that access takes. The FCC affirms its use of a case-by-case complaint activated approach to implementation of the reasonable access provisions. Were the FCC to abandon consideration of individual complaints in favor of a policy based on overall review at the time of licensee renewal, the timely resolution of access disputes would be impossible. Congress also intended such enforcement as it included the access provisions in the revocation section of the Act, *Reasonable Access Implementation*, 53 RR 2d 89 (1983). The Democratic National Committee requested the FCC order time on the basis of reasonable access to respond to pro-Reagan ads sponsored by Republican National Committee. To prove that CBS and NBC did not provide reasonable coverage of conflicting viewpoints a survey was taken which showed that views favorable to the administration received twice as much airtime on news shows and when the RNC ads were added the program imbalance was three-to-one. The FCC held that this disparity did not warrant an investigation. The Ct. of App. held that broadcasters are required only to program with reasonable good faith and the FCC standard of reasonableness is a lenient one. Licensees have wide discretion in determining how to fulfill their fairness obligations and may choose to present opposing viewpoints in any one of a number of programming modes. The Ct. noted that "Fairness Doctrine" complaints may arise from political ads if audience disparity were shown, however, to prevent the chilling effect that the "Fairness Doctrine" may have there is a formidable barrier in proof, *DNC v. FCC*, 717 F 2d 1471, 54 RR 2d 941 (DC Cir. 1983). The appearance of an announced Presidential candidate during a news documentary for one minute and twenty seconds, where no political comment was made, did not cause an equal opportunity obligation as news documentary is exempt, *Avery Productions*, 55 RR 2d 646 (1984). A new weekly news show to premiere during the Presidential primary is not subject to equal opportunities. Policy had been that must have been regularly scheduled news show before campaign before exempt status acquired, *CBS, Inc.*, 55 RR 2d 864 (1984). The Compliance Branch has ruled that ads for <u>Time</u> magazine, consisting of individual shots of candidates for periods no longer than two or three seconds were fleeting uses which would not give rise to equal opportunity obligations, *Time, Inc.*, 55 RR 2d 581 (1984). FCC, when abolishing the "Fairness

Doctrine" held that Teletext did not constitute "broadcasting" and content regulations, other than equal opportunity, would not apply to that service, *Telecommunications Research and Action Center v. FCC*, 801 F 2d 501 (D.C. Cir. 1986). (See "Subscription TV").

Ex Parte Rules—Conflict of Interest. (§1.1202); An investigation revealed FCC Commissioner Mack involved in illegal ex parte (contact by one party of interest without notice to other parties of interest). Lowest rated applicant awarded license causes extensive hearings and revocation of license after remand, *WKAT*, 22 FCC 117 (1957); *WKAT v. FCC* (Ct. App. DC) 258 F. 2d 418 (1958); 17 RR 997 (1960); 296 F. 2d 375 (1961); 368 US 841, Cert. denied (1961). Fine of $6,000 for contact by one party without notice to other or without giving opponent an opportunity to be heard is ruled not unreasonable nor excessive, *Desert TV*, 88 FCC 2d 1413, 50 RR 2d 1283 (1982). Ex parte rules requiring all written or oral contacts to be made part of record reaffirmed. To make all contacts illegal would inhibit policy making process, *Ex Parte*, 53 RR 2d 1337 (1983). Congressional expression of concern with administrative delay will not be treated as ex parte but as status inquiries if no view as to merits or outcome of proceeding, *Ex Parte Rules*, 63 RR 2d 1723 (1987); 64 RR 2d 1554 (1988). FCC employees may accept free meals (but not one-on-one from reporters), "not lavish in kind," at business-related group functions, if Office of General Counsel has first made written determination that attendance is desirable to assist employees in performing their official duties. Commissioners and staff may accept gifts of nominal value for participation in programs, seminars and conferences, if of the type usually given by sponsor and provided to all participants, *Acceptance of Gifts and Meals by Commission Employees*, 62 RR 2d 158 (1987); 64 RR 2d 1653 (1988). A further overhaul of the ex parte rules to govern communications by decision-making personnel (any person who is or may reasonably be expected to be involved in the decisional process in a proceeding) as well as communications to decision-making personnel restricted a wider range of proceedings than just "on the record" hearings. Speeches, panel presentations and other communications concerning non-restricted rulemaking will only prohibit presentations to FCC personnel and not from FCC personnel. An expanded "sunshine period" which bars all presentations (except Congressional and other federal agencies), ex parte or otherwise during the period between placement of a matter on the Sunshine agenda and final decision or other disposition is adopted to provide a period of repose from distractions and external pressures, promoting calm deliberation and well-reasoned decisions, *Ex Parte Rules*, 62 RR 2d 1755, 63 RR 2d 1275 (1987). Requests that the FCC staff mediate disputes or initiate settlement discussions require ex parte notification of all parties as may affect outcome in favor of one or another party, *Michael L. Glaser*, 66 RR 2d 991 (1989).

Fairness Doctrine. (§315); The FCC, from 1949 to August 1987, enforced the "Fairness Doctrine." What led to the repeal of the doctrine was the first "Fairness Doctrine" decision holding there had been a violation in ten years by the FCC. A Syracuse TV station was ruled to have failed to comply with its obligation to present fair and balanced programming relating to the issue of the soundness of the public investment in a nuclear power facility. The FCC rejected the licensee's claim that the actual issue involved was US dependence on foreign oil and the need for electricity and that its coverage of that issue was sufficiently balanced. While different parties may reach different conclusions concerning the issue addressed by a broadcast, and unless the facts are so clear that reasonable people could not differ as to the issue, the licensee's characterization will govern. Nevertheless, three commercials which described the proposed nuclear plant and concluded with the line "Nine Mile Point...a sound investment for New York's future" could only lead reasonable people to conclude that the issue discussed was whether the plant was a sound economic investment and, therefore, an answer to the state's economic and energy problems. The FCC also ruled that this was a controversial issue of public importance as evidenced by the public debate in numerous newspaper articles, by stated concerns of public and political figures, and by the filing of 20,000 petitions opposing the plant. The FCC had determined the imbalance of coverage was manifest: a ratio of 9:1 was further aggravated by a frequency ratio of 13:1. The licensee presented compensatory programming, and appealed, *Syracuse Peace Council,* 57 RR 2d 519 (1984), 59 RR 2d 179 (1985), 65 RR 2d 1759 (DC Cir. 1989). The FCC had sent a report to Congress recommending Congress abolish the doctrine, *Report Concerning General Fairness Doctrine Obligations of Broadcast Licensees,* 102 FCC 2d 143 (1985). The report concluded the doctrine was no longer necessary due to competition within each market; thereby relieving broadcasters of the requirement that they present controversial issues of public importance in a balanced fashion. The Ct. then remanded the *Syracuse* case to the FCC, declaring FCC had right to abolish the doctrine, 63 RR 2d 1073 (1987). The U.S. Ct. of Appeals had also held that the fairness doctrine did not apply to teletext, and that Congress had not mandated the "fairness doctrine" in 1959, and reaffirmed in *Telecommunications Research and Action Center v. FCC,* 801 F 2d 501 (D.C. Cir. 1986). An order from the US Ct. of Appeals remanded the Syracuse Peace Council case, *Meredith v. FCC,* 809 F. 2d 860 (DC Cir. 1987), which had challenged the constitutionality of the "Fairness Doctrine," in which the Ct. noted the previous opinion of the Ct. which had held the "Fairness Doctrine" to be an administrative policy and suggested that the Commissioners would be violating their oath of office if they continued to enforce the Doctrine despite their belief (as stated in their 1985 Fairness Report) that it was inconsistent with the First Amendment. The opportunity now apparently existed for the FCC to rule on the "fairness doctrine" itself. Congress ordered the FCC to study alternative means of enforcement of the "Fairness Doctrine," with the goal of telling the FCC not to change the doctrine. The FCC, had determined that the 1969 *Red Lion* decision, which had ruled the Doctrine constitutional, had also noted that significant technological advances or evidence that the Doctrine stifled rather than promoted controversial programming would warrant reappraisal of its constitutionality. The FCC then studied the scarcity rationale which underpinned the *Red Lion* decision and determined it could no longer serve as a foundation for conferring upon broadcasters a lower degree of First Amendment protection than is enjoyed by the print media. (See "First Amendment Rights for Broadcasting"). The FCC then sent Congress its' report on alternatives to the "fairness doctrine" to Congress, while emphasizing that it believed no alternative was superior to outright abolition of the Doctrine. The FCC found worthy of legislative consideration: (1) elimination of the personal attack rule; (2) elimination of the "Cullman Doctrine"; (3) repeal of the balanced coverage requirement; (4) adoption of a marketwide approach to enforcement of the balance requirement (under which one station's programming may be deemed to have balanced the programming provided by another station in the same market); (5) termination of all "Fairness Doctrine" enforcement in larger markets; (6) elimination of "Fairness Doctrine" obligations for radio stations only; and (7) implementation of an experimental moratorium on "Fairness Doctrine" enforcement, *Fairness Doctrine Alternatives*, 63 RR 2d 488, 64 RR 2d 1069 (1987). In the same meeting where it sent its' report to Congress, the FCC ruled that the Doctrine "chills speech and is not narrowly tailored to achieve a substantial government interest" and, thus, "under existing Supreme Court precedent...contravenes the First Amendment and thereby disserves the public interest." Along with the "Fairness Doctrine," the "Cullman Doctrine" corollary was also abolished except as it applies to political matters. Congress vigorously protested the FCC action and passed legislation reinstating the "fairness doctrine". President Reagan then vetoed the bill.

However, the personal attack and political editorial rules, the "Zapple Doctrine" as applied to ballot issues, and other aspects remain for the present. The Supreme Ct. declined to hear an appeal on the FCC action abolishing the "Fairness Doctrine," (Jan. 1990). Congress may yet be successful in codifying the "Fairness Doctrine" in the future. Given the significance of the "Fairness Doctrine" and that elements still remain and the volatile state currently on its reinstatement, an examination of its impact is necessary.

"The Fairness Doctrine" had two basic obligations. First, a broadcaster had to devote a significant amount of time to coverage of "controversial issues of public importance." Second, a broadcaster had to ensure that its coverage of any given "controversial issue" is not out of balance; and that a "reasonable opportunity" is afforded in overall programming for the presentation of significant contrasting or opposing viewpoints on each issue. (See "Editorializing"). Lawyer Banzhaf petitioned FCC to take cigarette advertising off radio-TV; FCC ruled equal time for anti-smoking spots not required, but some fair balance on controversial issue needed, *Banzhaf v. FCC*, 405 F. 2d 1082 (1968), 14 RR 2d 2061. Congress then passed law ruling Cigarette Ads off the air. Law bans cigarette ad on TV-Radio only, 15 USC 1335 (1971). Congress then added smokeless tobacco products (chewing tobacco, snuff, etc.), *Comprehensive Smokeless Tobacco Health Education Act of 1986*, Pub. L. No. 99-252. The law does not prohibit advertising of such tobacco products as pipe tobacco or cigars (not defined as little cigars). It is permissible for a program to mention the name of a cigarette product as part of a program title, i.e., "Salem Golf Classic," if kept to a minimum. DC App. Ct. ruled that Banzhaf decision can be extended to other issues even though FCC stated was "unique" situation. Must decide whether licensee has otherwise met its fairness obligations, *Friends of the Earth v. FCC*, 449 F.2d 1164; 22 RR 2d 2145 (DC App. 1971). In a major case relating to the Personal Attack Rule the Supreme Ct. upheld FCC's constitutional right to impose the "Fairness Doctrine." When a station broadcasts a personal attack they must allow a response from the individual attacked. Broadcast frequencies are scarce and there are legitimate claims by those unable without government assistance to gain access. Broadcaster's First Amendment rights are abridgeable, as different, *Red Lion v. FCC*, Sup. Ct. 395 US 367; 16 RR 2d 2029 (1969). Exempted from the "Fairness Doctrine" product commercials which do not obviously and meaningfully address a controversial issue of public importance even if the product is controversial in the minds of some viewers. (See "Defamation," "Editorializing," "Equal Opportunity," "Balanced Program Structure").

Federal Preemption of State Laws. *Public Notice* with respect to preemption of local laws by the *Communications Act of 1934*, as amended, 41 RR 2d 248 (1977); Example: FCC's preemption of regulation of special pay cable programming rendered invalid NY price regulation on such programming, *Brookhaven Cable TV v. Kelley*, 573 F.2d 765, 42 RR 2d 1185 (CA 2d 1978).

Filming US Currency for Ads. The filming of U.S. currency and obligations for advertising purposes is a criminal offense, 18 USC 474, 504. However, filming may be done for the purposes of philatelic, educational, historical or newsworthy purposes. The Supreme Ct. upheld a ruling that barring magazines from doing so constituted overbroad subject matter regulation that interfered unduly with protected speech. The government may restrict the size and color of reproduction and if in larger or smaller sizes than actual bills or coinage. Also, the government cannot regulate the reproduction according to purpose, such as advertising, *Regan v. Time, Inc.*, 539 F. Supp. 1371 (1982); 52 USLW 5084 (1984).

Financial Qualification. (§73:24(c), §73:4100, §73:4101); FCC does not require a legally binding commitment when a loan is used to finance a station, but a reasonable assurance the loan will be available, 44 RR 2d 487 (DC App. 1978). Applicants for new stations were required to certify that they were financially able to construct the facilities and operate the station for three years (what was then one license term) without reliance on advertising revenues. The FCC then announced a new financial qualification standard for radio and TV applicants and transferees of three months, without relying upon advertising or any other revenue, 69 FCC 2d 407, 43 RR 2d 1101 (1978); 72 FCC 2d 784, 45 RR 2d 925 (1980), 87 FCC 2d 200, 49 RR 2d 1291 (1981). In a TV renewal proceeding the FCC Review Board upheld the dismissal of a competing applicant who withdrew his initial certification of financial qualification and replaced it with a statement that "G-d would provide him the necessary funds." The Board rejected claims that this was no more fanciful than other applicants' certification and the contention that a dismissal amounted to deprivation of First Amendment right to religious freedom, *Central Alabama Broadcasters*, 55 RR 2d 1637 (1984). New applicants were then permitted to simply certify they possessed the financial ability to meet the financial qualification standard. The substantive financial standard remained and they had to do all necessary paperwork if asked to prove, *Dutchess Communications*, 58 RR 2d 381 (1985). Increased frequency of violation of financial certification requirements caused FCC to authorize staff to initiate a program of random checks and also to non-randomly verify applicants who have a large number of pending broadcast applications. If certification is determined to be false, financial and misrepresentation issues will be designated, *Verification of Financial Certification*, 62 RR 2d 638 (1987).

Financial Report. Form 324 eliminated as lack of public interest for financial information (AM-TV); Cable financial information eliminated, *Annual Financial Report,* 51 RR 2d 135 (1982); 54 RR 2d 799 (1983).

Fines and Short—Term License Renewals. (§503, §1:80, §76:9); Until 1960, the FCC could only use revocation or denial of license for violations and they were reluctant to use that massive power for "minor" infractions. With the power to levy fines the FCC was also given the power of short-term license renewal so as to have an early opportunity to review alleged past deficiencies. The first short-term renewal was for a licensee's failure to give enough supervision, *Eaton,* 20 RR 1074 (1960). The first fine was for $2,500 for failure to reduce power at night, *Crowell-Collier,* 21 RR 921 (1961). Some examples: a license is renewed short-term where broadcast unsubstantiated weather reports, lottery promotion, contest disrupted traffic, violated technical rules, failed to supervise, lacked due care in correspondence with FCC. Revocation too harsh as broadcast significant public service programming, *Action Radio,* 51 FCC 2d 803, 33 RR 2d 51 (1975). Fine of $8,000 against KIQI-AM for repeated violations of tower lighting rules (§73:1213), (Feb. 1990).
§503(b)(2)(A) then amended raising the maximum fine power of the FCC to $20,000 for willful or repeated violations, also see *Lenawee Broadcasting,* 42 RR 2d 390 (1978), *Pub. L.* 95-234.
Congress then authorized FCC to raise maximum fine power from $20,000 to $250,000 per violation, (Feb. 1990).

First Amendment Rights for Broadcasting. The Supreme Ct. noted: "We have no doubt that moving pictures, like newspapers and radio are included in the press whose freedom is guaranteed by the First Amendment," *US v. Paramount Pictures,* 334 US 131, 4 RR 2022 (1948). The FCC issues *Public Notice,* 28 FCC 2d 409 (1971), stating that licensees must make reasonable efforts to determine before broadcast the meaning of music containing drug oriented lyrics. After many comments about whether prior censorship (§326) and procedures which would be considered reasonable, FCC issues *Second Memorandum and Order*, 31 FCC 2d 377 (1971), clarifying and modifying: (1) FCC not prohibiting playing songs, (2) no reprisals against stations which did play drug oriented songs, but (3) licensee responsibility to know content and make judgment regarding wisdom of playing such songs. Appealed to Ct., which stated that purpose and actual result was to remind the industry of a pre-existing duty to assume responsibility for all material which is broadcast and not an issue to adjudicate as no case had yet been presented of license revocation on this issue, *Yale Broadcasting v. FCC*, 478 F. 2d 594 (DC App. 1973); 414 US 914, Cert. denied (1973); 28 RR 2d 938; 21 RR 2d 1576; 21 RR 2d 1698; 31 FCC 2d 385, 22 RR 2d 1808 (1971). The Recording Industry Association of America, announced a voluntary plan to identify albums containing explicit lyric references to sex, violence or substance abuse in response to concern expressed by the PTA and Parents Music Resource Center. Either label with a warning or print song lyrics on the album cover, (1985). In 1975, the NAB adopted a "family viewing policy" providing that entertainment programming inappropriate for viewing by a general family audience should not be broadcast during the first hour of network programming in prime time and in the immediate preceding hour. The policy also required the use of advisories to alert viewers to any prime time programs containing material that might significantly disturb significant segments of the audience. The three major TV networks had previously indicated their willingness to comply with such a policy. The Writers Guild, Directors Guild, Screen Actors Guild and Norman Lear's Tandem Productions brought actions against the NAB, the three networks and the FCC contending that the policy violated the First Amendment, *Administrative Procedure Act*, Antitrust laws, and §326 of the FCC Act. Tandem sought damages as <u>All in the Family</u> was moved to a less desirable time slot due to the policy. A Federal District Ct. in California concluded that the Family Viewing Policy had been adopted by the NAB and networks in response to threats, influence and pressure of the Chairman of the FCC; that the improper pressure was a _per se_ violation of the First Amendment; that the FCC had violated the *Administrative Procedure Act* by using the "raised eyebrow" to foster public policy instead of procedure; that action by the networks and NAB was "governmental action" under the 1st Amendment claim because of the pressure and because the networks, NAB and FCC had participated in an unprecedented joint venture to effect the independent judgments of other broadcast licensees; the networks and the NAB had violated the 1st Amendment by becoming surrogates in the enforcement of government policy. However, a Federal Ct. of Appeals vacated on technical grounds that the doctrine of primary jurisdiction requires the FCC to consider the claims prior to any court action. The doctrine of primary jurisdiction' generally applies when a court is presented with issues involving a regulatory scheme. The judicial process is suspended pending referral of such issues to the appropriate administrative body, presumably in order to achieve uniformity and consistency in regulation and to allow the court to benefit from the expertise and insight of the agency. A similar doctrine, requiring the "exhaustion of administrative remedies" prior to judicial review, applies when a claim must be heard in the first instance by an administrative agency first. The District Ct. had felt that the FCC was already biased and it would not serve any purpose for the FCC to review their own pressure efforts. The Ct. of Appeals disagreed and utilized the doctrine of primary jurisdiction to request a determination by the FCC of whether it had properly walked the tightrope. The Ct. also noted that informal procedures of a government agency (the raised eyebrow) resulting in self-regulation by an industry often avoided the need for formal government intervention. Even if such procedures were characterized as official action by the agency, the Ct. of Appeals concluded the District Ct. should not have thrust itself so hastily into the delicately balanced system of broadcast regulation and should have deferred initially to the FCC. After four years of reconsideration during which the NAB Code was declared a violation of Antitrust law, the FCC concluded that the Family Viewing Hour policy adopted by the NAB was voluntary. There was nothing, according to the FCC, inherently wrong with "jawboning" [which is what Samson did when he smote the Philistines with the jawbone of an ass], *Writers Guild of America, West v. FCC,* 423 F. Supp. 1064 (US Dist. Ct. Cal. 1976), 36 RR 2d 711 (oral opinion); 38 RR 2d 1409 (written opinion); overruled and remanded to FCC, 46 RR 2d 813 (CA 9th, 1979); 55 RR 2d 1064 (1983). Congress approved a resolution calling upon the media to refrain from projecting or characterizing election results as long as polls are open and requested guidelines to assure that exit polls are not used before all polls have closed. The measure, which does not have the force of law, developed from a confrontation between the right to vote and First Amendment freedom of the press. There is concern that announcing election results before all the polls across the country close decreases voter turnout and undermines the electoral process, *H. Con. Res. 321* (1984). Broadcasting film which dramatized the real-life experiences of an American student imprisoned in Turkey for drug smuggling was a form of speech protected by the First Amendment. Dismissed discrimination suit as too large a group, *Federation of Turkish-American Societies v. American Broadcasting Co.,* 620 F. Supp. 56 (SDNY 1985). (See "Fairness Doctrine," "Cable Regulation," "Censorship by State").

Foreign Language Broadcasts. Extensive use of foreign language programming is not private communication nor earns extra credit for being in the "public interest"; but illegal transfer of control to buyer of block time gets license nonrenewal, *WARD-United States Broadcasting Co.,* 2 FCC 208 (1935). In 1976, license revoked for numerous violations including, promoting a lottery abdication of control to time brokers, improper logging. Ct. told FCC to review giving greater consideration to multi-language public service programming. FCC revoked license anyway as (1) record was vague, often not logged and not sufficient to mitigate, and (2) three other stations in market broadcast 23 foreign languages, so revocation not detrimental to the "public interest," *Cosmopolitan Broadcasting*, 581 F.2d 917 (DC Cir. 1978); 75 FCC 2d 423, 46 RR 2d 1285 (1979). Policy statement §73:4105 eliminated and licensees are no longer subject to specific guidelines for monitoring foreign language programs. Instead, the same general standards applicable to all programming applies, *Underbrush Broadcast Policies*, 54 RR 2d 1043 (1983). D.J. used some Spanish words and phrases during his English-language program. Station, initially agreeing to allow him to do so, asked him to stop and he refused. He was fired. Upheld station's right as a programming decision of station and protected by the First Amendment and *Communications Act, Jurado v. Eleven-Fifty Corporation*, 630 F. Supp. 569 (CD Ca. 1985), aff'd, (9th Cir. 1987).

Fraudulent Billing. The FCC had rules prohibiting licensees from issuing to advertisers or program suppliers any bills, invoices, or affidavits containing false information or misrepresentations or to draft or supply such documents in a fashion where they easily could be misused by those parties (double-billing), 23 RR 175 (1962), 1 FCC 2d 1068 (1965), 38 FCC 2d 1051, 25 RR 2d 1759 (1972). Double-billing revocation, *Berlin Communication, Inc.*, 68 FCC 2d 923, 42 RR 2d 1513 (1978); aff'd, 46 RR 2d 621; 626 F.2d 869 (DC App. 1979). FCC did not renew license when stations had engaged in 5 1/2 years of double-billing with knowing participation of licensee's sole shareholder. The station would send two bills to local advertisers—one for true cost of ads and other for higher amount which local advertiser sent to national advertiser for reimbursements under cooperative shared—cost ad plan, *White Mountain Broadcasting v. FCC*, 598 F. 2d 274 (DC Cir.), 45 RR 2d 681 (1979). The FCC eliminated the fraudulent billing rule as licensees can be prosecuted under federal or state laws of fraud, misappropriation, etc. and are subject to private litigation by the injured parties, *Unnecessary Broadcast Regulation (Business Practices)*, 59 RR 2d 1500 (1986).

Handicapped. Ct. had held that FCC, in renewal, had to consider whether it was in the "public interest" for a public TV station not to show program captions for the deaf based on *Rehabilitation Act of 1973* (§504); non-discrimination of the handicapped in any federally assisted activity. Supreme Ct. ruled that while a public TV station has the duty to comply the FCC may find the licensees' efforts adequate since Dept. of Education, which was the proper agency to consider discrimination under *Rehabilitation Act*, found no adverse result. The FCC has no enforcement responsibilities in relation to that law and there was no need to treat noncommercial broadcasting more stringently than commercial stations, *Community TV of Southern California v. Gottfried*, 459 US 498, 53 RR 2d 271 (Supr. Ct. 1983). In a subsequent case, Ct. ruled that the FCC is not required, under the same law, to issue regulations to increase broadcast participation by the handicapped. The FCC agreed in 1980, to appoint a coordinator for broadcasting and the handicapped and stated it would consider findings of illegal discrimination against the handicapped in reviewing applications for new licenses and license renewals, *Cal. Assoc. of the Physically Handicapped v. FCC*, 721 F. 2d 667, 55 RR 2d 1 (9th Cir. 1983). However, when the same group petitioned FCC to deny Metromedia transfer of TV station licenses to Rupert Murdoch for not fulfilling its public duty to the handicapped by showing closed captioning and hiring handicapped Ct. ruled not an injury in fact established and, if injury, could not be traced to approval of the transfer application, *Cal Assoc. of the Physically Handicapped v. FCC*, 59 RR 2d 710 (1986); *Metromedia Radio &*

TV, 59 RR 2d 1196 (1985), stay denied, 59 RR 2d 1209 (1986); reconsideration denied, 59 RR 2d 1211 (1986). The DC Circuit Ct. then held that, in reviewing TV renewal and assignment applications, the FCC was under no duty to consider the extent to which the applicant has captioned its programming for the hearing-impaired or whether the applicant has an equal opportunity program covering the handicapped, *Cal. Assoc. of the Physically Handicapped v. FCC*, 840 F. 2d 88, 64 RR 2d 757 (DC Cir. 1988). (See "Equal Employment").

Home Recording and Viewing. Ct. overturned lower Ct. decision that recording at home on VTR constituted copyright infringement. Sony maintained no direct involvement with purchasers and the equipment has significant noninfringing uses. There is significant programming where copying is authorized. When used for noncommercial or nonprofit activity, even when the whole work is reproduced, the Ct. ruled "fair use" if the viewer might otherwise have watched in the home without charge when the program was originally broadcast. Congress would have to determine if royalties should be assessed.

The *1971 Home Recording Act* allows for home audio recording where it is for private use and with no purpose of reproducing or otherwise capitalizing commercially. Home video recording is permitted under same constraints, *Sony v. Universal*, 659 F. 2d 963 (9th Cir. 1981); 52 LW 4090, 55 RR 2d 156 (US Sup. Ct. 1984). The key is whether commercial use. An educational cooperative did large-scale off-air videotaping of copyrighted films and distributed them to schools in NY. The Board argued it was making "fair use" and repeated showings permitted time-shifting to allow more flexible viewing for teachers and students. Since taping interfered with marketability of the copyrighted works (Learning Corporation of America no longer allows telecast of its educational films because of declining film sales believed due to such taping); taping was massive and highly sophisticated; licensing agreements are available from educational film companies for limited taping; taping was substantial and verbatim; was not "fair use" and permanent injunction granted, plus damages, *Encyclopedia Britannica Educational Corp., v. C.N. Crooks*, 542 F. Supp. 1156 (WDNY 1982).

The Record Rental Act was extended for another eight years. It was originally passed in 1984, in response to the growing trend of commercial record rental outlets, whose primary purpose was to encourage customers to tape rented recordings instead of buying them. The act prohibits record rentals for direct or indirect commercial advantage, unless otherwise authorized by the copyright owners of the sound recording. It specifically exempts libraries and educational institutions and amended §115(c) of the *Copyright Act* to allow record companies to authorize the rental of their records of nondramatic musical works, subject to the payment of an additional royalty, *Record Rental Amendment Act*, 17 USC §109(b), 1989.

The Satellite Home Viewer Act of 1988, attempts to deal with issues raised over new technology. Amends the Communications Act to make it clear that over-the-air and cable networks may legally scramble their signals. Provides for stiffer penalties for piracy of satellite signals with a fine of up to $500,000 and prison for up to five years. Adds a new §119 to the Copyright Act giving satellite carriers a limited right to retransmit the signals of broadcast network affiliates if they pay a cable compulsory license fee, *Satellite Home Viewer Act*, effective Jan. 1, 1989 for six years, PL 100-667. (See "Subscription TV").

Imitation of Violent Act. Generally, network broadcasters have been immune from liability for imitative acts of violence resulting in injury. In order to be held liable in negligence, the requirements of a four-part test must be met; the plaintiff must have a duty to use reasonable care, that duty must be breached, a causal connection must exist between the broadcast and the injury, and an actual injury must occur. The courts have generally refused to apply negligence as to violence in broadcast programs. The producer, syndicator and broadcaster of the Mickey Mouse Club were found not liable for injuries sustained by an 11-year old boy who attempted to duplicate a demonstration which required placing a BB pellet inside a balloon, which he swallowed. The demonstration did not create an unreasonable risk of harm and was not an invitation to act in such a way as to pose a clear and present danger of injury, *Walt Disney v. Shannon*, 276 S.E. 2d 580 (Ga. 1981); also, Cts. have found the First Amendment bars recovery. In 1979, a 13-year old Rhode Island viewer hanged himself after watching a stuntman apparently hang Johnny Carson on The Tonight Show. The stuntman and Mr. Carson gave the "remember kids, don't try this at home" warning. The parents claimed NBC was negligent in broadcasting this type of stunt and in not providing adequate warning. The Ct., however, held as a matter of law that the First Amendment's freedom of speech barred recovery, *DeFilippo v. NBC*, 446 A.2d 1086 (RI 1982). In another case it was alleged that a rape scene in movie Born Innocent motivated a similar attack on a nine-year-old girl in San Francisco. Ct. granted a nonsuit on grounds that NBC did not encourage or advocate violent acts so broadcast was protected speech. Ct. refused to impose liability on basis of simple negligence as would lead to self-censorship seriously inhibiting broadcasters, *Olivia N. v. NBC*, 126 Cal. App. 3rd 488 (Cal. Sup. Ct. 1981), Cert. denied. A TV advertiser has no duty, under Florida law, to warn an audience of young viewers against imitating dangerous activity depicted in a TV ad. A 14-year old rode his bike off a ramp and broke his neck. The product had nothing to do with the activity depicted, *Sakon v. PepsiCo*, (Fla. Sup. Ct., 11/30/89).

Indecency—Obscenity. (§303, §326); Skit with Mae West and Don Ameche, written by Arch Oboler on Charlie McCarthy show about Adam and Eve vulgar and indecent. Warning; it's network and station's responsibility for objectionable language, *Broadcasting*, (12/20/37, p. 25). Broadcasts of indecent language in DJ program caused hearing order, *Mile High Stations*, 28 FCC 795; 20 RR 345 (1960). Profane and indecent materials, but denial based on misrepresentation, *Palmetto*, 23 RR 483 (1962); 33 FCC 250 (1962). Violence and mayhem are not obscene, indecent or profane as defined in §303 (m)(1)(D) of the Act, or 18 USC 1464, *Polite Society*, 35 RR 2d 39 (1975). In 1973, the FCC announced an inquiry into the broadcasting of obscene, indecent or profane material. Radio shows were asking sexual questions on talk-in shows. A $2,000 forfeiture was levied on *Sonderling*, 27 RR 2d 1508 (1973). Ct. affirmed FCC on merits, and upheld standing of Citizens Committee and Am. Civil Liberties Union to appeal as "public interest in free flow of information" would not be vindicated if licensee alone finds burden too great to contest FCC action, *Illinois Citizens Comm., v. FCC*, 31 RR 2d 1523 (1974) 515 F. 2d 397 (DC App. 1975). Broadcast of indecent language, not necessarily obscene, can be regulated because: (1) Children have access and are unsupervised; (2) received in home-people's privacy interest involved; (3) No warning possible; (4) licensing power of government. §326 of Comm. Act prohibiting censorship by FCC does not limit the FCC from imposing sanctions on licensees who engage in obscene, indecent or profane language <u>after</u> it has been broadcast. "We simply hold that when the FCC finds that a pig has entered the parlor, the exercise of its regulatory power does not depend on proof that the pig is obscene." For the first time allows the government to prevent minors from gaining access to materials that are not legally obscene, and are therefore protected by the First Amendment. [A work is obscene if a reasonable person would find the work, taken as a whole, lacks serious literary, artistic, political, or scientific value, *Miller v. Calif.*, 413 US 15, (1973) see also, *Pope v. Illinois*, (US Sup. Ct. 1987)] The community whose standards are applied are the local, (statewide) communities where the work is displayed or uttered. *FCC v. Pacifica*, 98 S. Ct. 3026 (Sup. Ct. 1978); 43 RR 2d 493, 438 US 726 (1978). A Utah statute banning indecent, although not necessarily obscene, material on cable was unconstitutionally overbroad as invaded area of free speech by failing to incorporate any reference to contemporary community standards, *Home Box Office v. Wilkinson*, 531 F. Supp. 987 (D. Utah, 1981); 555 F. Supp. 1164 (ND.Utah 1982), Upheld, 611 F. Supp. 1099, 61 RR 2d 1 (1986), aff'd, 107 S. Ct. 1559 (1987). A complaint alleging that obscene, indecent and profane material had been broadcast deemed to warrant no action. The FCC noted §326 prevents censorship. The material failed to meet the definition of obscenity or indecency. The *Pacifica* precedent does not require the FCC to intervene in every case where words similar or identical are broadcast. The staff concluded that the language was not profane and any sanction would not be judicially upheld, *Decency in Broadcasting*, 53 RR 2d 1370 (1983). Indecent speech is not obscenity and an ordinance prohibiting indecent material on cable was overbroad and facially defective. Miami law did not regard time of day or other variables and *Pacifica* only covered broadcasting, not cable. The enforcement procedures in the law also created a high risk of arbitrary or capricious governmental action, *Cruz v. Ferre; HBO v. Ferre*, 571 F. Supp. 125, 54 RR 2d 1541 (SD Fla. 1983); aff'd, 755 F. 2d 1415, 57 RR 2d 1452 (CA 11th 1985). FCC deleted cable obscenity rule as duplicative of statutory provisions which provided greater protection to the public. (See "Cable Regulation"). FCC ruled that cable operator must provide a lockbox (locking out certain channels) upon request of subscriber, *Cable Communications Policy Act Rules*, 58 RR 2d 1 (1985), amends, 63 RR 2d 1141 (1987). Multipoint distribution service carriers can, and probably should, deny access to customers seeking to transmit what carrier reasonably believes to be obscene or otherwise unlawful material. However, FCC notes, as a common carrier they may be subject to court-ordered damages and injunctions if it is in fact not unlawful, *MDS Transmission of Obscene Material*, 62 RR 2d 1517 (1987). It is improper for the FCC to issue declaratory rulings on how to apply its indecency standards to programming. Such a ruling would be the functional equivalent of prior restraint on expression and be a system of censorship in contravention of the First Amendment and §326. Impracticable nor administratively desirable because one cannot anticipate the overall context in which the material will be broadcast, which is a crucial factor in making indecency determinations. Mass Media Bureau, therefore, refused to determine in advance whether a licensee would be subject to sanctions if it aired a reading of passages from Ulysses, *William J. Byrnes*, 63 RR 2d 216 (1987). The FCC has authority to exercise concurrent jurisdiction to enforce federal anti-obscenity statutes, and has in the past exercised that authority. But, the FCC initially decided the "community standard" approach to obscenity in the *Miller* case made it more desirable to leave to local prosecutors the responsibility to identify situations perceived as a threat to "local community standards" and to leave the initial determination of "obscenity" to local juries, *Video 44*, 60 RR 2d 21 (1986). Two years later, FCC decided it will no longer defer initially to local prosecutors and courts when confronted with allegations of obscene broadcasting. The FCC cautioned that it will not entertain allegations that a licensee has broadcast obscene material unless evidence in form of video or audio tape or transcript presented soon after the time of the broadcast. Complaints must be acted upon so as to be timely and prevent a chilling effect on protected speech; and timely review will allow referral of complaints to the Dept. of Justice for criminal prosecution before the statute of limitations runs and, guarantees that the community standards are truly contemporary, *Video 44*, 64 RR 2d 378 (1988). The FCC, under Congressional pressure, then put broadcasters on notice that it would employ new, more stringent standards in enforcing the prohibition of obscene and indecent programming. FCC will use the definition of indecency upheld in *Pacifica*, "language or material that depicts or describes, in terms patently offensive as measured by contemporary community standards for the broadcast medium, sexual or excretory activities or organs." Application will not be limited to the seven "filthy words" which was the focus of that litigation. The repetitive use of those expletives will no longer be a pre-requisite to sanctions; other terms and types of material may also subject broadcasters to sanctions. The fact that an inde-cent transmission occurs after 10 P.M. and is preceded by a warning no longer serves to insulate the broadcaster auto-matically from enforcement action. The "indecency policy" should be viewed as a reasonable time, place, and manner restriction based on a nuisance rationale consistent with First Amendment precedent in the print context, *Indecency Enforcement Standards*, 62 RR 2d 1218 (1987). First sanctions with this statement were moderate as past pronouncements may have led licensees to believe they did not violate policy: Pacifica Foundation station aired dramatic play "Jerker," dealing with AIDS crisis, homosexual fantasies and con-tained language graphically describing sexual and excretory activities that were patently offensive. Although broadcast after 10 P.M. and preceded by warning did not insulate li-censee, *Pacifica Foundation*, 62 RR 2d 1191 (1987). Noncommercial station played song, "Makin' Bacon." As with other broadcasts noted did not contain any of the "seven filthy words" but it made several clearly discernible and patently offensive references to sexual organs and ac-tivities. Survey information indicated children might be in the audience even though after 10 P.M., *Regents of the University of California*, 62 RR 2d 1199 (1987). Howard Stern, "in a pandering and titillating fashion, made explicit refer-ences to masturbation, ejaculation, breast size, penis size, sexual intercourse, nudity, urination, oral-genital contact, erections, sodomy, bestiality, menstruation and testicles." While subjects not indecent per se, the overall context offen-sive, *Infinity Broadcasting*, 62 RR 2d 1202 (1987). The FCC then attempted to once again define a "safe harbor," of 12 Midnight to 6 A.M., *Infinity Broadcasting Corp. of Pennsylvania (Indecency Policy Reconsideration)*, 64 RR 2d 211 (1987). Congress, by voice vote, then passed a statutory directive codifying the definition of indecency from *Pacifica* in

§73.3999. The rationale for a "safe harbor" was that under previous interpretations of 18 USC 1464, the law prohibited the broadcast of <u>obscene</u> programming during the entire day but <u>indecent</u> programming was prohibited only when there was a reasonable risk that children might be in the audience. Because of the codification of indecency by Congress, FCC stated prevents any "safe harbor," *Broadcast Obscenity and Indecency,* 65 RR 2d 1038 (1988). The FCC, in the midst of this activity announced a fine against a TV station for presenting prime time broadcast of unedited film <u>Private Lessons</u>. Explicit nudity and scenes depicting sexual matters were dealt with in a pandering and titillating manner which were neither isolated nor fleeting. Nudity is not indecent <u>per se</u>, but it was the nude scenes, coupled with the depiction of the seduction of a teen-age boy by an older woman that "would have commanded the attention of children." FCC vacated their order of violation when the US Ct. of Appeals overturned "no safe harbor" part of FCC policy and held that the FCC may not bring enforcement actions against evening broadcasts until it had conducted an inquiry on children's viewing and listening habits, *Indecency Enforcement Standards; Action for Children's TV v. FCC,* 852 F. 2d 1332, 65 RR 2d 45 (DC Cir. 1988). FCC then sent to the Justice Dept. cases on three stations held having broadcast indecent programs during daytime. One of the stations had fired its "shock jock" four months prior to the FCC action because of his unwillingness to accept direction in matters of program taste and judgment, (1989). FCC gets about 6,000 complaints annually on indecency. Decision on "no safe harbor" policy after public comments will be made late 1990. (See "Profane Language," "Offensive Advertising").

International Copyright Agreements—Moral Rights. A step toward world-wide cooperation in the international protection of copyrighted programming carried by satellites has been ratified by Congress. The Treaty provides that signatory nations will take adequate measures to prevent the distribution on or from its territory any program-carrying signal to any distributor for whom the satellite signal is not intended. The unauthorized interception and distribution of American programming via satellite has occurred throughout the Western Hemisphere and as more powerful satellites are launched the problem has global proportions. Efforts to develop an agreement began in the late 1960's through the United Nations. Developed in 1974, the Convention does not apply to satellite signals intended for direct reception by the general public or for private viewing. These broadcast signals are generally already regulated under copyright or neighboring rights laws of most countries. A "fair use" provision enables an otherwise unintended distributor to carry short excerpts, for informational purposes, of a satellite-conveyed program reporting on current events, or to carry a program which might be used for educational or scientific research purposes in a developing country. A "first-sale" type provision permits the distribution of derivative signals used by a distributor for whom the original emitted signals were intended. The Convention declares that it does not limit or prejudice the protection secured to authors, performers, producers of phonograms, or broadcasting organizations, under any domestic law or international agreement, *Sen. Doc. 98-52* (1985).

The US has been a signatory to the *Universal Copyright Convention* since the 1950's, which has not been very universal. The major international copyright treaty is the *Berne Convention*. The US has joined with the passage of the *Berne Convention Implementation Act of 1988,* which amends the *Copyright Act of 1976*, as our law had not met some minimum standards. The most dramatic change made by the Implementation Act is the elimination of the requirement that published works bear a copyright notice. Such notice will be permitted but is not necessary for protection. Those who affix a notice will have the advantage of being able to prove that an infringer was not innocent as given notice. Berne generally prohibits mandatory formalities. The *Berne*

Implementation Act contains one provision specifying that it does not expand or reduce any right of an author to claim what are commonly known as "moral rights." This was the most controversial issue faced by Congress. Berne requires that authors be granted moral rights as well as economic rights. Opponents of colorization lobbied for an express moral rights provision, but were opposed by copyright owners of older films. A court in Paris, for example, initially barred the telecasting of colorized versions of any of the late John Huston's films as this might cause irreparable harm to the integrity of the films and his reputation. An appeal court then ruled that colorization did not violate moral rights as merely an adaptation rather than a desecration, *Turner Entertainment v. Huston*, Ct. of Appeal of Paris, 4th Chamber, Sec. B (July 6, 1989). Turner announced they would not colorize <u>Citizen Kane</u> as the contract between RKO, Orson Welles, and Mercury Productions specifically referred to the use of black and white, and provided Welles with almost total creative control of the film. ABC's plan to cut six minutes and 25 seconds from Warren Beatty's <u>Reds</u> for time format purposes was found to violate producer, director and star Beatty's contractual right of final cut on the film. Network had right to cut for censorship reasons. Film was licensed to ABC by Paramount for $6.5 million for three broadcasts over four and one-half years with grant allowing the right to edit the film "for purposes of time segment requirements." Oral agreement was that Paramount would reaquire TV rights from ABC in the event Beatty was not satisfied. After disagreement over cuts complaint was brought before the Producers Arbitration Tribunal of the Directors Guild of America. The arbitrator, using the "Monty Python" case, *Gilliam v. American Broadcasting*, 538 F. 2d 14 (2d Cir. 1976), ordered ABC not to telecast <u>Reds</u>. Two days later Warren Beatty was appointed to the Guild's Creative Rights Committee, and the Guild announced it would seek the contractual right for all directors of feature films to have their films exhibited on TV in the same version as released theatrically, allowing cuts only for network standards and practices, *In the Matter of the Arbitration between Directors Guild of American, Warren Beatty and JRS Productions and Paramount Pictures Corporation and American Broadcasting Companies,* Case No. 01738 (April 1985). With this controversy between creators and owners, Congress decided to consider express moral rights at a later date, *Berne Convention Implementation Act of 1988,* (effective date: March 1, 1989).

Judicial Coverage. TV Coverage of trial prejudicial; sentence reversed under Due Process Clause of 14th Amendment, *Billy Sol Estes,* 381 US 532; 85 S. Ct. 1628; 6 RR 2d 2104 (1965). Jury exposure to massive publicity of information not introduced at trial required new trial, *Sheppard v. Maxwell,* 384 US 333, 86 S. Ct. 1507 (1966). Led to American Bar Association and Cts. instituting stricter rules against broadcast coverage of trials. Network edited interview stemmed from appropriate concern of effect on a pending trial. FCC will not intrude in this sensitive area if good faith application by licensee, *Letter to Ottinger,* 31 FCC 2d 852, 18 RR 2d 1031 (1970). Orders of a Federal District Judge which not only forbade in-court sketching, but publications of sketches wherever made constitutionally overbroad. Sketching not shown obtrusive or disruptive, *US v. CBS,* 497 F.2d 102, 30 RR 2d 1349 (CA 5th 1974). No liability for truthfully publishing the name of a rape victim mistakenly released to the public in official court records. Only three states, Florida, Georgia and South Carolina have such a law now, *Cox v. Cohn,* 420 US 469; 32 RR 2d 1511 (1975). Prior restraint prohibiting broadcasting facts about confessions unconstitutional, *Nebraska Press Assoc. v. Stuart,* 427 US 539 (1976). Common law right of access to judicial records did not entitle TV networks and others to copy White House tapes used in criminal trial of Watergate defendants, *Nixon v. Warner Communication,* 435 US 589 (1978). Press not entitled to access to prison conditions any more than general public, *Houchins v. KQED,* 438

US 1 (1978). Convicted murderer Arnay contacted TV show, Lie Detector, which administered polygraph exams and showed results on show. Producers requested permission to enter prison to tape examination and spent $30,000 to prepare. Permission was denied and petition filed. Ruled that no affirmative duty to permit access even if show was news program as inmate's right of access is qualified, not content-based discrimination, and producer has no right of visitation, *Arney v. Director, Kansas State Penitentiary*, 671 P. 2d 559 (Kans. 1983). Supreme Ct. holds that press may be barred from a pretrial hearing of a motion to suppress evidence; however the Constitution guarantees the public and press the right to attend criminal trials. However, this is not an absolute right as the judge may choose to close trial when "overriding circumstances are present and articulated," *Gannett v. De Pasquale*, 443 US 368 (1979). Held that unless an overriding State interest the trial of a criminal case must be open to the public led to ABA reducing severity of previous rules on trial coverage, *Richmond Newspapers v. Virginia*, 448 US 555 (1980); *Chandler v. Florida*, 101 S. Ct. 802 (1981). A qualified privilege permits stations to report legal proceedings provided publication is fair and accurate statement and made without malice, *Mark v. KING Broadcasting*, 618 P. 2d 512 (Wash. App. 1980) and *Mark v. Fisher's Blend Station*, 621 P 2d 159 (Wash. App. 1980); 635 P 2d 1081 (Wash. 1981). In the Abscam trial, held, tapes entered into evidence may be copied and televised; however, the Fifth Circuit refused to allow the media to copy tapes admitted into evidence at the trial of the speaker of the Texas House of Representatives which came from a similar FBI sting operation. KSTP sought to copy and televise three hours of videotape received in evidence about the kidnapping of the wife of a clergyman which had been taped by the kidnapper and which included repeated rapes of the victim. The Ct. denied the station request as no "public interest" would be served as in the case where political corruption was involved, *US v. Myers*, 635 F.2d 945 (2d Cir. 1980); *Application of KSTP*, 504 F. Supp. 360

(D. Minn. 1980); *Belo Broadcasting v. Clark*, 654 F. 2d 423 (5th Cir. 1981). A one sentence order, not limited to time or geographic area, prohibiting a TV station from broadcasting a news segment concerning a criminal trial is too restraining. Alternatives to prior restraint were considered; and defendants had only asked for segment to be withheld until after the trial and then, only in that area, *US v. McKenzie v. CBS*, 697 F. 2d 1225, 53 RR 2d 301; 570 F. Supp. 578 (5th Ct. App. 1983). Between access and fair trial concerns there is a strong presumption that access should be allowed. Only if there is a substantial probability that there will be harm to the right of a fair trial can this presumption be overcome, *US v. Mouzin*, 559 F. Supp. 463 (CD Ca. 1983). Removed at emergency appeal a restraining order prohibiting CBS from broadcasting tapes of John DeLorean allegedly involved in drug-money deal. No reason to impose prior restraint on the First Amendment rights of the broadcaster when it was not clear that publicity would impair potential jury selection and the tapes were not lurid or inflammatory, *CBS, Inc. v. US Dist. Ct.*, 729 F. 2d 1174, 55 RR 2d 1557 (9th Cir. 1984). A segment of 60 Minutes involved the prosecution of seven New Orleans police officers. The officers attempted to enjoin CBS from broadcasting the segment in the Dallas area where the trial had been moved. CBS refused to give a copy of the script prior to broadcast to the Ct. which then ordered CBS to not broadcast. The Ct. of Appeals stayed the injunction as too speculative as to impact on potential jurors. After broadcast the District Ct. asked the US Attorney to institute contempt proceedings, but the Justice Dept. refused as not appropriate in light of substantiality of CBS' First Amendment defense. District Ct. then appointed private prosecutors to seek order requiring CBS to show cause why it should not be held in contempt. This was denied by a judge from the Western District of Louisiana as unconstitutional. Upon appeal, Ct. of Appeals ruled dismissal revoked private prosecutors appointment and thus no right to pursue, *US v. McKenzie*, 735 F. 2d 907 (5th Cir. 1984). Ct. allows copying of audiotapes by broadcaster admitted into evidence at racketeering and extortion trial of seven former Philadelphia police officers, *US v. Martin*, 746 F. 2d 964 (3rd Cir. 1984). NBC granted permission to copy audio tapes admitted into evidence and played to jury in trial of former Secretary of Labor Raymond J. Donovan. Rejected Donovan's argument playing tapes would create prejudicial publicity, *People v. Schiavone Construction*, NYLJ (Bronx Cnty., 1986). NBC's broadcast of the docudrama, "Billionaire Boys Club," did not violate Joe Hunt's Sixth Amendment right to a fair trail in a second murder case and the appeal on his first conviction, *Hunt v. NBC, Case No. 87-6625 (9th Cir., Apr. 1989)*.. Supreme Ct. reaffirms its ban on broadcast coverage of its proceedings (Oct. 1989).

House Rule XI(3)(f)(2) permits subpoenaed witnesses to deny radio and television coverage of their appearances before House committees. The Senate has a similar rule. U.S. District Ct. refused permanent injunction against rule requested by ABC, NBC, CBS and CNN as within legislative sphere. (Oct. 1989). (See "News Sources").

Lea Act Repealed. (§506); The 34-year old amendment which prevented unions from coercing broadcasters to hire and maintain staff they did not need was repealed by Congress. Provision was in reaction to 1946 "featherbedding" by American Federation of Musicians, *P.L. 96-507*, 1980.

Licensee Control Over Programs. Contract giving individual other than licensee complete control over content of news improper, but since could be terminated at any time by either party not illegal transfer of control, *KVOS*, 6 FCC 22 (1938). Contract giving manager all profits and requiring him to pay any losses is transfer of control. However, hearing proved owners actually retained general control and supervision so license renewed, *Federated Publications*, 9 FCC 150 (1942). Incentive Pay Contracts might lead to over-commercialization. Station renewed but had to promise in future no compensation on incentive pay basis for operating management, *WTOL-Community*, 12 FCC 85, 3 RR 1360 (1947). Illegal transfer of control; but when contract cancelled to preserve license then licensee liable for contract violation, *Georgia Tech*, 3 RR 47 (1945), *Regents of Georgia v. Carrol*, 338 US 586, 11 FCC 71, 5 RR 2083 (1950). As a condition of a station sale the former owner reserved program time on station. Station sued for later refusing to honor the contract. The station must, regardless of contract provisions, control its own time, *Regents-N.M.*, 158 F. 2d 900; 5 RR 976; 6 RR 131 (1947). Broadcast that amoeba was loose caused substantial disturbance and licensee should have maintained greater control, *WIST*, 2 FCC 2d 597, 6 RR 2d 793 (1966). Network-owned TV station broadcast a pot party, prearranged by one of its reporters. Lack of policy deprived licensee of control, *WBBM*, 15 RR 2d 140 (1969). Short-term license renewal of CBS owned station because network misrepresented "winner-take-all" tennis matches. Network misrepresentation hereafter attributed to licensee corporation operating network and could have resulted in revocation or hearing for all their licensed stations, *CBS*, 69 FCC 2d 1082, 43 RR 2d 1085 (1978). WABC staff members broadcast letters purporting to be from viewers, fictitious interviews and questions supposedly from studio audience actually written by staff. License informed FCC upon disclosure, instituted corrective procedures, dismissed or forced to resign those involved. FCC admonished licensee for failure to exercise reasonable diligence, supervision and control to insure that no matter that would deceive or mislead public is broadcast. License renewed but full Commission would review next renewal application, *American Broadcasting Company*, 52 RR 2d 1378 (1982). A university turned over its station to students, who then violated many FCC rules and policies. The FCC initially revoked the license but upon promises to adopt stricter controls, reinstated. The standard of adequate control and supervision is a strict one, but it is not one of strict liability for every employee peccadillo. Supervision must, however, be reasonably diligent, *Trustees of U. of Penn.*, 69 FCC 2d 1394, 44 RR 2d 747, 46 RR 2d 565 (1978). Failure of control by absentee licensee when promotional hoax aired about "missing DJ." Serious, prolonged event involved police and led to inaccurate news broadcasts, *Walton (KIKX)*, 47 RR 2d 1233 (1980), also *WMJX*, 85 FCC 2d 251, 48 RR 2d 1339 (1981). Mere inclusion of incorrect information cannot lead to conclusion deliberate and petition for full hearing against TV network denied, *Yellow Freight v. FCC*, 49 RR 2d 1663; 656 F. 2d 600 (1981). Music Service Program Contracts that unduly restricted licensees independent programming judgment caused rule §73:4145, which spelled out elements of such a contract that were impermissible. Rule eliminated but licensee still required to maintain control, *Underbrush Broadcast Policies*, 54 RR 2d 1043 (1983). College broadcast station fired two insubordinate employees. Employees do not have a First Amendment right to broadcast. The fact that the licensee was a governmental educational institution was not relevant to the requirement to retain programming control, *Schneider v. Indian River Community College Foundation*, 684 F. Supp. 283 (SD Fla. 1987).

Licensee Discretion to Censor. Smothers' Bros. program producers cannot sue network because of its' censorship under the *Communication Act of 1934*, unless network activities constituted governmental or State action, *Smothers v. CBS* (CD Calif.), 25 RR 2d 2099 (1972). Deleting Crest's name from Johnny Carson monologue for humorous but critical comment is licensee decision, *National Citizens Committee*, 49 FCC 2d 83, 31 RR 2d 293 (1974).

Licensee Discretion on Selling Time. There should be no station policy barring sale of time to unions for discussions of controversial issues as, absent a compelling state interest as corporations cannot be barred from influencing a public issue. However, neither unions nor businesses may compel members or employees to contribute money for such purposes, *United Broadcasting*, 10 FCC 515 (1945); *First National Bank of Boston v. Belloti*, 435 US 765 (1978). Union dues cannot be used to influence electorate, but union members may contribute to a fund as state is barred from restraining labor unions and others from expressing viewpoints, *Fed. Corrupt Practices Act, US v. UAW*, 138 F. Supp. 53, reversed 352 U.S. 567; 15 RR 2018 (1957). Station is not a common carrier (public utility) which must sell its services to anyone who wishes to buy; instead, the licensee is free to make own choice of what programs are broadcast, to sell time as they see fit and to allow free time on the same basis or refuse to sell time, *McIntire v. William Penn Broadcasting*, 151 F. 2d 597 (1945); 327 US 779, Cert. denied (1946). Licensee can refuse to sell time and can restrict free time for religious programs, *NJ Council of Churches*, 5 RR 1014a, 14 FCC 370 (1949). Licensee has right to refuse to broadcast programs it considers unsuitable and has final decision as to what programs best serve the "public interest," *Mass. Universalist v. Hildreth*, 183 F. 2d 497, 5 RR 2073, (1950). Licensee has right to refuse ads from union urging boycott as this did not violate "Fairness Doctrine," *Oil, Chemical & Atomic Workers Union*, 18 FCC 2d 501, 17 RR 2d 153; 20 RR 2d 2005; 48 FCC 2d 1, 30 RR 2d 1261, 436 F.2d 248 (1969). Broadcast licensee's general policy of not selling ads to individuals or groups wishing to speak on issues does not violate the FCC Act or First Amendment. The Ct. will not apply the "Fairness Doctrine" to editorial advertising; however if such time is sold, "Cullman" fairness aspect (see "Fairness Doctrine") must be observed, *CBS v. Democratic National Committee*, 412 US 94 (Supr. Ct. 1973), 19 RR 2d 977 (1970), 27 RR 2d 907 (1973). Product advertising per se is not a statement on a controversial issue so long as the ad merely extols the virtues of the product and takes no explicit position on matters of public controversy. No right of reply required. No scheme of government-dictated access (free or paid) for discussion of public issues is practicable or desirable, 48 FCC 2d 1; 30 RR 2d 1261 (1974). TV station which had entered into contract to carry basketball games from TV syndicator and which failed to do so must perform, *William B. Tanner v. Briarcliff,* 50 RR 2d 737 (1981). Held there is no absolute right to reject commercials once contract signed. Only reasonable grounds such as technical quality, obscenity, libelous content, etc. Therefore, station should not have rejected commercials containing price comparisons just because prices could not be checked as accurate after broadcast of first announcement, *Sam's Style Shop v. Cosmos Broadcasting,* 696 F. 2d 128, 52 RR 2d 1533 (5th Ct. App. 1982). The FCC admonished a TV station which had refused to sell advertising to a local FM station where that TV station had previously sold time to other FM stations in that market including its own. The TV station was held to have discriminated in an improper attempt to influence or penalize the other licensee and by refusing to permit it to advertise over their TV station had attempted to gain a competitive advantage for its own FM station, *Midwest Communication,* 53 RR 2d 993 (1983). The Katz Agency, acting as the exclusive national advertising sales representative for a broadcast station, was ruled entitled to damages for breach of contract. The station was sold without notice to Katz, and the new owner cancelled their contract without giving a required one year's notice, *Katz v. Evening News,* 705 F. 2d 20, 53 RR 2d 815 (1983). ABC may refuse to broadcast TV commercial incorporating a recording for editorial reasons. The *Communications Act* does not provide for a private right of action, and neither the Act nor the First Amendment requires ABC to sell commercial time to persons seeking to discuss "controversial issues." Does not have to broadcast even though portions deleted such as name of recording, as requested, *Rokus v. American Broadcasting Co.,* 616 F. Supp. 110 9S.D.N.Y. 1984). (See "Editorializing").

License Terms Extended. (§73:1020); Legislation extended license terms to <u>five years for television stations</u>, <u>seven years for radio</u>, 8/13/81—Signed by President.

Lotteries. (§73:1211, §76:213); Broadcasting information concerning any lottery was a violation of criminal law and the *Communication Act, WRBL,* 2 FCC 687 (1936). License renewal denied, in part, due to carrying information concerning lottery, *Metro,* 5 FCC 501 (1938). Supreme Ct. ruled that consideration was payment of money in any way or thing of value, but not post card or listening to station, *ABC v. US,* 110 F. Supp. 374 (1953), *FCC v. ABC,* 347 US 284 (1954). Calling at place of business to play game does not constitute consideration, *Caples, v. US,* 13 RR 1154 (1956), 15 RR 2005 (1957). Congress in enacting criminal law statute 18 USC 1304 empowered FCC and Justice Dept. to regulate and enforce Federal Lottery Laws. This preempted state law in field, *Miss. Broadcasters Assoc. v. Danforth* (Mo. Cir. Ct.), 26 RR 2d 967 (1973). Congress changed law, 18 USCA 1307 (1976), to exempt broadcasts about legal State Lotteries in state or adjacent state if own state has lottery. Announcing a winning number is news on the day drawn and can be broadcast. Can do advertising, prize list, or information. Supreme Ct. decision allowed any state with or without lottery to broadcast about lottery as news, *NJ State Lottery Comm. v. US,* 29 RR 2d 157, 491 F.2d 219 (CA 3rd, 1974), 34 RR 2d 825. Consideration is not: postage, watching, writing for tickets, going to station, going to business, etc., *KCOP TV,* 59 FCC 2d 1321, 37 RR 2d 1051 (1976). The fact that proceeds of lottery held at local fair were given in part to local civic and charitable organizations did not absolve licensee which carried, but warranted reduction in fine, *Smith Broadcasting,* 87 FCC 2d 1132, 50 RR 2d 356 (1981). Congress passed the *Charity Games Advertising Act of 1988,* effective May 7, 1990 and the *Indian Gaming Regulatory Act..* Prohibits gambling casino advertising. The present exemption for advertising State-conducted lotteries is expanded so a station may advertise State-conducted lotteries in any other state. Stations can advertise lotteries and other games of chance conducted by not-for-profit organizations or government organizations if the lottery or other game of chance is either authorized or not otherwise prohibited by the State in which it is conducted. Stations can advertise a lottery or other game of chance that is conducted as a promotional activity by a commercial organization which is clearly occasional and ancillary to the primary business of that organization, but only if the lottery or game of chance similarly is authorized or not prohibited by the State. Almost all States have statutes that prohibit chance promotions if a purchase or payment is required in order to participate, unless by charitable organizations. Broadcasters will still be subject to FCC policies on advertising a contest in which a prize is offered to the public based upon chance or skill. A lottery is based on prize, chance and consideration. In advertising contests, broadcasters are advised to disclose all rules and all material terms; conduct the contest in accordance with pre-announced terms; supervise employees responsible for conducting the contest; and avoid misleading the contestant about the prizes offered. The *Indian Gaming Act* permits the broadcast of information concerning certain Indian gaming activities, but broadcasters are obligated to ascertain that any such activity advertised on the air meets specified federal standards: (1) on Indian lands; (2) owned by tribe or grandfathered; (3) permitted by law in state where held; and (4) in games played against the house there is a compact to permit such games and all requirements of the compact are met. Broadcasters may contact the Indian Gaming Commission for guidance, *Charity Games Advertising Act of 1988*, (1988); *Indian Gaming Regulatory Act*, (1988). (See "Station Promotions").

Mechanical Reproduction Announcement. (§73:1208); Al Jarvis in the early 1930's in California and Martin Block at WNEW in 1935, did DJ shows entitled "Make Believe Ballroom." Described as "creating the illusion that the country's foremost dance bands are performing on four large stands in a glittering, crystal-chandeliered ballroom." Until the end of 1956, to make sure the public was not deceived into believing it was hearing or seeing live talent, all recorded programs and records had to be identified as such at the beginning and end of such programs and at certain specified intervals. The "mechanical reproduction" announcement is now only required if time is of special significance, or an impression is affirmatively made that the tape, film or recording is an event occurring simultaneously with the broadcast, 14 RR 1541 (1956).

Minority Ownership. (§73:4140); It is upon ownership that diversity of content rests and greater weight should have been accorded minority ownership; remanded to FCC. Dealt with issues of experience, participation in local affairs, etc., 495 F. 2d 929 (DC App. 1973); 419 US 986, Cert. denied; 28 RR 2d 1115 (1973), 69 FCC 2d 607, 43 RR 2d 811 (1978); Ownership and management by blacks deserves more credit in a competitive hearing than such involvement by women, *Radio Gaithersburg, Md.,* 72 FCC 2d 821, 45 RR 2d 1709 (1979). Female participation, while not as significant as other minority participation, merits more than a slight preference, and where things are equal can be determinative. Issue must be certified to be considered. Minority policy is not dependent upon proof that minority-owned station will specifically program to meet minority needs. In an effort to increase opportunities for minority ownership the FCC issued a supplemental policy statement, *1978 Policy Statement* (68 FCC 2d 979, 42 RR 2d 1689); *North Carolina Radio Service,* 52 RR 2d 993; *Horne Industries,* 52 RR 2d 1009, 54 RR 2d 249 (1983); *Waters Broadcasting,* 52 RR 2d 1063; *Minority Ownership in Broadcasting,* 52 RR 2d 1301 (1982). FCC ruled that integration (active participation) of minority owners is equal to that of applicant proposing equal percentage of local owner integration. Minority ownership is of significance only in the context of active participation in ownership and management and not to be considered in diversification as well, *Radio Jonesboro,* 57 RR 2d 1564 (1985). When Congress passed the "Random Selection Licensing Lottery Statute" it limited eligibility for minority ownership preference to a specific list of racial and ethnic minorities, and did not have on the list a separate preference for women. Women were within each of the enumerated groups. The FCC interpreted Congress to mean that the FCC was without authority to enact a women's preference, *Lottery Selection (Preference for Women)*, 58 RR 2d 1077 (1985). Also, ruled that policy of extending preferential treatment to female applicants for FM radio stations in comparative hearings exceeded statutory authority, *Steele v. FCC*, 770 F. 2d 1192 (DC Cir. 1985). However, Congress then mandated the granting of preferences to minorities or females in licensing proceedings, *House Joint Resolution 395* (1987). (See "Equal Employment").

Misrepresentation. (§73:1015); License denied for lying on application, *WSAL*, 8 FCC 34 (1940). FCC has right to revoke license for false statements on ownership, *WOKO v. FCC*, 153 F. 2d 623, 329 US 223, Upheld FCC; 3 RR 1061 (1946). License denied for misrepresentations, attacks on other religious groups and other station's programs, *Independent*, 6 RR 383 (1950), 193 F. 2d 900 (1951), 344 US 837, 14 FCC 72 (1949). License revoked for falsifying logs, *WMOZ*, 36 FCC 201, 1 RR 2d 801 (1964). The submission of a misleading and untruthful response to an interrogatory served by competing applicant is as serious as lying to the FCC as ultimately it deceives the FCC, *WNST*, 70 FCC 2d 1036, 44 RR 2d 492 (1978). Applicant, not its legal counsel, is responsible and application is denied for misrepresentation and withholding of substantial information, *WADECO, Inc. v. FCC*, 628 F.2d 122, 47 RR 2d 177 (DC App. 1980). National Telecommunications and Information Administration of the Department of Commerce grants federal funds for construction of public broadcasting stations. Two universities contended winner of funds had misrepresented information. The statute authorizing the Secretary of Commerce to distribute such grants is in the *Communications Act of 1934*, but does not provide for judicial review other than by FCC, *Xavier University v. NTIA,* 656 F. 2d 306 (5th Cir. 1981). FCC must be able to rely upon representations in hearing process, and failure to provide complete and accurate information may always be examined even if not designated as separate issue, *William M. Rogers,* 52 RR 2d 831 (1982). Peoria radio station denied license renewal due to misrepresentations regarding changes in ownership and control of the corporate licensee, *Peoria Community Broadcasters, Inc., and Central Illinois Broadcasting Co.,* 79 FCC 2d 311, 48 RR 2d 1164 (1982). License revoked for numerous violations, including making flagrant misrepresentations, *Catoctin Broadcasting of NY,* 62 RR 2d 1132 (1987), 66 RR 2d 131 (1989). FCC ordered to hold hearing on renewal of three noncommercial broadcast licenses on basis of misrepresentations in connection with operation of KQEC-TV, *KQED,* 59 RR 2d 721 (DC Ct. of App. 1986). FCC then denied license renewal of KQEC-TV for saying it went off-the-air for technical reasons, but actually going silent because of financial problems. Renewed licenses of its two other principal stations, KQED-FM-TV San Francisco, (Feb. 1990). FCC denied license renewal of WBBY-FM, Westerville, Ohio, for mispresenting how much time a one-fourth owner would spend in managing the station in order to win "integration" credit. The FCC stated record shows "a pattern of deliberate concealment and false statements regarding a matter of potentially crucial importance." (Feb. 1990). (See "RKO Revocation").

Multiple Ownership Regulations. (§73:3555, §76:501); In 1953, the FCC proposed to limit ownership of TV to five VHF stations. Storer Broadcasting's application for a sixth station was dismissed. Supreme Ct. deferred to the FCC's right to decide if it was necessary to limit the number of stations owned by one owner, *Storer,* 220 F. 2d 204, 11 RR 2053 (1955), *US v. Storer,* 351 US 192; 13 RR 2161 (1956). Subsequently, the number of stations which can be owned by majority active ownership was revised. From 7 AM, 7 FM, and 7 TV (of which 2 had to be UHF) entities may now own 12 AM's, 12 FM's and 12 to 14 TV's as of April 2, 1985. TV station ownership is restricted to cover no more than 25% of the nation's television homes. UHF-TV's are assessed at only half of their market's TV homes to encourage UHF purchases. Group owners who buy into stations more than half owned by minorities are able to own up to 14 TV stations and are permitted to reach 30% of nation's TV households, as long as two stations are controlled by minorities. The networks then owned stations that reached about 20% of the national audience, 57 RR 2d 966 (1985). The FCC also did away with the prohibition of anyone owning, operating or controlling three commercial stations where any two were located within 100 miles of the third, and where primary service overlapped. The increase in media outlets made it highly unlikely, the FCC stated, that any single owner would be able to exercise undue sway over public opinion and broadcasters could take advantage of increased operating efficiencies from regional group ownership, *Regional Concentration of Control*, 55 RR 2d 1389, 55 RR 2d 1465 (1984). The "duopoly" section of §73.3555(a) which prohibited any party from owning two or more stations in the same service if there is a prohibited amount of signal overlap was liberalized to permit commonly owned radio stations to be located in closer proximity to each other within the same Area of Dominant Influence market or geographic area, *Multiple Ownership of Broadcast Facilities*, 65 RR 2d 1676 (1989). The "one-to-a-market" rule prohibited an entity from having an attributable interest in more than one each AM or FM and a TV station in the same community. Such ownerships prior to this rule were grandfathered until they were sold. In a measure that should increase the value of at least some major market broadcast properties, the FCC has relaxed §73:3555, specifying that the agency will look with favor at requests for waivers of the rule under certain conditions. Broadcasters in the top twenty-five markets may now apply for a waiver, so long as there are at least thirty separately owned licensees in the same market, and certain other criteria are met. Smaller markets may also request a waiver. Also, if "failed station" not operated for a substantial period of time or in a bankruptcy proceeding may be granted a waiver. The FCC will consider the number of stations owned by the applicant, financial status of the stations, and the availability of cable in the market. Applicants must show that the "public interest" benefits of the proposed cross-ownership, such as viewpoint diversity and economic competition, would be maintained, *Broadcast Multiple Ownership Rules*, 65 RR 2d 1589 (1989). Ruled FCC acted arbitrarily and capriciously in denying a request for an evidentiary hearing (§309) before agreeing to waiver authorizing the transfer of a "failing" UHF station to the licensee of AM-FM stations in the same market. The licensee of the radio stations was controlled by the father, sister and brother-in-law of the TV licensee and TV licensee held a 5% interest in the radio stations prior to filing the transfer application. Issues which should have been settled were (1) had radio stations' licensee exercised <u>de facto</u> control; (2) would this be anti-competitive concentration of media ownership and control; (3) were misrepresentations made as TV licensee had agreed to divest holdings in AM-FM; and (4) had licensee intentionally caused TV to fail to justify UHF exception to one-to-a-market rule, *Astroline Communications v. FCC*, 857 F. 2d 1556, 65 RR 2d 538 (1988). The FCC has decided to reduce the scope of its "cross-interest policy." This policy was devised to reach certain business relationships not proscribed by §73:3555, but which might have had an adverse impact on economic competition and programming diversity. Three specific instances of an individual or firm with a consulting arrangement, advertising agency representation, or time brokerage agreement are no longer essential. However, in comparative settlement situations, consulting arrangements will still be reviewed to see if possible attempt to obtain "greenmail" to drop application. (See "Comparative Qualifications"). Antitrust laws and the availability of civil remedies for breach of contract are available to deter and redress abuses stemming from such relationships. Being considered for removal but remaining in force for now are three situations: (1) where a "key" employee of one station services as a "key" employee or has ownership interest in another station in the same market, (2) owners of different stations in the same market are in a joint venture to build to buy another in the same market, (3) an individual or entity has an attributable or controlling ownership interest in one broadcast property in a market as well as substantial equity in another in the same market not falling under multiple ownership rules, *Cross-interest Policy*, 65 RR 2d 1734 (1989). Prior to 1977, an AM station owner could not duplicate (simulcast) his programming on his co-owned and located FM station for more than 50% of the time. After 1977, 25% duplication in markets over 100,000, and in 1979, in markets over 25,000. This rule was based on assumption that it would foster separate FM program development. Now it is AM that is in trouble, and FCC has eliminated this restriction. Successful FM stations can now simulcast 100% on AM sister stations, thereby keeping costs down and preserving AM broadcasting to the benefit of the listening public, *AM/FM Program Duplication*, 59 RR 2d 1611 (1986).

Multiple Violations. Revocation affirmed on the ground that a long history of persistent violations of FCC operating rules was sufficient, *United v. FCC*, 34 RR 2d 1465, 55 FCC 2d 416, 40 RR 2d 1646 (DC App. 1977). Renewal denied where majority stockholder unlawfully transferred control, made misrepresentations, willfully violated technical rules, lacked candor, *Stereo Broadcasters*, 87 FCC 2d 87, 49 RR 2d 1263; 50 RR 2d 1346 (1981). License revoked for repeatedly and willfully violating the public file and community ascertainment rules, harassing persons attempting to review the station's public file, making flagrant misrepresentations, engaging in racially discriminatory hiring practices, conducting fraudulent contests, *Catoctin Broadcasting of NY*, 62 RR 2d 1132 (1987), 66 RR 2d 131 (1989).

Network Regulation. (§303 (i), §73:132, §76:501, §73:658, §76:92); "Territorial Exclusivity Rule" (no station may affiliate with any network owning more than one network) forced NBC to sell Blue Net; Sale conditions: Couldn't have a policy barring sale of time for controversy, *RCA and ABS*, 10 FCC 212 (1943). Supreme Ct. held FCC has a right to exercise control over network-station business arrangements, *NBC v. US*, 47 F. Supr. 940 (1942), 319 US 190 (1943). FCC §73:132, §73:658 (b) also prevents any station from having a contract with a network which prevents any other station in the same area from broadcasting that network's shows if affiliated station declines to run. As network radio declined, FCC waived and then eliminated Rule §73.137 to permit ABC to operate four radio networks, 11 FCC 2d 163, 12 RR 2d 72 (1967), 17 FCC 2d 508, 16 RR 2d 84 (1969). Statement of Policy on Network Radio allowed multiple radio networking; §73:132; *1977 Report & Order*, March 23, 42 FR 16415, 63 FCC 2d 674, 40 RR 2d 80 (1977). (See "Multiple Ownership Regulations"). CBS proposed more pay to its affiliates the more programs they carried. This was declared violation of prohibition of exclusive affiliation, §73:658(a), by FCC after pressure from Justice Dept., *CBS*, 23 RR 769 (1961); 24 RR 513 (1962). Again, under pressure from the Justice Dept. which felt option time was antitrust violation, FCC ruled TV Networks could not option time in affiliation contracts, §73:658(d), *FCC Rept. & Order*, 34 FCC 1103, 25 RR 1951 (1963). Radio station filing of network agreements with the FCC eliminated, but TV licensees are still required to file network affiliation agreements with the FCC, based on the limited number of networks available to TV as opposed to radio stations (§73:3613). Since regional and other non-national TV networks do not provide substantial programming these agreements need not be filed, 101 FCC 2d 516, 58 RR 2d 815 (1985). The FCC deleted two year limitation on the duration of affiliation agreements between TV networks and stations citing changes in the TV industry, and competition in the mass media marketplace generally, that have occurred since the rule was instituted in 1945. FCC has concluded it is no longer necessary to promote competition among networks and that it may actually serve to stifle such competition. The FCC also expressed concern that the rule prevented networks and stations from entering into long-term relationships that would facilitate extended planning by both parties, *Network Affiliation Agreements (Two-Year Rule)*, 66 RR 2d 190 (1989). Network definition §73:658(j)(4) is any organization offering interconnected programs on regular basis for 15 or more hours per week to at least 25 affiliated TV licensees in 10 or more states. Waived to permit interconnected religious programming of up to 30 hours per week in more than 10 states, *Christian Broadcasting Network*, 87 FCC 2d 1076, 50 RR 2d 359 (1981). Also, Home Shopping Network and Univision (84 hrs. of Spanish-language programs to 28 stations in 14 different states) are deemed not TV networks for regulatory purposes. Low powered TV stations are not to be counted. Therefore not subject to §73:568(k) "prime-time access" rule, §73:658(j)(1)(ii) "Financial interest" rule, §73:658(j)(1)(i) "syndication" rule, and §73:658(g) "dual network" rule, *Home Shopping Network*, 66 RR 2d 175 (1989). "Network Syndication and Financial Interest Rules." Public Notice eliminated networks from distribution and profit-sharing in domestic syndication and restricted their activities in foreign markets to distribution of programs of which they were the sole producers, *Amended 73.658 (j)*, 23 FCC 2d 382, 18 RR 2d 1825 (1970).

"Prime-time Access Rule" was passed by FCC in 1970, prohibiting networks from using more than three hours of prime-time each night on affiliated stations in order to give independent producers prime-time access on affiliated stations. Held constitutional and consistent with FCC obligations under First Amendment to promote diversity of program sources, *Mt. Mansfield v. FCC*, 442 F. 2d 470; 21 RR 2d 2087 (1971); *National Assoc. of Ind. TV Producers and Directors v. FCC*, 516 F. 2d 526 (1975); Ct. remanded for rule changes,

33 RR 2d 2087 (1975); *Exemptions and Waivers*, 50 FCC 2d 829, 32 RR 2d 697, 1975; *2nd Report and Order*, FCC; 53 FCC 2d 335, 33 RR 2d 1089 (1975). Policy which had prohibited affiliated network stations from using off-network and feature films which had been on the network within past two years has been eliminated as part of the prime-time access rule, *Underbrush Broadcast Policies*, 54 RR 2d 1043 (1983).

"Network Antitrust." Consent judgments were entered against ABC and CBS to restrain monopolization of prime time TV entertainment programs in violation of *Sherman Antitrust Act*, based on an NBC Consent Decreeentered into earlier. Affiliated and owned-and-operated stations of the networks were found to depend upon the networks for virtually all their entertainment programming. The commercial value of such control over programming, in addition to the first network showing, includes stripping (broadcasting program series episodes five days a week after initial network exhibition), syndication, foreign distribution, merchandising, literary and musical rights, etc. During the 1950's many advertisers purchased programs from independent suppliers (producers and production companies) for showing on networks. By 1967 only 11% were advertiser supplied and as of judgment no prime-time shows were advertiser supplied. The FCC, in response to network dominance of production or subsidiary rights adopted rules forbidding networks from demanding financial interests or syndication rights from producers, §73:658(j), but networks continued to seek such rights as long-term renewal options with preset license fee escalation rates; exclusive options on spinoffs; creative program control; right to all profits from network exhibition; and right of first refusal at end of option period. The consent judgment, certain provisions which will be in effect until 1991 and others until 1995, enjoined networks from acquiring syndication and other distribution rights or profit shares in non-network exploitation of entertainment programs produced by others. Domestic syndication was prohibited by the networks but would allow network-produced and certain foreign programs to be distributed in foreign markets. In order to increase competition networks may produce no more than 2 1/2 hours per week in prime time (with similar restrictions in other time periods). Other practices prohibited are purchasing exhibition rights not incident to network use; a ban on requiring a program supplier having to use network production facilities; a prohibition against purchasing another network's programs when there is a condition that the other network purchase similar rights; and no exclusive yearly options for more than a total of 4 years. The networks may not have exclusive rights in connection with exhibition of feature films either theatrically, nontheatrically, on discs, cartridges or cassettes, or on closed circuit TV in certain situations. The networks are barred from retaining rights to option program pilots not selected for broadcast beyond 35% of the pilots produced so as to allow other networks and stations access to remaining product. If a spinoff depicts a non-continuing character, the network may contract only for first negotiation and a limited first refusal right and the use of repeat broadcasts of series episodes is curtailed. With respect to talent agreements, individuals performing continuing or essential creative services on a prime time series licensed to a network are barred from entering agreements which prevent them from providing their services to the series if it is later licensed elsewhere. The judgment does not affect network ability to acquire certain rights for non-network broadcast (49 RR 2d 1343; 1981) distribution of programs abroad and they may recover money advanced for development, *US v. CBS*, Civil Action No. 74-3599-RJK; *US v. ABC*, No. 74-3600-RJK (C.D. Calif. 1980); *US v. NBC*, No. 74-3601-RJK (C.D. Calif. 1977). Ct. of Appeals ruled that costs studios incurred in responding to pretrial discovery subpoenas of $650,000 may be awarded to Columbia Pictures, Gulf & Western, MCA, 20th Century-Fox and Warner Communication from ABC and CBS, 666 F.2d 364 (1982), Cert. denied; *US v. CBS*, 103 F.R.D. 365 (C.D. Ca. 1984.)

Then in 1983, the FCC attempted to eliminate the rules which prohibited network entry into the independent production and syndication markets since 1970. The rules applied only to prime time entertainment series and only to domestic distribution of such series for non-network exhibition. To reduce the possibility of warehousing, a TV network would be required, within six months of the completion of a series' network distribution to transfer its rights relating to syndication to an unaffiliated syndicator. The rules also would require networks to transfer all syndication rights no later than the fifth year of the series' network run. Passive financial interests could have been maintained by networks. This proposed change ran into some conflict with the above consent decrees which would expire, in part, by 1991, *Syndication and Financial Interest Rules (Tentative Decision)*, 54 RR 2d 457 (1983). Congressional hearings were held after considerable pressure from syndicators, producers and stations not to eliminate rules. Then Chairman Fowler stated, "...we believe that Congress should permit us to reach a final decision— under the "public interest" standard by which we are governed—and to conclude this proceeding without further delay." However, an effort to achieve a compromise on the rule changes between the networks and Hollywood producers fell through and therefore no action, (1983). Since the provisions prohibiting networks from producing more than five hours week of primetime programming will soon be expiring, networks and producers are now again attempting to arrive at an agreement. Although the financial and syndication exclusivity rules still would prevent the networks from taking any financial interest in the programs they carry— whether produced in-house or by other production companies—the networks theoretically would be able to produce all 22 hours in-house, thus shutting out outside producers. One proposal from the producers is that the network get a 25% financial interest in income from domestic syndication if they agree to cover 90% of a show's debt financing; the production costs that exceed the license fee paid by the network, (1990).

Network Service Rights. Station cannot compel a network to provide service, *WSAY-Federal Broadcasting Co. v. ABC*, 167 F. 2d 349, 4 RR 2019, 335 US 821 (1948). Change in affiliation not contrary to Antitrust laws, *Van Curler v. FCC* (DC App.), 12 RR 2040 (1955); *Rosenblum*, 22 FCC 1432; 11 RR 825, 12 RR 283; 13 RR 49 (1957). Cancelling affiliation to transfer to a new network owned station no violation of Antitrust laws, *Poller, WCAN-TV v. CBS*, 22 RR 2080, 174 F. Supp. 802, aff'd, 109 US App. DC 170, 284 F. 2d 599, rev. 368 US 464 (1962). No FCC rule or policy prohibits networks and their subsidiaries from acquiring independent stations or stations affiliated with other networks, even if another station in the market is affiliated with the acquiring network. GE (NBC) approved to acquire CBS affiliate WTVJ-TV even though current NBC affiliate is WSVN-TV. CBS would terminate affiliation at end of current contract and WTVJ will then become NBC affiliate. Until then station, although owned by GE (NBC) will carry CBS network and will seek to increase ratings, which means no preemption of CBS network fare, *WBC Associates*, 63 RR 2d 1179 (1987). KMTC-TV, Springfield, MO purchased for $13 million. ABC informed potential purchaser they was considering changing affiliation to another station. Purchaser went ahead, but included contract clause that price would be reduced by $5 million should ABC terminate. ABC cancelled and new owner sued. Ct. ruled not fraud or false misrepresentation as could not establish he relied on ABC affiliation in buying station or making improvements, *Charles Woods v. Cap. Cities/ABC*, 869 F. 2d 1155 (8th Cir. 1989).

Newspaper Ownership. (§73:3555, §76:501); FCC denies newspaper applicant on desirability of diversity of ownership, *Arkansas-Oklahoma Co.*, 3 RR 479 (1946). Daily News-NY loses license in comparative hearing because of newspaper ownership. FCC goal is diversity, also residents of community preferred, etc., *News Syndicate*, 12 FCC 805, 4 RR 205

(1948). Right to consider monopolistic and unfair ad practices of newspaper applicant, *Fostoria*, 3 RR 2014a (1948); *Mansfield v. FCC*, 180 F. 2d 28, 5 RR 2074e, 13 FCC 23 (1950). Injunction against unfair competitive methods not violation of Freedom of Press, *WEOL v. Lorain Jr.*, 92 F. Supp. 794, 6 RR 2037 (1950); *US v. Lorain Jr.*, 342 US 143, 7 RR 2078 (1951). FCC consideration of diversification in mass media within scope of agency, *Scripps-Howard*, 4 RR 525 (1949); 189 F. 2d 677, *Scripps v. FCC*, 342 US 830, Cert. denied, 13 FCC 473 (1951). Even superior performance insufficient for newspaper applicant in competitive hearing, *McClatchy*, 9 RR 1190 (1954); 239 F. 2d 15, 13 RR 2067 (1956); 353 US 918, Cert. denied (1957). Newspaper guilty of unfair practices divested of stations, *Kansas City Star*, 240 F. 2d 643 (1957); 354 US 923, Cert. denied. (1957). Revocation based on concentration in media of mass communications, *Indianapolis Broadcasting*, 22 FCC 421 (1957); *WIBC*, 104 US App. DC 126, 259 F.2d 941, Cert. denied. 359 U.S. 920, 22 RR 425 (1961). Herald-Traveler station in Boston was filed against by a group which promised better programming, integration (ownership involvement) and diversity of local media control. Newspaper claimed not fair as only promises and paper would fold. FCC revoked license and newspaper ceased publication shortly thereafter, *WHDH*, 444 F. 2d 841, DC App.(1970); 403 US 923, Cert. denied, 15 RR 2d 411 (1971). (See "Comparative Qualifications"). FCC proposed prohibiting commercial licensee owning more than one full-time station of different broadcast services (AM, FM, TV) in the same market, 8 RR 2d 1735 (1970). Not passed, except for divestiture of cable systems owned in the same market with broadcast station. Supreme Ct. upheld FCC policy grandfathering most existing media cross-ownerships, disallowing future cross-ownerships and requiring break-up of egregious' cross-ownership situations (§76:501), *National Citizens Comm. v. FCC*, 555 F. 2d 938 (1977); 98 S. Ct. 2096 (1978); 436 US 775, 43 RR 2d 152 (1978); 51 RR 2d 449 (1982). Petition-to-deny renewal of WSYR-TV, Syracuse, NY on grounds station part of a group of holdings owned by Newhouse Broadcasting. Newhouse owned AM, FM, cable, two major newspapers, ALL in Syracuse. Without a hearing FCC renewed and ruled that citizens group had failed to show; (1) specific abuses attributable to common ownership, or (2) that common ownership created economic monopolization violating *Sherman Antitrust Act*. One of these elements must be present before FCC will consider cross-ownership in a license proceeding. At the time of renewal FCC had cross-ownership rule requiring Newhouse to divest itself of cable, but this rule was modified so as to be inapplicable to pre-existing systems, *Syracuse Coalition for the Free Flow of Information in the Broadcast Media v. FCC*, 593 F. 2d 1170, 44 RR 2d 581 (DC Cir. 1978), see 73 FCC 2d 186, 46 RR 2d 35 (1979). Multiple media ownership rules are not contingent upon how many signals received in market, but whether local issues can be covered with diversity, *Petitions for Waiver of §73:35, §73:240 and §73:636*, 74 FCC 2d 497, 46 RR 2d 684 (1979). Practice of newspaper with local license to list programs out-of-channel sequence and give itself preferential photos constitutes cross-ownership abuse, *KHQ*, 87 FCC 2d 705, 50 RR 2d 21 (1981). Connecticut Supreme Ct. rules that State's body which governs cable was not barred by federal preemption from revoking the franchises of a company which refused to divest itself of ownership of a statewide newspaper having significant circulation in the cable areas involved, 56 RR 2d 639 (1984). FCC finds owner of small free weekly circulation newspaper, of specialized nature, which is only one out of three weeklies in a community which has a daily newspaper of general circulation, does not suffer a diversification adverse effect in applying for an FM license, *Barton Broadcasting*, 60 RR 2d 322 (1986).

News Piracy. Decision by Supreme Ct. that while there could be no copyright of news as such, "piracy" by one newsgathering organization of the news items collected by another was "unfair competition," (*International News Service* *v. Associated Press*, 248 US 215, 1918) was applied to broadcasting, but damages not substantiated, *Associated Press v. KVOS*, 299 US 269 (1936); Use by station of newspaper items for newscast may be "unfair competition" if station is competing with newspaper for advertisers or subscribers' and news is fresh and of commercial value to paper, *Comm Broadcasting*, 6 RR 2d 589 (1965). State has jurisdiction concerning "unfair competition." Use does not violate copyright act if factual content only, *Pottstown*, 6 RR 2d 2027, 247 F. Supp 578 (ED Pa. 1965). Although the government may deny access to information it generates and punish its theft, government may not prohibit or punish the publication of that information once it falls into the hands of the press unless the need for secrecy is overwhelming, *Landmark Comm. v. Virginia*, 435 US 829, 98 St. Ct. 2588 (1978). ESPN Cable Network enjoined from using on cable sports news highlights of Boston Red Sox and Bruins games without consent of either team. Not "fair use" under *Copyright Act* and video taped from WSBK which sells use. Although only 2 minutes in length from complete game Ct. stated it was the quality of use and highlights were substantial as networks had paid for such use, *New Boston Television, v. ESPN*, Civil Action 81-1010-Z (D. Mass. 1981). TV News Clips Co. sold copies of news video to those mentioned at $35 per clip. WXIA-TV sued for copyright infringement. Station had copyright and registered pretaped version of feature as well as later broadcast. News Clips tape was a <u>total</u> reproduction of a particular feature and did not qualify for First Amendment protection or "fair use" as not satire, parody or comment, and not partial, noncompetitive use. Injunction granted, *Pacific & Southern v. Duncan*, 744 F. 2d 1490 (CA 11th 1984). Docudrama titled <u>Murder in Texas</u> did not infringe book <u>Blood and Money</u> although both works recounted events surrounding death of Houston socialite Joan Hill as factual news event. Only expression can be protected by copyright, not facts or ideas, *David Merrick v. Dick Clark*, Case No. 80 Civ. 5877 (SDNY 1980). (See "Copyright—Broadcast

Rights").

Newsroom Security. Legislation passed Congress in 1980, requiring all federal, state and local law enforcement agencies to obtain a subpoena before searching newsroom or newsperson unless person involved is suspected of crime; information necessary to prevent death or serious bodily injury; imminent destruction or concealment of material not produced in response to a Ct. order or if contraband material. Law came about to overturn *Zucker v. Stanford Daily*, 436 US 547 (1978). CBS required to turn over out-takes from report on fast-food franchises. A month after aired a federal grand jury returned indictments for conspiracy and fraud against the company involved and defendants served CBS with subpoena. Appeals Ct. recognized needs of news gathering, but has to be weighed against defendants' need and judge would have to view before invoking journalists' privilege. Later ruled judge erred in scope of release of some material to defendants, *US v. Cuthbertson*, 630 F.2d 139 (3rd. 1980); Rehearing (3rd Cir. 1981).

News Sources. Walter Roche of WBZ-TV refused to reveal confidential sources consulted for investigative report on local judges. Held although sources could be identified from other testimony by other witnesses object was to use interviews to reveal inconsistent statements and order not oppressive, unnecessary or irrelevant, *In the Matter of Roche*, 411 NE 2d 466 (Mass. Sup. Judicial Ct. 1980). New York has a shield law protecting journalist from having to disclose information gained in newsgathering. There is a requirement that the reporter must get the story with the understanding of confidentiality, but if not so obtained the First Amendment provides an independent basis, *Wilkins v. Kalla*, 459 NYS 2d 985 (NY Cnty 1983); *Grand Jury Investigation*, 460 NYS 2d 227 (Co. Ct. 1983); *People v. Bova*, 460 NYS 2d 230 (Kings Co. Sup. 1983). CBS's KMOX-TV received subpoena for all tapes of conversations between reporter and individuals interviewed on story about illegal placement of video poker games. CBS claimed disclosure would interfere with its ability to collect the news and its editorial process. Since Missouri does not have a shield law and request was for grand jury secret proceedings; there was no potential for harm. Reporter had not promised secrecy, *CBS v. Campbell*, 645 SW 2d 30 (Mo. App. 1982). Car dealer claimed documentary defamed him and obtained court order for outtakes and other material used in the making of the program. Ruled Pennsylvania shield law protects broadcaster from a court order requiring material to be produced even where it is the station being sued on content, *Hatchard v. Westinghouse*, 504 A. 2d 211 (Pa. App. 1986). TV reporter Bradley Stone was found in contempt of court for failure to comply with a subpoena issued by a county grand jury. The videotapes were sought in connection with the investigation of the murder of a state police officer. Held that reporters do not possess a qualified testimonial privilege, and even if so, would have to disclose tapes as clear and convincing that he had information that was clearly relevant to a specific violation of criminal law which was not available from other sources and the state had a compelling and overriding interest in obtaining the information. A state shield law does not pertain to broadcast reporters, and a statute granting newspaper reporters a privilege against grand jury testimony did not include broadcast media, *In re Grand Jury Proceedings (Storer)*, 810 F. 2d 580 (6th Cir. 1987). (See "News Piracy").

NonCommercial Donor Announcements. (§73:503); Public broadcast stations are prohibited from broadcasting announcements which promote the sale of goods and services of for-profit entities in return for anything of value paid to the station, its principals or employees, including programming material and funds, and services or goods used for programming. However, contributors of funds and other items of value may be donated for on-air acknowledgements in order to give noncommercial broadcasters the means to exploit revenue sources. FCC has authorized noncommercial stations to include in their underwriting announcements the brand, trade names of products, listing of products and services, and/or promotional logos of donors. Rules governing interruption of regular programming for underwriting and donor acknowledgments are limited to the regular schedule, but not to fund-raising activities that suspend or alter normal programming. Public broadcasters are still not permitted to substantially alter or suspend regular programming to raise funds for any entity other than the station itself, *Noncommercial Educational Broadcasting*, 55 RR 2d 1190 (1984). Spots for program-related materials sold by non-profit organizations and to raise funds for station or non-profit performing arts organizations in connection with programs furnished allowed; so long as spots do not interrupt other regular programs, *Educational Promotional Announcements*, 90 FCC 2d 895, 51 RR 2 1567 (1982). FCC staff admonished Xavier University FM for making impermissible promotional and qualitative underwriting credit announcements. Exception was taken to using word "discount" to describe Jiffy Lube shop. Also challenged was policy of allowing underwriters to state the number of years they were in business, and for permitting descriptions of underwriter's services as, "fresh and original foods," an art gallery's "timeless traditional truths in contemporary visual vocabulary," and an ad company's "creative services." Commissioner James Quello has stated that other than "discount," the staff was not reasonable and FCC may overrule, (WVXU, Nov. 1989).

Offensive Advertising. Birconjel contraceptive copy read, "to avoid the consequences of moral impropriety" and was also misleading, *Knickerbocker*, 2 FCC 76 (1935). When AIDS became public issue and NAB Code, which discouraged such advertising, was discontinued in 1982, some networks and stations ran condom public service and commercial ads. (See "Antitrust—Broadcasting").

Overcommercialization. No renewal because insufficient public service and overcommercialization, *Public Service Responsibility of Broadcast Licensees*, p. 41 (1946). Incentive pay contracts led to over-commercialization and although station renewed it had to promise in future no such compensation arrangement for operating management, *WTOL-Community*, 12 FCC 85, 3 RR 1360 (1947). (See "Licensee Control Over Programs"). FCC has right to consider overcommercialization as part of programming in the "public interest," *WREC*, 10 RR 1323; 14 RR 1262; 22 FCC 1572 (1960). Excessive Commercials (av. 15 per hour); lack of program balance gets short-term license renewal, *WESY-Miss-Ark Broadcasting*, 22 RR 305 (1961). Past record and local program service superior even though overcommercialization, *Kentucky Broadcasting v. FCC*, 12 FCC 282, 3 RR 1547 (1947); 174 F. 2d 38, 4 RR 2126 (1949). In the 1960's the FCC had issued a "Notice of Proposed Rulemaking" to consider a formal rule limiting commercial time, but industry and Congress upset over issue; so FCC released Policy Statement which became basis for §0.281(7)(i,ii,iii). Commercial AM-FM stations exceeding 18 minutes per hour, or 20 minutes per hour for 10% or more total weekly hours of operation and which, during political campaigns or seasonal business markets exceed 22 minutes for 10% of total hours could not be renewed routinely by FCC staff. TV stations could not exceed 16 minutes per hour, but during high demand political campaigns could go to 20 minutes for 10% of total hours of operation, 36 FCC 45 (1964). Subsequently, noting the growth in the number of competing radio stations the FCC decided to rely upon market-place forces to achieve balanced programming and abolished rule. In the area of programming the FCC stated that official amounts of certain programming would be censorship, *Hubbard*, 48 FCC 2d 517 (1974); but unofficial processing guidelines for the FCC Staff continued: Non-entertainment had to be more than 8%, 6% and 10% respectively for commercial AM, FM, TV. TV had to show more than 5% local programming and 5% or more informational programming—6 a.m. to 12 midnight, *FCC Report No. 14173*, May 12, 1976, see 37 RR 2d 144 (1976). Then the unofficial guidelines requirement for TV stations was eliminated in 1981. Policies on limiting commercial time were eliminated with the expectation that audiences, advertisers and individual station owners would act to curb abuses or excesses. This cleared the way for program-length commercials previously disapproved, *Public Notice*, 44 FCC 2d 985, 29 RR 2d 469 (1974). There is no rule or policy which proscribes the type announcement for which a licensee may charge-obituary-dedication, etc., *La Fiesta*, 59 FCC 2d 1175, 37 RR 2d 983 (1976).

Petition—to—Deny. (§73:3584); FCC had held that members of the listening public did not suffer any injury peculiar to them and they did not have standing to participate in hearings as this would pose great administrative burdens. The theory was that the only effects sufficient to support standing were economic injury and electrical interference. The FCC therefore could react or not on comments and complaints from the public. Most often the FCC aligned itself with the interests of the broadcast industry it was established to regulate. The WLBT case radically changed that policy. The FCC turned down an organized protest group as not having standing to be heard even though detailed information was provided by the group that the only VHF TV station in Jackson, MS had discriminated against the very significant black audience. Remanded back to the FCC holding that responsible spokesman for representative groups in the listening community pursuing broad "public interest" have standing as petitioners to deny license renewal and should be heard. The FCC then held the required hearing but placed the burden of proof on the public group instead of the renewal applicant and renewed license. Ct. took unusual step of vacating the renewal and ordered the FCC to consider new applicants for the channel. Thus began a period of public activism in the license renewal process with over 500 petitions-to-deny in the 1970's alone, *Office of Comm. of United Church of Christ v. FCC*, 359 F. 2d 994 (1966). The FCC has subsequently implemented a rule allowing anyone who resides within the station's service area to file a petition-to-deny against renewal applicant. The petition must contain specific allegations of fact sufficient to demonstrate that the petitioner is a party in interest and that the grant would be prima facie inconsistent with the "public interest, convenience and necessity requirement." The allegations must be supported by the affidavits of a person or persons with personal knowledge of the facts. Licensees then began to negotiate agreements with groups to not file, or to drop opposition. KCOP had petition-to-deny filed by an association of citizens which claimed deficiency in programming and breach of agreement. The FCC denied the petition without holding an evidentiary hearing, pursuant to §309(d) of *Communications Act*. The Ct. noted that the criticisms of the quality of programming were imprecise and unspecific and no material questions of fact or prima facie evidence offered. Ct. stated that the FCC has discretion to pursue or not pursue allegations of excessive violence in programming. The Ct. found that FCC decision was, however, garbled on question of an agreement breach. The agreement with the group had been incorporated into the license renewal application. These become representations to FCC and should be treated as promises of future performance. FCC declined to conduct a hearing on the grounds it would not arbitrate vague terms and KCOP had satisfied its obligations, *National Association for Better Broadcasting v. FCC*, 591 F. 2d 812, 44 RR 2d 793 (DC Cir. 1978). The FCC has reaffirmed its policy of voiding citizen agreements that restrict a licensee's control over its station. (See "Comparative Qualifications").

Point—to—Point Communication. (§73:1250 (a)); Horse racing results in code not understandable by all listeners are private communication, not broadcasting. Licensees may address messages to a particular individual (e.g., a person in public life) if the message is an integral part of the program format and its meaning is clear to the audience, *Bremer*, 2 FCC 79 (1935). A radio station may not transmit announcements asking a Dr. (identified by code number) to call the Physician's Bureau. This is point-to-point communication, not broadcasting and other services available, *KFAB*, 1 RR 2d 403 (1963), and see *WANV*, 27 RR 2d 1607 (1973). Certain emergency situations may justify an exception to the prohibition on point-to-point communication. At the request of responsible public officials a station may air messages to request or dispatch aid in rescue operations. However, immediately after such broadcast, the licensee must notify the FCC, stating the nature of the emergency, *Rule §73:1250(e)*.

Political—Sponsorship Identification. (§73:1212, §76:221); The FCC requires licensees to identify sponsors of paid advertising, commercial or political, on the air, at the time the ads are run. Licensees are under an obligation to make reasonably diligent inquiries to learn the true sponsor when they have reason to suppose it may be someone other than the apparent sponsor. Station cannot refuse <u>all</u> political ads because of difficulty in determining source, *KOB-Albuquerque*, 3 RR 1820 (1946). In a paid political campaign for a proposition requiring separate smoking and non-smoking areas a group asked the FCC to order broadcasters to display "paid for by the Tobacco Industry." Licensees, in this case, had exercised reasonable diligence as the tobacco industry, although supplying the funds, did not have editorial control over ads. A more stringent duty to investigate would create administrative and constitutional difficulties, *Loveday v. FCC*, 707 F. 2d 1443; 53 RR 2d 1452; 55 RR 2d 1086 (DC Cir. 1983).

Political Time Limits. (§315); Station has right to limit the amount of time used by political candidates as long as all are treated equally, *Homer P. Rainey*, 11 FCC 898, 3 RR 737 (1947). Station not required to sell time to one candidate if hasn't sold time to other candidates for same office, *Grommelin*, 19 RR 1392 (1960). §312 amended adding (a)(7), requiring broadcasters to allow "reasonable access" to or permit purchase of reasonable amounts of time by a legally qualified candidate for <u>Federal</u> Elective Office on behalf of his candidacy. Does not apply to local or state races, *P.L. 92-225* (1972). Since networks are licensees and their affiliates' programming agents, they are covered by political broadcasting sections of *Communications Act*. The Presidential nominating process is not isolated state primary/caucus campaigns, but a nationwide effort and networks cannot base their acceptance or rejection of requests for time upon the date of a national nominating convention. With respect to requests for time, requests for equal time must be submitted within one week of day reply proposed and candidate must be legally qualified at time of the proposed broadcast, but does not need to be qualified when request is made, §73.120; §1940(e). Federal candidates desires for specific time periods and length of time should be honored whenever possible and an arbitrary ban on the use of a particular class or length of time is not reasonable. Stations must honor candidates' assessment of his or her media needs and request for time cannot be met with just news coverage or other exposures exempt from §315. Each candidates' request is to be considered individually, not against backdrop of campaign as whole, or multiplicity of candidates *Carter-Mondale*, 74 FCC 2d 631, 46 RR 2d 829; aff'd, 46 RR 2d 1711 (Ct. App. 1980); aff'd, in *CBS v. FCC*, 453 US 367, 49 RR 2d 1191 (Supr. Ct. 1981). (See "Equal Opportunity")

Privacy. In a dramatized crime story a named individual has a right of privacy when the former news event has faded and is no longer news, *Mau v. Rio Grande Oil Co.*, 28 F. Supp. 845 (1939). Person involved in current newsworthy event does not retain right of privacy, *Elmhurst v. Pearson, et. al.*, 153 F. 2d 467 (1946). Broadcasting old fight film not dissemination of news; former professional boxer has not completely lost right of privacy and can challenge unauthorized use of name and picture for ad purposes, *Sharkey v. NBC*, 93 F. Supp. 986, 6 RR 2070 (1950). Gene Autry dramatized inaccurately a news event of an actual air-sea rescue. Invaded the privacy of the actual hero, *O'Brien v. Autry, Variety*, (3/8/50). Gossip program informational and Chaplin a public figure subject to legitimate public interest, *Chaplin v. NBC*, 9 RR 2051 (1953). Widely publicized criminal proceeding does not lose its status as matter of legitimate public interest even after eight years; dramatization permitted, *Bernstein v. NBC*, 129 F. Supp. 817, 11 RR 2091 (1954). Spectator shown on TV at news-worthy event (gambling raid) loses right of privacy, *Jacova v. Southern*, 83 So. 2d 34, 13 RR 2001 (1955). Names of rape victims not used, but occupations and pictures of car which were readily identifiable. Name is interpreted as equivalent of identity, *Nappier*, 1 RR 2d 2012, 322 F.2d 502 (1963). Nothing in First Amendment requires showing of malice as prerequisite to recovery for violation of right of privacy of person not public official. Negligence sufficient, *Yousoupoff v. CBS*, 265 NYS 2d 754 (NY Sup. Ct.), 6 RR 2d 2033 (1965). Capone, deceased, has no right of privacy and right cannot be asserted by next of kin, *Maritote v. Desilu*, 345 F. 2d 418; 5 RR 2d 2077 (1965). Docudrama <u>Tail Gunner Joe</u> about the late Senator Joseph McCarthy, did not defame or invade the privacy of Roy Cohn or David Shine, former aides. Subject matter still a matter of public interest and unless the promotional advertising was false or published with reckless disregard for the truth, or unless the selection of actors was done in a defamatory manner, NY's *Right of Privacy* statute was not violated, *Cohn v. NBC*, 414 NYS 2d 906 (1979), aff'd, 430 NYS. 2d 265 (NY 1980). Not liable for invasion of privacy when prison inmate incidentally appears in the background of a news report, *Cox Communication v. Lowe*, 328 S.E. 2d 384 (Ga. App. 1985). Footage of an accident scene never made the news, but was used in promotional spots advertising a special report about emergency medical help. Individual shown bleeding and in pain. Ruled that pictures were newsworthy, even if not promptly published. Did not claim spots implied he endorsed the station's program about medical services, *Anderson v. Fisher Broadcasting*, 712 P. 2d 803 (Ore. 1986). People who objected to being filmed dining in a private or secluded section of a restaurant, even when permission for filming from owner, have a right of privacy, *Stressman v. American Black Hawk Broadcasting*, 416 NW 2d 685 (Iowa 1987). (See "Trespass—Intrusion—Consent," "Defamation," "Right of Publicity").

Profane Language. (§303); FCC attempts to hold license renewal hearings on fourteen network affiliates for profane language used in network program <u>Beyond the Horizon</u> but drops idea after an editorial protests over interference with work of art, *Broadcasting*, (10/15/38, p. 22). Profane and indecent materials (off-color jokes and remarks) broadcast by DJ Charlie Walker, but denial based on misrepresentation, *Palmetto*, 23 RR 483 (1962); 33 FCC 250 (1962); *Edward G. Robinson v. FCC*, 334 F. 2d 534 (D. C. Cir. 1964). Westwood One-owned NBC Radio News fired anchorman for saying on-air "What the <u>hell</u> was that?" when computer glitch occurred. Producer received 4-week suspension without pay, *Variety*, (12/6/89, p. 5.) (See "Indecency—Obscenity").

Program Logs. Claiming stations for years have performed at levels considerably higher than those required by rules the FCC eliminated program log requirements as a paperwork burden on stations, *Federal Communications Commission, Deregulation of Radio*, 84 FCC 2d 968, 49 RR 2d 1 (effective April 3, 1981); 53 RR 2d 805; 53 RR 2d 1371; aff'd, 706 F. 2d 1224, 53 RR 2d 1501; 707 F. 2d 1413, 53 RR 2d 1371; 719 F. 2d 407, 54 RR 2d 811, 1151 (DC Cir. 1983); *Deregulation of Radio*, 55 RR 2d 1401; *Deregulation of Commercial Television*, 56 RR 2d 1005. Eliminated noncommercial Radio-TV program log requirements to bring into line with commercial licensee requirements, 56 RR 2d 1157 (1984).

Program Service Contracts. Tanner (now Media General) and other companies provide promo material (jingles) for cash and use of station's commercial time which it brokers to others. Contracts stated use of time valid until used. In Oklahoma, Ct. ruled that spots unused were forfeited after reasonable time had passed. Station had made all necessary cash payments and no longer used material supplied by Tanner. In Minnesota ruled contract did not specify the time for performance and held reasonable time was seven-year term of the contract. In Utah, ruled that there was no time limitation and Tanner was entitled to fair market value of spots and time credits. There station still owed on contract and was still using material. The Ct.'s have not reached consistent results, but generally feel "valid until used" is not ambiguous, *Tanner v. Plains,* 486 F. Supp. 1313, 47 RR 2d 519 (WD Okla. 1980); *Tanner v. KOWO,* 549 F. Supp. 411 52 RR 2d 317 (D. Minn 1982); *Tanner v. Granite,* 49 RR 2d 219 (Utah Dist. Ct. 1980); *Sparta-Tomah,* 716 F. 2d 1155, 54 RR 2d 769 (7th Cir. 1983); *Tanner v. Mesa,* 571 F. Supp. 28 (D. Colo. 1983). A former radio station employee who purchased prerecorded music and program materials acted within scope of employment and authority so station is obligated to pay on contract. The supplier had no notice of, and no reason to inquire about, any limitation on employee's authority. Station continued to use and pay for contracted materials, thereby approving contract, *White River Valley Broadcasters v. Wm. B. Tanner Co.,* 487 F. Supp. 725 (ED Ark. 1979). Station changed from beautiful music syndicated taped format to top forty. Contract with Stereo Radio Productions for beautiful music format tapes was for three years. New York law applied as contract executed, Stereo located and tapes made in New York. Fixed damages at amount music syndication company would have received under the contract less the amount they would have had to spend to perform. Since Stereo only saved $100 per month total breach was for $25,792, *Schulke Radio v. Midwestern Broadcasting,* 453 NE 2d 683 (Ohio 1983).

Promise v. Performance. FCC calls for programming to be in line with application promises, *KIEV-Cannon System Ltd.*, 8 FCC 207 (1940). Public Interest Requirements which would be considered as basic in serving the "public interest" listed. However, never evenly enforced, nor officially repudiated, *Public Service Responsibility of Broadcast Licensees*, [Blue Book] Mar. (1946). Cited in <u>Blue Book</u> and given a short-term license renewal and then challenged for its license, upgraded programming. Renewal given on providing a well-rounded program presentation and preference for past record, *Hearst*, 6 RR 994, 15 FCC 1149 (1951). Stations put on notice that to give renewal FCC would look at promises versus performance, *KORD*, 21 RR 781; 31 FCC 85 (1961). Short-term renewal granted for commercial station not meeting promises, *Loyola*, 24 RR 766 (1962). Petitioner must make specific allegations of fact, which, if true, would establish that overall programming could not have reasonably met needs and interests of community including substantial minority. Licensee not required to program in proportion to minority numbers in population, *Newhouse*, 53 FCC 2d 966, 33 RR 2d 1514 (1975). All minority programming done just on Sunday morning—licensee should present when reasonably could be expected to be effective, *Sonderling Broadcasting*, 68 FCC 2d 752, 43 RR 2d 573 (1978). FCC decided station did not intend to fulfill its promises when initially made and did not show good faith efforts as little news, no public affairs, insufficient staff, unresponsive to problems, needs and interests of community. Promise vs. performance inquiry is directed toward determining whether licensee made reasonable and good faith efforts and an examination of the licensee's efforts is material, *West Coast Media*, 47 RR 2d 109 (1980); 695 F. 2d 617, 52 RR 2d 1295 (1982); After exhausting all legal appeals West Coast then asked FCC for permission to distress sell the station to a minority group. (See "Sale or Transfer of License"). Denied; the licensee had pursued the renewal application to its unsuccessful conclusion and no longer possessed a license to transfer. Permitting a distress sale would signal other licensees not to opt to sell to a minority group until the ultimate outcome of their attempt to renew, which would not encourage the early entry into broadcasting of minority owners, 56 RR 2d 483 (1984). (See "Minority Ownership"). In 1985, FCC eliminated the promise vs. performance standard by requiring only a brief narrative statement of proposed programming when applying for a license. This was clarified by the FCC in a statement that applicants for new broadcast station permits, transfers or assignment need not include detailed information on proposed programming concerning community issues, including information as to the duration, type and time of presentation of such programming. Detailed information is not necessary to a determination as to whether grant would serve the "public interest," and to impose such a requirement would be inconsistent with recent deregulatory efforts, such as the deletion of formal ascertainment requirements, and the quantitative programming guidelines. There need be "only a brief description, in narrative form, of the planned programming service relating to the issues of public concern facing the proposed service area." This requirement is intended, essentially, to satisfy the FCC that applicants know of the policies regarding the obligation to present programming responsive to the community's needs, and to serve as a representation that licensees will comply with those policies, *Programming Information in Broadcast Applications*, 65 RR 2d 397 (1988).

Public Disclosure of FCC Records. Supreme Ct. required public disclosure except where FCC determines not in "public interest," *MCA v. FCC*, 85 S. Ct. 1459; 381 US 279 (1965). A radio station proposal to FCC to move to another city obtained an order against a potential competing applicant which had copied their application documents made available for public inspection. Five months after the original filing the identical engineering report was filed by the competing applicant. Suit for copyright infringement, "unfair competition," and fraudulent and corrupt practices upheld, *WPOW v. MRLJ*, 584 F. Supp. 132, 55 RR 2d 934 (DDC 1984). (See "Copyright—Broadcast Rights")

Public File. (§73:3526, §73:3527, §73:1202, §76:305); The FCC requires that certain records be maintained for public inspection during regular business hours within the community of license. Deregulation or "reregulation" of broadcasting has made the public file even more important. With the discontinuance of logs and other record keeping requirements the public must have continued reliance on the public file as an index to the general programming responsibilities of licensees. Prior to 1952, the *Communications Act* dictated extensive procedures for granting and renewing licenses. In 1952, an amendment substituted the lengthy review with the "public interest, convenience and necessity" standard. This and Congress's failure to include programming in a list of suggested renewal application questions convinced the Ct. that there was no mandate to inquire into programming. A postcard short-form license renewal form which contains no program related questions, with long-form renewal applications sent at random to a small (5%) percentage of radio and TV renewal applicants, does not render the FCC incapable of weighting the "public interest" in renewal activities. The intent of the FCC's action is to reduce regulatory burdens. The Ct. noted that the renewal form is not the only source of information to determine "public interest" as there is monitoring, random station inspections and public response, *Black Citizens for a Fair Media v. FCC*, 719 F. 2d 407, 54 RR 2d 1151 (DC Cir. 1983). When the FCC went from a long form license renewal form, which required detailed statistical analysis of "promises v. performance" to a short-form "postcard" license renewal, they again focused on the public file. Broadcasters must certify that the file is complete, up-to-date, and timely. Members of the public have an absolute right to inspect the file during normal business hours and the FCC publishes a manual which must be in the public file to inform the public of procedures available such as personal attacks, equal opportunity, petitions-to-deny, petitions-for-rulemaking, and informal complaints, *Broadcast Procedure Manual* (1972), 37 FCC 2d 286, 25 RR 2d 1901 and revised 49 FCC 2d 1, 31 RR 2d 224 (1974). TV licensees are not required to place new statement of program service in public file at renewal time if the statement on file is current, 87 FCC 2d 1127, 50 RR 2d 704 (1981). License revoked for harassing persons attempting to review the station's public file, repeatedly and willfully violating the public file and community ascertainment rules, and other abuses, *Catoctin Broadcasting of NY*, 62 RR 2d 1132 (1987), 66 RR 2d 131 (1989). Applications and related material must be maintained in the public file for one license term or until grant of the first renewal application, whichever is later, *Public File Requirements (Record Retention Periods)*, 64 RR 2d 1016 (1988). (See "Ascertainment of Community Needs").

Public Issue Program Recordings Unconstitutional. Held that Section §399(b) requiring all noncommercial educational radio and television stations to record all broadcasts in which any issue of public importance was discussed violates 1st and 5th Amendments of Constitution. Purposes unsatisfactory; no legitimate government interest; and difference in treatment between public and commercial broadcasters involved fundamental First Amendment rights, *Community-Service Broadcasting of Mid-America v. FCC*, 593 F. 2d 1102, 43 RR 2d 1675 (DC Cir. 1978).

Public Notice. (§73:3580); Requirement that applicants submit proof of publication of local notice of applications removed and replaced by single certification of compliance with notice requirement, 51 RR 305 (1982).

Racetrack Broadcasts. Racetrack broadcasts not desirable programming if promotes gambling, *Capitol*, 4 RR 21, 12 FCC 648 (1948). Racetrack information aiding illegal gambling grounds for revocation, *Port Frere Broadcasting*, 5 RR 1137 (1950). License revoked when SCA Multiplex channel of FM station used to broadcast horse race results to be received by bookmaker's, *Carol Music*, 3 RR 2d 477 (1963), 8 RR 2d 93, Cert. denied. (1966). The FCC has removed policies concerning the broadcast of legal horse racing information and advertising. The absence of evidence of abuses, changes in attitude of the public and governmental authorities toward gambling, the administrative costs, and censorship concerns were reasoning. However, the FCC will refer activities which appear to violate criminal laws dealing with illegal transmission of gambling information to appropriate authorities, 56 RR 2d 976 (1984).

Random Selection Licensing. (§1:1601, §1:1623, §73:3572, §73:3584, §73:3597); The FCC did not think the "public interest" would be better served by a policy that substituted open bidding for licenses for the reasoned decision-making of an expert body accountable in its actions to Congress, *Letter to Hon. William Proxmire*, 27 RR 2d 1321 (1973). Congress thought otherwise and included a lottery procedure in its 1981 budget bill. The lottery procedure allowed the FCC, at its discretion, to use for initial grants of licenses. The Lottery Selection was again rejected by the FCC, 89 FCC 2d 257, 50 RR 2d 1503 (1982). Congress, increasingly unhappy with the independence of this "independent regulatory agency" retaliated by authorizing the FCC's budget for a limited two-year period to provide Congress with an opportunity for regular and systematic oversight of the FCC's implementation of Congressional policy. Congress then passed new lottery system legislation to meet some of the objections of the FCC. Selection between applicants may be made by lottery so long as the qualifications of the applicants thus selected are subsequently reviewed and approved by the FCC, *Cong. Rec.*, Vol. 128, No. 155, Signed by President (1982). (See "Minority Ownership"). When the FCC authorized low power TV as a primarily rural local and fill-in or specialized programming service, the imposition of multiple ownership restrictions was rejected to encourage participation by experienced broadcast operators and random selection was allowed for uncontested applications in the low power area, *Low Power*, 51 RR 2d 476 (1982); 53 RR 2d 1267 (1983).

Rebroadcasting. (§73:1207); Muzak used Mutual <u>World Series</u> program and sent by wire to its' clients. "Unfair competition" and violative of property rights to use play-by-play materials without permission, *Mutual v. Muzak*, 30 NYS 2d 419 (1941). Affiliate cannot refuse to permit rebroadcast for no reason, or upon unreasonable grounds, *In Re Amendment of FCC Rules* (Docket 9808), 1 RR 91 (1952). Broadcast of play-by-play cannot be used or resold as would violate property rights, *National Exhibition v. Fass*, 143 NYS 2d 767, 11 RR 2086 (1955). Station has right to refuse blanket rebroadcasting permission, 24 FCC 147 (1958); 26 FCC 178 (1959); 225 F. 2d 560 (1955); 14 RR 150 (1959). Reminder by FCC that licensees and cable systems cannot retransmit without permission summarized contents or texts of messages transmitted by others, *Retransmission*, 50 RR 2d 76 (1981). When the US invaded the small island of Grenada no newspeople were allowed to cover and news blackout. In desperation networks and various stations rebroadcast amateur transmissions of what was occurring. Rule §73.1207(c)(3) prohibited the rebroadcast of CB and amateur radio by broadcast stations. After consideration, and an initial denial of permission, the FCC determined that no prior authorization was required to air monitored CB or amateur transmissions, but broadcasters must advise the FCC of date and nature of such rebroadcasts and rule was changed, 54 RR 2d 1145 (1983). The Smith-Mundt Act of 1948 bans the dissemination of USIA material, including the Voice of America in the U.S. to prevent the party in power from using the agency as a propaganda organization to U.S. citizens. However, District Ct. ruled the act does not affect private parties re-broadcasting VOA. C-Span started using audio feed early morning hours February 1990, (Nov. 1989).

(See "Copyright—Broadcast Rights").

Religious Broadcasting. Applicant wished to broadcast only fundamentalist religious programs. FCC denies application as propaganda stations not in the "public interest" as should present both sides of controversial issues, *YPGA for Propagation of Gospel*, 6 FCC 178 (1938). Station has an obligation to air atheist Scott's unpopular views. Scott later sought to have four licenses revoked for not carrying his programs but refused. No obligation to grant the request of a specific person to state those views, *Scott*, 11 FCC 377, 3 RR 259; 5 RR 59 (1946). Commercial sponsorship of religious programs not inherently objectionable or against "public interest," *WKRG*, 10 RR 225 (1955). Station did not violate "Fairness Doctrine" by refusing to carry religious program, *RKO General*, 46 FCC 2d 240, 29 RR 2d 1459 (1974). Oregon State, licensee of TV station, is not barred by the Constitution from broadcasting religious programs, *Corvallis TV*, 59 FCC 2d 1282, 37 RR 2d 1045 (1976). In a civil action against licensee Faith Center Church, claims were rejected that investigation of the president and pastor of his personal church donations by the FCC, disclosure of the investigation to the press and public, and sharing of the information with state law enforcement authorities violated his First Amendment and Civil Rights. The investigation of his personal donations (in the context of investigating solicitation for religion on broadcast stations) violated his First Amendment right to exercise his religion freely, since his faith requires that his donations remain secret in order to retain their sacred character. However, the FCC's duty to protect the public from misuse of funds solicited through the broadcast media are sufficiently compelling to justify. Also rejected Civil Rights claims, holding that mere sharing of information does not suggest conspiracy, *Scott v. Rosenberg*, 702 F. 2d 1263, 53 RR 2d 127 (9th Cir. 1983). His continued refusal to comply with discovery order then caused the FCC to deny renewal of his station, *Faith Center*, 53 RR 2d 797 (1983). A station's religious format was the focus for much of the Review Board's attention. Rejected were challenges to renewal based on alleged violation of the "fair break doctrine" (restatement of propaganda argument). No licensee may appropriate and monopolize a frequency or convert it to its own private purpose by transforming that frequency into an exclusive extension of its own church. The policy does not require a religious-oriented station to present any particular cleric, variety of cleric or spokesperson for any particular religious viewpoint. The Board found that variegated views, religious and secular were broadcast, including views which were undoubtedly anathema. Dissent noted that no programs were directed to Jewish people other than to persuade them to become Christians, and that could cite no religious programs other than a Christian philosophy and presented no Catholic views, *Pillar of Fire*, 57 RR 2d 601 (1984). Denial of TV applicants for religious program service on channel reserved for noncommercial educational use. Must show they are broadly representative of educational, cultural and civic groups in the community. Trustees lived significant distances from license communities. Religious organizations which described themselves as "reaching and teaching about the gospel" do not qualify as educational organizations. No educational institution was identified which would use described "instructional programming." Religious entities are free to apply for nonreserved channels and, even though religiously oriented, on appropriate showing, reserved channels, *Way for the Cross of Utah*, 58 RR 2d 4555 (1985).

Reports to the FCC. (§73:3612; §73:3613; §73:3615); All stations must file an Annual Employment Report, FCC Form 395, on May 31st; an EEO Program Report, FCC Form 396, with renewal application, but reviewed annually. Commercial stations, if a corporate licensee, file an Annual Ownership Report, FCC Form 323. If individual or partnership file on application for assignment of license, due on anniversary date of renewal. Non-commercial stations must file Ownership Report, FCC Form 323-E, within 30-days of any change of information on boards or governing bodies and on licensee renewal date. Any contract, written or oral dealing with ownership or control of the station or any interest in it, including—organizational articles and bylaws, subscriptions, pledges, options, sale agreements, etc., general proxies and proxies valid for more than one year, and loan agreements restricting the licensee's freedom of operation. Certain personnel—management agreements providing for a sharing of profits and losses, and management contracts with consultants or independent contractors who are not officers, directors or regular employees must be filed, and national network TV affiliation contracts. Available at the station, but not in public file—time brokerage contracts, subchannel and Vertical Blanking Interval leasing contracts, bulk sponsorship contracts for 4+ hours per day, and contracts with chief operators. (See "Network Regulation", "Equal Employment").

Rights of Performer. Promoter has right to sell Broadcast rights of fight to TV if nothing in fighter's contract to contrary, *Chavez v. Hollywood Post 45 & Don Lee Stations.*, 16 USL Week 2362 (Cal. Superior Ct. 1947). No violation of employed entertainers property rights by broadcast of film of act if broadcast rights not retained by entertainer, *Peterson v. KMTR*, LA Sup. Ct. 557555 (1949). Roy Rogers and Gene Autry could not prevent Republic Pictures from releasing their old theatrical films to TV once they had become popular stars in their own TV series without specific clauses restricting the use of their films for television. The fact that commercials were inserted in the films did not result in the audience assuming the stars endorsed the products, *Rogers v. Republic Pictures.*, US Dist. Ct. (S.D.-Calif.), 7 RR 2072; *Autry,* (CA 9th), 213 F. (2d) 662, 10 RR 2059 (1954); *Autry,* 213 F. 2d 667, 10 RR 2063 (1954); *Rogers,* 348 US 858, Cert. denied (1954). First Amendment does not immunize the media from liability for damages when station broadcast without consent a performer's entire Human Cannonball Act on newscast, *Zacchini v. Scripps-Howard*, 433 US 562, 40 RR 2d 1485 (1977). In 1973, agreement signed with performer for commercial to be used in 1974. Screen Actors Guild put the company on notice that term of employment contract had expired after that use. In 1975, commercial was used again. $1,000 compensatory damages and $15,000 punitive damages were awarded, *Welch v. Mr. Christmas, Inc.*, 454 NYS 2d 971; see also *Dzurenko v. Jordache*, 451 NYS 2d 102 (App. Div. 1982). MGM-TV agreed in 1976, to give William Smithers up-front billing and no other performer would get better compensation in series <u>Executive Suite</u>. For this most-favored credit arrangement Smithers agreed to less than his usual fee. After airing he learned his agreement had been changed on an unsigned form contract which he had declined. Blacklist threats were evidence of tortious breach of contractual duty of good faith and fair dealing. Damages for breach of contract, tortious breach, fraud, punitive damages for emotional distress settled for $2.4 million, *Smithers v. MGM*, 2 Civ 65508 (Cal. App. 1983). In the absence of an express written agreement to the contrary, under the copyright law, major league baseball players do not own any interest in the broadcast rights for major league baseball games and the clubs may retain the revenue from such broadcasts, *Baltimore Orioles v. Major League Baseball Players Association*, 805 F. 2d 663, 61 RR 2d 543 (7th Cir. 1986).

Right of Publicity. An individual has the right to control the commercial exploitation of his or her name, face, talents, and fame. Record included one-minute excerpt of CBS announcer's voice reporting Kennedy assassination. No property rights in news as now history, but in announcer voice and style, *CBS v. Docu. Ltd*, 2 RR 2d 2011 (NY Sup. Ct. 1964). Johnny Carson's right of publicity was invaded. Company may not use the phrase "Here's Johnny" as a corporate or trade name in connection with the advertising or sale of portable toilets, 498 F. Supp. 71 (ED Mich. 1980); Reversed,

698 F. 2d 831 (6th Cir., 1983), 810 F. 2d 104 (6th Cir. 1987); A preliminary injunction was obtained barring the use of Johnny Carson's name, portrait or picture for advertising purposes in connection with the movie The Eileen Ford Story. Newspaper articles had displayed his photo and indicated he would make his movie debut in the film which he denied, *Carson v. King*, (NY Cnty., 1984). Ads using real personalities and some look-alike models was challenged by Jacqueline Kennedy Onassis as unauthorized misappropriation for trade purposes under Section's 50 and 51 of *NY Civil Rights Law*. Deceptive by confusing identification and is commercial exploitation of a person who did not authorize or consent to endorsing the product. The model argued that she could not be prevented from using her own face. She may continue to capitalize as long as not deceptive or confusing and if not in commercial ads. She may appear on TV in dramatic works, but not pass herself off for what she is not. Mrs. Onassis has not forfeited her right of privacy even though public figure and does not become subject to commercial exploitation. If model identifies herself, or is used in accurate manner to recreate event, in satire or parody than no false implication, *Onassis v. Christian Dior*, 472 NYS 2d 254 (1984). Celebrity Look-Alikes supplied a Woody Allen look-alike for a video rental service company's commercials. Since his actual picture was not used no *Civil Rights* violation. Difference between Onassis case was the effort in that case to obtain realistic tone through use of real personalities as well as some "look-alikes." Ct. granted Allen's claim under §43(a) of *Lanham Act* as creating impression that Allen endorsed product. Although all but one ad had a disclaimer of "Celebrity Look-alike" was not sufficient. Should have made clear and bold statement that Allen did not endorse, Settled for $425,000. *Allen v. National Video*, 610 F. Supp. 612 (SDNY 1985). There is a trend toward protecting an original performer's rights, and to prevent what might be considered misappropriation. Winston used photograph of racing driver (with features not visible) but in his distinctive car. Signs and

symbols to convey the impression of association, *Motschenbacher v. R.J. Reynolds*, 498 F. 2d 821 (9th Cir. 1974). Like *Motschenbacher*, but based on 1985 California statute protecting the picture, signature and likeness of a person, living or dead, Bette Midler possesses a protectible common law property right in her voice. Approached to sing on Ford commercial she declined and "sound-alike" used with song associated with Midler. Ct. cautioned that did not hold that every imitation of a voice to advertise merchandise is actionable, but rather "that when a distinctive voice of a professional singer is widely known and is deliberately imitated in order to sell a product, the sellers have appropriated what is not theirs and have committed a tort in California." Ford dismissed from suit but Young and Rubicam, ad agency, held to damages of $400,000, *Midler v. Ford Motor Co.*, 849 F. 2d 460 (1989).

For some time there was a question of whether the right of publicity was inheritable after death. The majority of jurisdictions have begun to recognize that if a prominent person promoted and commercially exploited his name and likeness during his lifetime; that is a property right which can be inherited. Involved are considerations of fundamental fairness for an entertainer or athlete who has devoted his or her life to attain celebrity status. It would be unfair to permit a commercial enterprise to reap windfall benefits from those labors at the expense of the performer or that celebrity's heirs or beneficiaries. The ability to leave a valuable property interest to one's heirs also serves the "public interest" by encouraging enterprise and creativity. (See "Privacy," "Copyright—Broadcast Rights," "Advertising"). NY has had a statute protecting such rights for some time. California enacted statute establishing descendible right of publicity, *Calif. Civil Code*, §990, 3344 (1984). Tennessee adopted a statute establishing descendible right of publicity after conflicting decisions by State Cts. on such protection for the Elvis Presley estate, *Personal Rights Protection Act of 1984*, Senate Bill 1566. Kentucky enacted statute recognizing descendibility of right of publicity with no use by others for commercial profit for 50 years without written consent, *Chapter 263*, 1984 Kentucky General Assembly. The son of the late Bobby Darin is suing McDonald's for more than $10 million, alleging they copied his father's singing style in the "Mac Tonight" commercials, infringing on rights to Darin's 1959 hit song <u>Mac the Knife</u>. (1990).

RKO Revocation. The beginnings of RKO's troubles are noted in "Comparative Qualifications." However, other problems surfaced which finally resulted in the FCC revoking all RKO's licenses. WNAC, KHJ and WOR were revoked on the grounds that RKO's Broadcast Division, in cooperation with its' parent corporation RKO-General, participated in illegal trade scheme (see "Antitrust—Broadcasting"); filed inaccurate financial reports and misrepresented facts (see "Misrepresentation"). Ct. noted that illegal trade practice could not be retroactively applied; that inaccurate financial data was insignificant and not allowing a hearing on intent was unlawful. The Ct. requested the FCC clarify if they were holding corporate licensees to a higher standard than individual owners. Ct. then upheld FCC's WNAC revocation on basis of lack of candor. Station worth $400 million. Although KHJ and WOR renewals were conditioned on WNAC-Boston decision, these cases did not illustrate direct misconduct and, on remand, each station was entitled to distinguish its policies. The FCC then denied RKO's license renewals upon rehearing. The FCC then ordered <u>noncomparative</u> hearings on RKO's remaining 13 licenses. Ct. overruled so companies who would seek to obtain RKO's licenses could file competing applications at once. Congress then passed §331, modifying the *Communications Act of 1934*, which states that it shall be FCC policy that if a licensee of a commercial VHF station agrees to reallocation of its channel to a state where there was no VHF commercial TV channel (NJ, Delaware, Rhode Island, at that time), the FCC, notwithstanding any other provision of law shall issue a license for a five-year term. (See §307(b)). RKO then moved WOR to NJ in 1983. RKO allowed to retain WOR for five years; 62 FCC 2d 604, 39 RR 2d 137 (1976), aff'd, 574 F. 2d 1119 (1978), 670 F. 2d 215, 50 RR 2d 821 (1981); 685 F. 2d 708, 52 RR 2d 1 (1982); 53 RR 2d 469 (1983); 728 F. 2d 1519, 55 RR 2d 911 (DC Cir. 1984); approved by App. Ct. against challenge. The FCC then commenced hearings in 1985 with 149 competing applications for RKO's 12 radio stations and for WHBQ-TV, Memphis. An agreement was reached whereby RKO was allowed to sell its remaining licenses and divide the proceeds with the competing applicants who would drop their applications in favor of the highest bidder. RKO could retain no more than 65% of sales price, 60 RR 2d 1694 (1986). WOR-TV was sold, 61 RR 2d 1069 (1986). ALJ ruled RKO exhibited unprecedented dishonesty in that the RKO Radio Network had overstated its audience and thereby overcharged advertisers by as much as $7.9 million since 1980, had engaged in fraudulent billing practices and gave the FCC misleading financial reports, 63 RR 2d 866 (1987). KHJ-TV Los Angeles was sold to Disney (call letters changed to KCAL) and WHBQ-Memphis to Flinn Broadcasting at less than market value, 65 RR 2d 192, 65 RR 2d 245 (1988). WRKO-AM, WROR-FM-Boston and Bethesda stations sold, 65 RR 2d 837 (1988). WRKS-FM sold with RKO retaining no more than 65% of sales price, 66 RR 2d 851 (1989). WHBQ-TV was sold for $39 million, of which RKO received $25.35 million and eight challengers shared $13.65 million. WAXY-FM, Fort Lauderdale was sold for $21 million with RKO getting $12.6 million, and four challengers splitting $8.4 million (1990).

Sale or Transfer of License. (§310 (b)); When a license was to be sold or transferred, the FCC required the licensee to advertise and permitted open-bidding by any qualified applicant. The FCC reasoned that it had chosen among competing applicants originally and should have a choice between subsequent owners as well. Industry pressure had Congress changing the FCC's rule with an amendment to the Act prohibiting competing applications in transfer and assignment cases, but still requiring the FCC to pass on the qualifications of those seeking to buy stations to determine if the sale would serve the "public interest,"*Crosley*, 11 FCC 3, 3 RR 6 (1945); *MacFarland Amendment*, FCC Act (1952). In 1962, FCC adopted rule requiring license to be held for at least three years or face hearing for trafficking. Eliminated to allow unfettered marketplace forces; however, the amount of funds receivable for purchasing another's construction permit is restricted and a one-year holding period is required for a construction permit obtained through a comparative hearing or with minority tax certification or through distress sale to prevent profiteering, 52 RR 2d 1081 (1982); 57 RR 2d 1149 (1985). The "minority distress sale" policy of the FCC (§73:4140) provided an exception to the rule that a broadcaster may not assign or transfer his license if issues concerning his basic qualifications to remain a licensee have been designated for hearing but not yet resolved. When faced with such a predicament, the applicant could apply to have the license assigned to a minority-controlled enterprise, provided the hearing had not begun and the licensee would receive no more than 75% of the fair market value of the stations assets and license. US Ct. of Appeals panel struck down the FCC's minority distress sale policy as violating the Equal Protection Clause of the Fifth Amendment. Such a policy must be narrowly tailored to remedy past discrimination or to promote programming diversity. The panel determined that the FCC, as they have applied their policy, has imposed an unconstitutional burden on a nonminority applicant because it deprived him of a unique opportunity to obtain a broadcast station solely because of his race. The Congress and FCC, according to the Ct., have never found any evidence to link minority under-representation in the broadcast industry to past discrimination by the FCC or to particular discriminatory practices in the industry. Assuming such evidence, the policy is still fatally flawed because it is not narrowly tailored to serve its intended purpose, *Shurberg*

Broadcast of Hartford v. FCC, 66 RR 2d 261 (DC Cir. 1989). The parties request to have the full Ct. review because the opposite was determined in *Metro Broadcasting v. FCC* was denied, *Shurberg v. FCC*, 66 RR 2d 846 (DC Cir. 1989). The Supreme Ct. then agreed to determine the constitutionality of government-sponsored affirmative action programs by combining these cases in 1990. This comes at the same time the Supreme Ct. issued two decisions tending to blunt what had been a steady expansion of minority and female rights in employment and commercial matters. Both involved employment disputes brought under *Title VII of the Civil Rights Act of 1964*. (See "Comparative Qualifications," "Equal Employment," "Minority Ownership").

Secondary Boycott Illegal. NLRB has ruled that it is illegal for AFTRA union of striking radio or TV announcers to pressure ad agencies to withdraw prerecorded "spot" announcements from a struck station. AFTRA violated the "secondary boycott and hot cargo" provisions of Federal labor law which prohibit the use of coercive tactics against the suppliers or customers of a struck business. AFTRA had contended that its tactics were lawful because sending a members' voice on tape to a struck station was the same as forcing him personally to cross a picket line, *NLRB,* 240 NLRB 40 (1979)

Separate Aural and Visual Transmission. (§73:653); The FCC changed the requirement that TV station could not operate their aural and visual transmitters separately to present different or unrelated program material, to may at any time of day for any duration. This allows video-only bulletin boards or non-associated audio-only services, *Television Broadcast Stations (Technical and Operational Regulations),* 65 RR 2d 1820 (1989).

Secret Recording. In some circumstances, secretly recording an interview through use of concealed microphones and/or cameras is illegal. Under the US Criminal Code, the consent of one-party (the reporter) is enough. This is less stringent than FCC rules which require all parties to consent if using a licensed device. Recordings without notification are allowed if ENG camera, wired microphone or tape recorder as these devices are not licensed. Reporters must make certain recorded conversations are carried on within earshot of others not engaged in the conversation or they may be violating a person's right of privacy. Some states may also require two-party consent, and their laws on invasion of privacy may affect use. A plaintiff consented to an interview in her house, but when the ABC crew arrived she refused permission. The journalists hid a camera and microphone, transmitting the interview to a van nearby. The Ct. of Appeals upheld dismissal of action as the Wiretap statute not in effect unless proven that ABC intended to use in a manner injurious to the plaintiff rising to the level of a crime or tort, *Boddie v. ABC, Inc.*, 731 F. 2d 333, 55 RR 2d 1145 (6th Cir., 1984). Generally, pictures may be taken by hidden cameras for news and public affairs programs, but not without permission of parties if for entertainment or commercial use. Must be what can be seen by others in public or semi-public place. Also, if your source for a recording was not a party to the conversation recorded must diligently check to assure the recording was legally obtained. (See "Broadcasting Telephone Conversations").

Sound Effects in Announcements. The FCC restricted the use of sirens and similar emergency warning sound effects in commercials and other announcements which might confuse drivers and be a hazard, *Public Notice*, 20 RR 2d 98 (1970). The FCC deleted this policy, noting, "Licensees' general obligation to operate in the public interest should preclude any misuse of sound effects which might threaten public safety," *Underbrush Broadcast Policies*, 54 RR 2d 1043 (1983).

Sponsor ID. (§317, §507, §73:1212(b), §73:4242, §76:221); Station's should have identified union as source of films of strike, *KSTP*, 17 RR 553; *Storer*, 17 RR 556a; *Westinghouse*, 17 RR 556d (1958). Teaser Ads are short announcements to arouse the curiosity of the public as to the identify of the advertiser or product to be revealed in a subsequent announcement. However, all announcements must carry a sponsor ID so teasers illegal, *FCC Memo:* 18 RR 1860 (1959). To prevent payola FCC requires Sponsor ID whenever station broadcasts any material for which it has or will receive any money, service, or other valuable consideration, including free records, etc., *FCC Rept & Order 601-1141*, 21 Sept (1960). Failure to fully identify any sponsor who has furnished valuable consideration may be considered as the taking of "payola" and can result in a fine and/or imprisonment. Sponsor ID rules apply to all commercial matter, including political broadcasts, teasers, and messages paid for by federal, state and local entities, and local public service organizations, as well as trade associations. It also requires an ID of the entity that "furnished" the material even if not aired on a "paid basis." Announcement must be comprehendible and clear. Program-length commercials are no longer prohibited so station can broadcast them if proper sponsor identification is made that "program" is a commercial, *Public Notice, Applicability of Sponsor Identification Rules*, 40 FR 175 (1975). FCC issued a public notice to remind licensees that the acceptance of "payola" by an employee is not only a violation of federal criminal law but can subject the licensee to administrative sanctions, fine or revocation. §507 requires that such payments or agreements for such payments be reported to the licensee. The licensee, in turn, is required by §317 to disclose that the matter contained in the program was paid for, and to disclose the identity of the person furnishing the consideration. Both §317 and §73:1212(b) require reasonable diligence in investigating payola. The reasonable diligence standard can require a higher duty of care by stations whose formats or other circumstances make them more susceptible to payola, such as a station that reports to record charting services and which might be asked to inflate reporting play of specific recordings. Compliance is more than simply requiring employees to sign affidavits promising, under oath, that they will not violate payola laws and regulations. Besides triggering an FCC investigation, evidence may be forwarded to the Dept. of Justice for possible prosecution. Licensees may call the FCC for informal advice on particular situations, *Payola and Undisclosed Promotions*, 64 RR 2d 1338 (1988). LA Grand jury returned a 57-count indictment charging three individuals with making undisclosed payola payments to radio stations for adding records to their play lists. The FCC stated, "The combination of drugs and payola, when shown to exist among broadcast licensees, involves a violation of the public trust which cannot be tolerated. The Commission will act with respect to its licensees to assure that our communications system remains free of these totally improper influences." (Nov. 1989). (See "Children and TV," "Conflict of Interest").

State Control of Interstate Advertising. Supreme Ct. ruled New Mexico station must obey New Mexico advertising statute even when carrying ads for nearby Texas firm, *New Mex. Board of Examiners v. Roberts*, 23 RR 2042; 70 NM 90; 370 P. 2d 811, aff'd, 25 RR 2087; 374 US 424 (1962); Supreme Ct. ruled that state retained jurisdiction over advertising, even though ads distributed on an interstate basis; indirect effect on commerce of country, *Head v. New Mexico Broadcasting.*, 23 RR 2042 (1962); 25 RR 2087, 374 US 424 (1963). (See "Alcoholic Beverage Advertising").

Station Identification. (§303, §73:1201); In 1970, the FCC consolidated separate rules for different broadcast services concerning station ID's, 17 RR 2d 1691. Station's must identify themselves at the beginning and end of each day of operation, and hourly, as close to the hour as feasible at a natural break in the programming. TV stations may make the required announcement either visually or aurally. The rule exists from the beginning of government regulation in order to provide the public with a means of identifying to the FCC which station is the subject of any complaints. The official announcement must contain the station's call letters followed by the name of the city of license as specified in the station license. The name of the licensee and that station's frequency or channel number may be included between the call letters and the city of license, but no other extraneous matter may be placed between the call letters and city of license. Additional communities may be included, but the community of license must come first. There are other provisions relating to specific situations. For examples of violations see, *Public Notice*, 10 FCC 2d 399, 11 RR 2d 1607, (§73:1201) (1967). Stations also use slogans, phrases and/or channel numbers to identify themselves to listeners at times other than when the legal station ID is required. They notify rating services of this use so as to be credited properly with listening or viewing. Station operating on 98.5 since 1982, ID'd as 99 FM. Another station in the market in 1985, on 99.7, began to use informal ID of "WARM 99 FM." Cox failed to prove confusion as other station used with "WARM," and Cox had created whatever confusion there might be by using number that another station could legally use, *Cox Communication v. Susquehanna Broadcasting*, 620 F. Supp. 143 (ND Ga. 1985). Ct. ruled that KABC had used "KABC—Talk Radio" for 17 years and enjoined KFI's use unless separated from the call letters, (1989). (See "Call Letters").

Station Promotions. (§73:1216); License revoked, negligent, guilty of fraud in conduct of promotion contests and logs altered with intent to deceive FCC, *Eleven Ten Broadcasting-KRLA*, 32 FCC 706, 33 FCC 92 (1962); 11-10 v. FCC, 25 RR 2128a, 320 F. 2d 795 (DC Cir.), Cert. denied, 375 US 904 (1963). Letter was sent to all licensees noting playing one song all day as promotion when format and call letters were changed did not qualify as inventive or in the "public interest," *Raleigh-Durham*, 24 RR 221 (1962). Repetitious broadcast of a single record or tape had raised questions as to basic qualifications, but now left to discretion of licensee, *Underbrush Broadcast Policies*, 54 RR 2d 1043 (1983). License revoked for Treasure not hid, *KWK*, 25 RR 577, 1 RR 2d 457 (1963), 34 FCC 1039, 35 FCC 561, 2 RR 2d 2071, US App DC (1964). Policy Statement, 6 RR 2d 671 (1966), cautioned against carrying contests and promotions adversely affecting the "public interest," including contests resulting in disruption of traffic, telephone service or public safety. Some examples of those promotions causing problems: Damage to public & private property, *McLendon*, 3 RR 2d 817 (1964); Trespassing, traffic congestion, *SIS*, 6 RR 2d 792 (1966). Rule §73:1216 was implemented requiring the broadcasting of the material terms of a contest, *Station Contests*, 37 RR 2d 260 (1976). The 1966 Policy Statement was then eliminated as existing civil remedies can be used, *Policy Statement and Order*, 57 RR 2d 913 (1985), aff'd, *Telecommunications Research and Action Center v. FCC*, 800 F. 2d 1181, 61 RR 2d 61,(DC Cir. 1986).

Hypoing is artificial inflation of audience through contests or promotions to affect ratings. Unfair trade practice complaints on use of survey and hypoing were to be sent to FTC by the FCC, (§73.4035; §73.4040), 58 FCC 2d 513, 36 RR 2d 938 (1976). Network clipping single unintentional instance of lack of candor, issuance of memo pertaining to a local tennis club that was arrears in ad payments not to cover in sports programming, serious exaggeration of station coverage area in promotional coverage maps overridden by forty-eight years of service and affirmative steps to correct practices upon discovery, *Gross Telecasting*, 52 RR 2d 851 (1982). In 1983, the FCC eliminated formal policy and rules on the use of distorted ratings information, misleading or inaccurate signal coverage maps and other misleading promotional materials. Complaints should be taken to Federal Trade Commission by the parties involved and FCC will consider upon license renewal, *Unnecessary Broadcast Regulation*, 94 FCC 2d 619, 54 RR 2d 705 (1983). Station ran a promotion that it would pay $25,000 to the first caller if they did not play three songs in a row. Jennings, in prison, contacted the station, but the station refused to pay him. Lower Cts. ruled an enforceable contract could exist because he could have listened to another station. The station benefitted because it gained new listeners. However, Jennings argument was that the station's receipt of records without charge was a valuable consideration amounting to payment to the station, and, thus, the announcing of the records titles and artists consti-tuted a paid commercial interruption entitling him to the $25,000. Ct. finally held that since Jennings had no personal knowledge of the business practices of record companies or of KSCS, found for station, *Jennings v. KSCS*, 708 SW 2d 60 (Tex. App. 1986), 745 SW 2d 97 (Tex. App. 1988), 750 SW 2d 760 (Tex. 1988). KABC rating data was eliminated from May 18-25, 1987, ratings book by Nielsen for violating guidelines. Ran series of reports during sweeps period about the Nielsen rating system. Nielsen families, whose viewing habits are being measured would be most likely to watch, thereby skewing ratings. KABC protested that Nielsen had helped prepare series and was aware would be broadcast during sweep period. Claimed cost $1 million in revenue. Case set-tled out of court, (1987). License revoked for conducting fraudulent contests (prize was not awarded but retained, and another in which a grand prize was withheld from drawing and given to a favored advertiser), and many other serious abuses, *Catoctin Broadcasting of NY*, 62 RR 2d 1132 (1987), 66 RR 2d 131 (1989). (See "Multiple Violations," "Advertising").

Stereo Broadcasting. FCC authorizes AM stations to provide stereo broadcasts but abandons its attempt to select a single approved transmission system, leaving to the marketplace the determination. Minimal technical standards are estab-lished to prevent interference, *AM Stereophonic Broadcasting*,

51 RR 2d 1 (1982), 64 RR 2d 516 (1988). The lack of a standard led to few AM stations selecting from among the competing standards as no manufacturers decided to gamble on which system their receivers should use, so the FCC selected a system standard for Television Stereo Sound. The TV aural baseband may also be used for other services such as multi-language sound and other purposes. The networks quickly converted to stereo TV sound and on Aug. 7, 1984, noncommercial WTTW Chicago became first station to regularly use stereo sound, *TV Aural Baseband Transmission*, 55 RR 2d 1642 (1984).

Subscription TV. (§73:641—§73:644, §73:4247); Broadcast TV campaigned against allowing the charging of a fee for over-the-air Pay-TV signals. In 1963, California voters outlawed over-the-air scrambled Subscription TV. The California Supreme Ct. overturned as unconstitutional but by that time this particular project had died, *Weaver v. Jordan*, 411 P.2d 289, Cert. denied, 385 US 844; 7 RR 2d 2166 (1966). FCC regulation of subscription TV relaxed to allow development. Eliminated requirement that there must be four conventional stations in market before one could convert to scrambled Pay-TV signal and a 28 hours' a week program limitation, *Subscription Television Service*, 46 RR 2d 460 (1979); 90 FCC 2d 341, 51 RR 2d 1173 (1982). Subscription TV stations petitioned FCC to require local cable systems to carry their scrambled signals along with other local TV stations. FCC refused to require carriage as no evidence needed for economic success of STV; would impose burden on cable operators; and could be done by contract, *WWHT v. FCC*, 656 F. 2d 807 (DC Cir. 1981). FCC declined to permit Public TV stations to engage in subscription TV operations on a general basis for the "public interest" would be adversely affected if this were to become the dominant form of delivery of for public broadcasting, but will accept requests for waivers which will be granted in appropriate individual circumstances, 56 RR 2d 311 (1984). UHF licensee entitled to renewal expectancy for past programming, even though at end of license period scrambled its signal and provided only adult-oriented subscription service with no non-entertainment programming, *Video 44*, 64 RR 2d 1517 (1988); 65 RR 2d 1512 (1989). FCC not required to apply broadcast regulation to Subscription TV and Subscription DBS, *National Association for Better Broadcasting*, 849 F. 2d 665, 64 RR 2d 1570 (1988).

Syndicated Exclusivity. (§76.151—§76.163); TV stations have no property rights in programs they broadcast other than those covered in *Copyright Act, Intermountain*, 196 F. Supp. 315, 21 RR 2084 (1961). Supreme Ct. decided that cable did not do performance within meaning of *1909 Copyright Act* and so no copyright infringement, *Fortnightly v. United Artists*, 88 S. Ct. 2084; 392 US 390; 13 RR 2d 2045 (1968). FCC rules passed in 1972, granted TV stations the exclusive right to broadcast their affiliated network programs in their market (non-duplication rule) and exclusive broadcast rights to the syndicated programs they had purchased in their viewing area (syndicated exclusivity rule). Cable had to "black out" non-local stations which carried network programs and programs for which local stations had contract exclusivity. In 1980, the FCC abolished both the distant signal limitations and the syndicated exclusivity rules, *Malrite TV v. FCC*, 652 F. 2d 1140 (2d Cir. 1981). The development of satellite delivered distant over-the-air TV to cable systems had created difficulties. Syndicated programs are sold, licensed, distributed and offered to stations in more than one market for non-network broadcast, not including live presentations. An example: WOTV had been granted exclusive rights by Multimedia to carry The Donahue Show on tape-delayed basis in Grand Rapids, MI. Show was produced and broadcast live in Chicago on WGN-TV; recorded and distributed. Two cable companies in Grand Rapids began carrying WGN's Donahue via satellite—live, several days before tape of show ever got to WOTV. Cable operators refused to give exclusivity protection and WGN had no contract with the satellite company to carry their programming to cable systems. No copyright violation as passive retransmission did not require WGN's permission once signal was broadcast, (*Fortnightly*). Multimedia then transferred program from WGN to WBBM (not on satellite) when contract with WGN expired, *In re Manhattan Cable Television*, Inc., 73 FCC 2d 25, 45 RR 2d 1695 (1979). This type of situation led to Copyright Agreement, in which cable systems were given right to carry—cable compulsory license, but required to pay copyright; *Cable TV Report and Order*, 36 FCC 2d 143, 25 RR 2d 1501 (1972); 37 RR 2d 213 (1976); 42 RR 2d 659, 45 RR 2d 581 (1978). Copyright owners contract with networks on the understanding that program will reach virtually all markets and local stations usually welcome their signal being carried on nearby systems. When the Copyright Law was revised, <u>cable systems</u> cable compulsory license included which allows them to carry distant TV signals without the permission of, or direct payments to, the television stations being carried. Cable pays royalty fees to the US Treasury and a Copyright Royalty Tribunal distributes the money to claimants. The cable fees are based on a percentage of gross revenue and the number and type of distant signals being carried (similar to blanket music licensing), *Copyright Act of 1976*, (effective 1978); USCA Title 17 (1976). Whether the cable compulsory copyright license applied to satellite distribution of broadcast programming to home satellite dish owners was an issue never before adjudicated until decided that a company which uplinked an NBC affiliate's signal for <u>direct</u> retransmission to home dish owners without obtaining consent of the network or station was guilty of copyright infringement, *Pacific & Southern v. Satellite Broadcast Networks*, 65 RR 2d 372 (ND Ga. 1988). Affiliates, to get blackout of distant signal network programs on cable systems in their market so they have exclusive first showing had to prove need for protection, *Spartan, <u>et. al.</u> v. FCC*, 47 RR 2d 1521; 619 F.2d 314 (4th Cir. 1980) (CA 4th, 1980). Eastern Microwave retransmited

WOR signal to cable systems, and Mets owner objected, contending violation of §106 of *Copyright Act*. Held retransmission exempt under §111(a)(3) as EMI is passive common carrier (does not convert or control signal). However, when United Video, a passive carrier, retransmitted WGN signal and replaced vertical blanking interval Teletext signal with Dow Jones Teletext, for which it charged, this was held not passive. WGN intended Teletext material to be an integral series of related works, even if not viewed without pay. Ct. felt technological advances motivated reform of new *Copyright Act* which required Ct. to use flexibility in decision, *Eastern Microwave v. Doubleday Sports*, 691 F.2d 125; *WGN v. United Video*, 693 F.2d 622 (1982); clarified, 692 F.2d 628, 52 RR 2d 1693 (1983); Cert. denied. The FCC then authorized TV stations to make expanded use of the vertical blanking interval in the "public interest" for franchised or leased secondary transmission of data, processed information or any other analog or digital material or paging services. These services are regulated as private or common carrier activities and were not to be subject to content controls as read rather than watched, except as relates to "use" for equal opportunities under §315, *Telecommunications Research and Action Center v. FCC*, 801 F. 2d 501, 61 RR 2d 330 (US App DC 1986). FCC not required to apply broadcast regulation to Subscription services, *National Association for Better Broadcasting*, 849 F. 2d 665, 64 RR 2d 1570 (1988). Public TV may lease subcarrier for such use, 53 RR 2d 1309 (1983); 57 RR 2d 832 (1985); 57 RR 2d 842 (1985), and Noncommercial radio stations are permitted to lease their subcarrier to commercial users for a profit to support their noncommercial service. Seeking to resolve a long-standing conflict the FCC issued a policy statement on §73:593, whereby, if a radio reading service for the blind requests subcarrier use any out-of-pocket costs may properly be charged, but not profit as "there is no allowable alternative usage for the subcarrier capacity if it is needed to provide a reading service to its community." Lost revenue from actual or potential alternative lessee may not be charged to the reading service, *Radio Reading Services*, 65 RR 2d 589 (1988). MGM, producer of <u>Chips'</u> sold exclusive local run to McGraw-Hill. NBC, which had original license to broadcast certain number of runs announced a concurrent network strip re-run schedule. McGraw-Hill sued on basis of no local exclusivity as contracted. Ct. issued decision same day NBC was to begin re-run that McGraw-Hill had not demonstrated probability of success of suit on merits; and did not show irreparable injury. NBC would suffer hardship if injunction requested was granted, *McGraw-Hill v. MGM*, 537 F. Supp. 954 (SDNY 1982).

In 1988, the FCC restored the syndicated exclusivity protection it had rescinded in 1980 (§76.151 through §76.163) except for cable systems of fewer than 1,000 subscribers (effective January 1, 1990). Broadcasters are allowed to purchase the same enforceable exclusive distribution rights in syndicated programming that all other video program distributors enjoy. Relatedly, the FCC modified network non-duplication and non-network territorial exclusivity rule. No distinction is made between off-network, first run, movies, non-series, etc., nor by age as older programs and movies may well have substantial value. Contract determines length of exclusivity. Only broadcasters may assert exclusivity, but a program supplier or syndicator may invoke exclusivity rights in those markets where syndication rights have not yet been sold, within one year from the first sale to a broadcaster in the US. Within 60 days of an exclusive contract, the language of which must be specific, and at least 60 days prior to having duplicative programming deleted by the cable system, the broadcaster must notify affected cable operators. Must also notify if exclusivity rights lost or when contingency contract ends (ex: three runs). The FCC also strengthened the network non-duplication rules (§73:92—§76.97) because of satellite distribution. An affiliate asserting exclusivity for the network shows it carries is protected for whatever length of time in contract. If a cable system can show no significant harm to a network affiliate it can request a waiver. Burden shifts to the affiliate to demonstrate harm. The "non-network territorial exclusivity rule" was modified to permit "Superstations" to obtain national exclusivity rights against all other broadcast stations for the exhibition of non-network programs and against cable systems for programs for which they have purchased nationwide broadcast exclusivity, *Program Exclusivity in the Cable and Broadcast Industries*, 64 RR 2d 1818 (1988), 66 RR 2d 44 (1989). (See "Network Regulation").

Tax Deductions. Newsman deducted as business expense wardrobe, laundry, dry cleaning, haircuts and makeup. The IRS disallowed the deductions. Tax Ct. held Revenue Code §262 specifically denies deductions for personal, living or family expenses and burden of proof is on taxpayer. Three tests must be met for clothing to be deductible (1) required or essential, (2) not suitable for general or personal wear, and (3) in fact, not worn for general or personal use, *Hynes v. Commissioner*, 80(10) CCH Standard Tax Reports, Para. 7932 (1980). Inaccurate filings, false information led to license revocation. $46M in legal fees for hearings are tax deductible, *BHA Enterprises v. Commissioner*, 74 T.C., No. 46 (1980). Freelance artists and authors are allowed to deduct work expenses during the tax year in which the expenses were incurred. This deduction applies to individuals whose personal efforts create or may reasonably expect to create a literary manuscript, musical composition, dance score, photograph, photographic negative or transparency, picture, painting, sculpture, statue, etching, drawing, cartoon, graphic design or original print edition. Further provides that individuals who are employees or owners of a personal service corporation and who are photographers, writers or artists, qualify if substantially all the stock of the organization is owned by the individual or members of his or her family. Factors such as originality and uniqueness together with balancing the work's aesthetic and utilitarian value will be considered. Not deductible are expenses incurred or paid for producing furniture, silverware and other household items, printing, photographic plates, motion picture films, video tapes or similar physical items. This traditional deduction had been removed in the *Tax Reform Act of 1986*, (PL 99-514) but is now reinstated in, *Technical Corrections Act of 1988*, (PL 100-647, 1988).

Taxes on Programming, Opinion of Att. Gen. Kentucky: Can't put local tax on TV programs & advertising revenue, 1 RR 2d 2058 (1963). A Pennsylvania statute authorizes City of Pittsburgh to levy tax upon "...all persons, transactions, occupations, privileges, subjects and personal property" except manufacturing. Radio and TV stations sought to enjoin collection on grounds they were manufacturers. Held that "despite complexity of changing sound and visual information into electronic signals, broadcasters do not change or produce new, different, or useful articles, but merely effect a superficial change in the original materials." Primary purpose of broadcasting was transmission of commercial messages and the sale of advertising, not translation of events into electronic impulses, *Golden Triangle v. City of Pittsburgh*, 397 A. 2d 1147 (Pa. Supr. Ct. 1979). In Indiana, closed circuit, simultaneous telecast promoters of boxing matches must pay 10% tax on gross receipts from ticket sales. Differentiated from subscription TV as not seen in home; over receiver which viewer does not control, and seen much as live boxing match, *Sunshine Productions v. Ridlen*, 483 NE 2d 761 (Ind. App. 1985). Many states are considering enacting taxes on professional services; advertising, doctors, lawyers, etc. Several states argue current state sales tax laws include advertising. Three months after a 5% services tax went into effect, and after intensive lobbying by the advertising industry, the Governor of Florida called a special session which repealed the tax. A provision taxed in-state advertising and taxed national advertising on an apportioned ratio calculated by the number of ads "seen" in Florida. The Florida Services Tax was the most comprehensive and far-reaching tax effort to date, December, (1988). Oklahoma legislature, after intensive lobbying, voted down tax on services which would have included advertising costs to businesses, (1989).

Trade—Service Mark—Unfair Competition. A "trade name" is a word, symbol, name, device or combination used to identify and distinguish a business, vocation or occupation. A "trademark" is a mark used to identify goods and distinguish them from another's goods. A "service mark" means a mark used in the sale or advertising of services to identify the services offered and to distinguish them from another's services. Company used the slogan, "Where there's life. . . there's bugs" in spots for combination floor-wax-insecticide, imitating Budweiser slogan, "Where there's life. . . there's Bud" in which over $40 million had been invested. Injunction granted not-with-standing the fact the products were noncompetitive, 306 F. 2d 433 (5th Cir. 1962), Cert. denied 372 US 965, 83 S. Ct. 1089 (1963). Florist Association of Greater Cleveland, during a one week local promotional campaign used the slogan, "This Bud's for You-and 11 more Rosebuds." Ct. noted Anheuser had not registered the slogan in connection with the sale of fresh-cut flowers, and consumer would not confuse beer with flowers. While intending to capitalize on slogan, did not intend to deceive the public that Anheuser had connection with their product, *Anheuser-Busch v. Florists Association*, 603 F. Supp. 35 (N.D. Ohio 1984). Producers register the names and generally own all rights to the service marks and all rights of publicity of the stars of the shows as the characters they play. Eighteen manufacturers licensed to merchandise products for $1,800,000 for Charlie's Angels; and exclusive license for T-shirt transfers. Defendants had, without a license, infringed on trademarks and rights of publicity and had competed unfairly under the *Lanham Act, Spelling-Goldberg Prod. v. Schneider*, Civil No. 78-1907 (DNJ. 1979). In 1974, Universal applied for several trademarks for The Six-Million Dollar Man and The Bionic Woman. The American Footware Co. did a trademark search and noted the term "bionic" had not been registered in relation to footwear and registered the trademark name, "Bionic Boot." Universal claimed the public would be confused as to the source but Ct. disagreed. The exclusive right to a trademark is derived from its actual use in the marketplace which Universal used in the area of TV and toys. Both companies could use term if one referred to TV show and the other to footware, *American Footwear v. General Footwear*, 609 F. 2d 655 (2d Cir. 1979). WISN obtained license to use "I Love You, Milwaukee" slogan. Slogan had been registered with Copyright & Trademark office as a service mark for entertainment services. Three months before end of campaign WOKY began to use "I Love You." Ct. reluctant to allow exclusive commercial use of a common phrase despite successful registration and cited lack of showing of confusion, *M.B.H. Enterprises v. WOKY*, 633 F. 2d 50 (7th Cir. 1980); see also *Invisible v. NBC*, 212 USPQ 576 (CD Cal. 1980). DC Comics licensed, on occasion, <u>Superman</u> for use by a consumer electronics retailer known as "Crazy Eddie." TV commercial for his business was nearly in every aspect copied in detail from the trailers' for the <u>Superman</u> TV series and had not obtained a license for that spot. The average lay person would instantly recognize the source. "Crazy Eddie" argued his commercial was a parody. [Jack Benny's TV parody of play <u>Gaslight</u>, was a copyright infringement as too substantial and divulged surprise ending, *Loew's v. CBS*, 131 F. Supp. 165, 12 RR 2077 (1955); *CBS v. Loew's* (C.A. 9th,) 239 F. 2d 532, 14 RR 2075 (1956); *CBS v. Loew's*, 356 US 43, all aff'd, (1958).] A parody or satirical use is entitled to greater freedom than other uses, but commercial would irreparably harm <u>Superman's</u> licensing value. Injunction granted, *DC Comics v. Crazy Eddie*, CCH Copyright Law Reports, Para. 25,097, 205 USPQ 1177 (SDNY 1979). "Parody in its proper role creates something new by drawing from the old; but when it has the effect of refashioning or destroying the old, it is not protected," *DC Comics v. Unlimited Monkey Business*, 598 F. Supp. 110 (N. D. Ga. 1984). Turn-around is fair play.

"Crazy Eddie" then got injunction on one commercial out of several parodies against advertising agency and Lafayette Stores which used his service mark and trade name. Set in a confessional booth, significant number of individuals might wrongly believe that "Crazy Eddie" was exploiting the confessional for commercial purposes, *Crazy Eddie v. Lois Pitts Gershon*, 600 F. Supp. 537 (SDNY 1984). Enjoined use of Sambo's commercials, based on finding that copied essence of copyrighted Dr. Pepper commercial and jingle, *Dr. Pepper v. Sambo's*, 517 F. Supp. 1202 (ND Tex. 1981). TV ad reported a consumer-survey comparing Body on Tap with competitive products. Vidal Sassoon, Inc., sued, contending that number of women reported did not participate in comparison; 1/3 were 13 to 18 years old and "may not be women"; and only 1% statistically insignificant difference between top four ratings. Granted motion to halt commercial on grounds that it was ambiguous and misleading, violating §43(a) of the *Lanham Act*. Upheld, *Vidal Sassoon, Inc., v. Bristol-Myers*, 213 USPQ 24 (2d Cir. 1981). TV ad parodied popular promotional characters used by Wendy's. Ad created likelihood of confusion. Survey's showed small group confused was a significant portion in that market, *Wendy's v. Big Bite*, 576 F. Supp. 816 (ED Ohio 1983). The US Olympic Committee under the *Amateur Sports Act of 1978*, has trademark protection for name and five-ring symbol. This law does not require confusion, just unauthorized use, *US Olympic Committee v. Intelicense Corp.* (2d Cir. 1984); *US Olympic Committee v. Union Sport Apparel*, 220 US PQ 526 (ED Va. 1983). Also, obtained permanent injunction barring organizers of "Gay Olympic Games" from using "Olympics," as all uses barred, *International Olympic Committee v. San Francisco Arts & Athletic*, 781 F. 2d 733; modified, 789 F. 2d 1319 (9th Cir. 1986), Upheld, US Sup. Ct. (1987). WSM used "Opry" in 1927 for Barn Dance radio show, and registered Grand Ole Opry in 1950. The word "Opry" itself was registered in 1982. The Ct. ruled that term was generic, no consumer confusion between Country Shindig Opry. Two marks, not distinctive, and used by others before 1927, *WSM v. Hilton*, 724 F. 2d 1320 (8th Cir. 1984). Permanent injunction restraining Gay Toys from marketing look-alike <u>General Lee</u> car featured on <u>The Dukes of Hazzard</u> TV show. Since consumers wanted the toy, in part, because of the identification with the series this was sufficient to establish a secondary meaning even though Warner is not a manufacturer of toy cars and no showing that consumers thought Gay Toys cars were sponsored or authorized by Warner. The toys flag emblem, numerals and color functioned as identification. However, no injunction for Mattel's <u>Masters of the Universe</u> figures against <u>War Lord</u> figurines. Claim torso had been copied was an unprotectable idea. Mattel had to prove the figures had secondary meaning and since Mattel was selling all they could produce they had not demonstrated an illegal trading upon their success, *Warner Bros. v. Gay Toys*, 724 F. 2d 327 (2d Cir. 1983), 598 F. Supp. 424 (SDNY 1984); *Mattel v. Azrak-Hamway*, 724 F. 2d 357 (2d Cir. 1983). <u>Star Wars</u> trademark not infringed by public interest groups' use of phrase in TV ads referring to Reagan's Strategic Defense Initiative as not confusing to public or attached to goods or services for sale, *Lucasfilm Ltd. v. High Frontier*, 622 F. Supp. 931 (DC Cir. 1985). T-shirts with cartoon <u>Miami Mice</u> dressed in <u>Miami Vice</u> style would not confuse consumers into believing items were sold with the authorization or consent of Universal. The word "Miami" is not proprietary when used with "Vice" or any other element of TV series, *Universal City Studios v. Casey & Casey*, 622 F. Supp. 201 (SD Fla. 1985). Showtime and The Movie Channel are barred from using slogans such as "Showtime & HBO. It's Not Either/Or Anymore," as violation of §1125(a) of the *Lanham Act* and infringement of HBO's servicemark. Ruled would create a likelihood of confusion that HBO and Showtime had merged or participated in a cooperative promotion campaign, *Home Box Office v. Showtime*, 832 F. 2d 1311 (2d Cir. 1987). (See "Advertising," "Copyright—Performance Rights to Music").

Treatment of Licensees. FCC can deal on case-by-case basis because lack information of all violations, but they cannot single out one transgressor for denial or hearing from among a number of licensees under scrutiny if the same issue or investigation (i.e., network affiliation contracts). Must explain the basis for differing treatment that are of legal significance to warrant disparity when licensees are in the same investigation, *George T. Hernreich, KAIT-TV*, 72 FCC 2d 511, 45 RR 2d 963, and *United TV*, 46 RR 2d 655 (1979). Clear and convincing standard of proof needed at agency level, *Collins v. SEC*, (562 F. 2d 823) which applies to FCC, where loss of livelihood is involved, *Sea Island Broadcasting v. FCC*, 46 RR 2d 1339, 627 F. 2d 240 (DC Cir. 1980). With the encouragement of Senator Edward Kennedy, a frequent target of the Boston Herald, Congress passed a proviso precluding the FCC from granting a temporary waiver to the newspaper/television cross-ownership rule. Rupert Murdoch, owner of the Boston Herald was the only licensee having such a temporary waiver, having recently purchased and needed time to divest either newspaper or station. Ruled that singling out one licensee for uniquely disfavored treatment implicated the First Amendment and Equal Protection Clause of the Constitution. Murdoch later sold WXNE Boston and retained the Boston Herald, *News America Publishing v. FCC*, 64 RR 2d 1309 (1988).

Trespass—Intrusion—Consent. Media invited to accompany police in a midnight raid of a school for delinquent children pulled children from their beds and photographed against them their will, *Green Valley School v. Cowles Florida Broadcasting*, 327 S. 2d 810 (Fla. App. 1976). TV reporters, without owner consent on announcement of a health code violation entered a restaurant with cameras rolling, disturbing patrons, *Le Mistral v. CBS*, 61 AD 2d 491, 402 NYS 2d 815 (1978). A TV newscaster was guilty of trespassing when he went on private property to film a police investigation of a reported shooting incident, *Prahl v. Brosamle*, 295 N.W. 2d 768 (Wisc. App. 1980). Reporters entered home with Humane Society investigator and took pictures protested by owner. Reporters have no special immunity or special privilege to invade rights and liberties of others, *Anderson v. WROT-TV*, 441 NYS 2d 220 (NY Sup. Ct. 1981). CBS' WCAU-TV broadcast a report on Ct. proceeding involving property and filmed on the property as tenants showed deficiencies. Covered by the fair report privilege in Pa. common law as a report on a judicial proceeding and tenant had given permission to reporter to enter the premises but otherwise defamatory, *Lal v. CBS*, 551 F. Supp. 356 (ED Pa. 1982); 726 F. 2d 97 (3rd Cir. 1984). NY *Civil Rights Law* not applicable when CBS documentary portrayed mentally incompetent patient who had signed consent form. Report was privileged as news as long as not used for advertising or trade purposes, *Delan v. CBS*, 445 N.Y.S. 2d 898 (NY Sup. Ct. 1981); 458 NYS 2d 608 (NY App. 1983). In 1979, an NBC TV crew filmed LA paramedics as they attempted to assist David Miller, who had suffered a fatal heart attack. NBC used the film on its nightly news and later used portions advertising a report about the paramedic's work. Held reasonable people could regard intrusion into the bedroom at a time of vulnerability and confusion as highly offensive conduct. Considerations of emotional distress, the intruder's objectives and motives, the setting, and the expectation of those whose privacy is invaded are relevant in considering whether or not an act is offensive enough to give rise to intrusion, *Miller v. NBC*, 232 Cal. Rptr. 668 (Ca. App. 1986). (See "Privacy").

INDEX

A/B switch 10, 27
Access to government information 145
Action for Children's Television 22, 40, 41
Administrative Procedure Act 107
Advertising 5, 11, 168, 178, 189
  agencies liable for payment 8
  alcoholic beverages 9
  astrology 22
  ban on cigarette ads 102
  clutter 14
  comparison ads 7
  copyright infringement 6
  defamation 6, 68
  disclosure of prize/odds 7
  endorsements 6
  false claims 7
  filming of U.S. currency 103
  fraudulent, misleading and deceptive 7, 40
  FTC 6
  Lanham Act 167
  legal racetrack information 161
  limits 14
  look-alike models 167
  NAB Code 14
  NY Civil Rights Law 167
  overcommercialization 149
  piggy-back spots 14
  pipe tobacco or cigars 102
  prior notice of nonliability 8
  promoting products to children 40
  responsibility of station 5
  smokeless tobacco products 102
  sound-alike 168
Advice programs 22
AFTRA 70, 83, 172
Alcoholic Beverage Advertising
  on broadcasting 9
  on cable TV 9
All—Channel TV Sets 9, 27
American Association of Advertising Agencies 8, 10